Clement Moore Butler

St. Paul in Rome

Lectures Delivered in the Legation of the United States of America...

Clement Moore Butler

St. Paul in Rome
Lectures Delivered in the Legation of the United States of America...

ISBN/EAN: 9783744766500

Printed in Europe, USA, Canada, Australia, Japan

Cover: Foto ©Suzi / pixelio.de

More available books at **www.hansebooks.com**

ST. PAUL IN ROME:

LECTURES

DELIVERED IN THE

Legation of the United States of America,

IN ROME.

BY THE

REV. C. M. BUTLER, D.D.,

PROFESSOR OF ECCLESIASTICAL HISTORY IN THE DIVINITY SCHOOL, PHILADELPHIA.

PHILADELPHIA:
J. B. LIPPINCOTT & CO.
1865.

PREFACE.

THE author of the following lectures has, as it will be seen, adapted himself, in their preparation, to the peculiar circumstances in which he was placed. Addressing a shifting audience of tourists, whose minds were absorbed in the monuments and memories and ceremonies of pagan and papal Rome, he desired to place before them the great Apostle of the Gentiles, as the embodiment of the truth as it is in Jesus, in the midst of pagan impurities and Christian superstitions; and to rally around the greatest presence that ever appeared in Rome some of the interest which is lavished on less worthy objects. Looking "on this picture and on that," he felt assured that his hearers could not but appreciate the divine purity and beauty of Pauline Christianity, in contrast with the disingenuous system which unwarrantably invokes the name of the single-minded Peter, and with the hideous heathenism of the Rome of Nero. Hence he has not hesitated to enter into historical details, which however unsuited, in ordinary circumstances, to the pulpit, might be at the same time peculiarly interesting to those who were sojourning in the scenes where they occurred, and would tend to deepen and fix the impressions which it was his purpose to convey. They are intended as the dark back-ground of his sketch, in order to bring it out with more distinctness.

In prosecuting his purpose, the author does not claim to have thrown any new light on the question of St. Paul's sojourn at Rome. He has only attempted to concentrate that light, and by its aid to look steadily at some of the details of that historical picture in which both Nero and Paul are introduced, which might easily escape a casual observation. Hence he has not felt it needful to encumber his pages with foot-notes of references to authorities. It will be sufficient to name the few authors who have furnished most of the materials which he has employed. They are the following: Tacitus; Suetonius; Les Césars par le Cte. Franz de Champagny, 3 vols., Paris, 1859; Storia degli Imperatori Romani da Augusto Sino Costantino de, Sigg Lebeau, Crevier, etc., 36 vols., Roma, 1857; Indicazione Topographica de Roma Antica in correspondenza dell' Epoca imperiale del Commendatore Luigi Canina, 1 vol., Roma, 1850; Gli Edifici di Roma Antica e sua Campagna, Luigi Canina, 6 vols. folio, Roma, 1851; the Life and Epistles of St. Paul, by the Rev. W. J. Conybeare, M. A., late Fellow of Trinity College, Cambridge, and the Rev. J. S. Howson, D. D., principal of the Collegiate Institute, Liverpool, two volumes, People's edition, London, 1863; Lectures upon the Ecclesiastical History of the first three centuries, by Edward Burton, D.D., Oxford, 1845. Baronius, Fleury, and the Papal Constitutions have been consulted in the library of the Convent of Minerva.

It would not interest the reader of these discourses to know the few modifications which they have undergone in preparing them for the press. They are published in substance as they were delivered.

The last Lecture, on the claims of the Church of Rome to exclusive sanctity, to infallibility, and to unity, has no immediate connection with the series upon St. Paul. It was delivered last year, after the hearing of a discourse by Monsignore Manning. I venture to publish it, because although hastily prepared, it contains a refutation of that one train of argument which is over and over again repeated, by the distinguished author, to the English and American auditors who crowd to listen to his Advent and Lenten Sermons.

The author cannot conclude this preface without the expression of his gratification at the favor with which the discourses were received by the congregation, of several nationalities and many denominations, to which they were delivered. It is but justice to himself to add that it is at the instance of many clerical brethren, English, American, and

Scotch, that he ventures to commit them to the press.

As he pens these lines, it is with a feeling of sadness that he remembers how many loved brethren and friends, who listened to these discourses, and with whom he has taken sweet counsel in the house of God, under circumstances well calculated to deepen and enrich all Christian sympathies and affections, are now dispersed and journeying far over sea and land. May grace, mercy, and peace attend them and abide upon them forever!

ROME, April 6, 1864.

CONTENTS.

I.

St. Paul's Relation to the Church of Rome as exhibited in his Epistle to the Romans.

The Papacy a gradual growth. Presumptions in favor of St. Paul's rather than St. Peter's headship of the church. St. Paul makes no allusion, in his Epistle to the Romans, to St. Peter's presence or official connection with them. He claims authority over them as the Apostle of the Gentiles. The same claim is implied in the whole tenor of the Epistle. The chief design of the Epistle was to show that man could not be saved by works, but by the faith which appropriates the finished work of Christ. Jewish misapprehension of the consequences of this doctrine corrected. St. Paul's salutations to the Christians at Rome. The profound interest connected with recalling them on the spot. Departure of the present Church of Rome from the doctrines and practices of St. Paul............... 13

II.

The Circumstances which preceded St. Paul's Journey to Rome.

Origin of the Church in Rome. St. Paul's visit to Jerusalem. State of the Church in Jerusalem. His reception. The Nazaritic vow. St. Paul's wise dealing with Jewish prejudices. The fanaticism of the Jews. Their misrepresentation of St. Paul. Their persecution of him. St. Paul before the Sanhedrim. St. Paul in prison. The appearance and promise of Christ to him. St. Paul sent by night to Cæsarea. Arraigned before Felix. Festus succeeds Felix. Paul's address to Festus and Agrippa. His appeal to Cæsar. Contrast of fanatical and persecuting zeal with the holy and loving zeal exhibited in the Jews and in St. Paul 36

III.

St. Paul's Journey to Rome from Puteoli.

St. Paul's entrance into the Bay of Naples. The splendor of the scene. The position, work, prospects, and feelings of St. Paul. His sojourn at Puteoli. His journey to Rome. The meeting of St. Paul with the brethren at the Appii Forum and the Three Taverns. View from the Alban Hills. The Appian Way. Appearance of Rome from Albano. The Roman custom of placing tombs upon the great highways. Its reason and its significance. St. Paul's passage through the city to the headquarters of the Prætorian prefect. Paul permitted to dwell by himself with a soldier that kept him. Paul in bonds preaching the Gospel. Reflections................................. 58

IV.

St. Paul and the Jews in Rome.

Locality of St. Paul's hired house. State of the Jews in Rome. Origin of the Jewish community at Rome. Causes of mutual animosity between the Jews and Romans. Caligula orders his statues to be worshiped. Tumults in consequence at Alexandria. Capito erects an altar to the god Caius. Order of Caligula to have his colossal statue set up in the Temple of Jerusalem. Violent excitement of the Jews. Their petition to the proconsul Petroniüs. Assassination of Caligula. The Jews protected during the first years of Nero's reign. Testimony of St. Paul to the Jews in Rome. Its reception by the Jews. Their judicial blindness. Their persecution and dispersion to continue so long as they reject the Gospel. Condition of the Jews in Rome since the time of Paul. The triumph of Vespasian and Titus. Treatment of the Jews by the Pope. The humiliation and degradation to which they have been subjected. Their present wretched condition in Rome. A striking fulfillment of prophecy and of St. Paul's declaration. The foretold restoration and conversion of the Jews................... 81

V.

St. Paul in his own Hired House.

Locality of St. Paul's house. St. Paul permitted to preach and teach. The fact explained by the influence of Seneca and Burrus, by ignorance of the essential antagonism of Christianity to all pagan systems, by the protection of the Empress Poppea, and by the then absence of any motive on the part of Nero for the persecution of Christians. St. Paul received all who came to him. Probable character of his assemblies. St. Paul preached the Kingdom of God and taught the things that concern the Lord Jesus. Importance of the visible church. Its peculiar adaptation to the wants of that era. The difference between the teachings of St. Paul and that of the Church of Rome.. 109

VI.

Cæsar's Household, and the Saints.

1. The house of Cæsar. The palaces of Augustus, Tiberius, Caligula, and Nero. 2. The household of Nero. Sketches of the family of the Cæsars. 3. The saints in Cæsar's household. Their position. Their fidelity. Their example. 4. The other saints in Rome. Epaphroditus, Tychicus, Onesimus, Aristarchus, Justus, Epaphras, Timothy, Mark, Luke. Contrast of the household of Cæsar, and of the saints in his household and the other saints in Rome.. 133

VII.

St. Paul's Position in reference to Established Customs and Institutions.

Delay in the trial of St. Paul. The principle of his procedure in relation to existing customs and institutions. Illustrated in reference to (1) the Jewish economy, (2) the family, and (3) the state. The Jewish economy no longer to be enforced as of divine institution. The family a divine institution. The purity of the Roman family during the Republic. The corruption subsequently introduced. St. Paul enjoins the duties of the family relation, but does not assail the prevailing corruptions of that relation. Purifying influence of the Gospel. The state divine. The relative duties of magistrates and citizens enjoined. Why the powers that be are said to be ordained of God, and obedience without limitation "unto the Lord," is enjoined. Conclusion.. 159

VIII.

St. Paul's Position in reference to Established Customs and Institutions.

St. Paul's method of dealing with established customs and institutions restated. Illustrated in the case of Caligula, Claudius, and Nero; and in reference to games and gladiatorial combats. The example of the Saviour followed by St. Paul. Reflections.. 179

IX.

St. Paul's Position in reference to Established Customs and Institutions.

St. Paul sometimes enjoins the relative duties of relations which are evil in their origin or themselves. This principle illustrated in the case of the marriage of Christians to heathens. The absence to condemn does not imply the approbation of a custom. Exhortations to masters and slaves. The case of Onesimus considered. 197

X.

St. Paul's Position in reference to Established Customs and Institutions.

The condition of slaves in Rome. The wisdom of St. Paul's treatment of the case of Onesimus. The emancipating influence of the principle of Christian brotherhood. System of slavery in the United States. Personal impressions in reference to the character of slavery in the United States. Comparison of American and Roman slavery. Mistaken extremes in reference to slavery in the United States........................ 214

XI.

St. Paul's Second Imprisonment at Rome.

St. Paul liberated from his first imprisonment. Preaches the Gospel in the East and in the West. His second imprisonment. Its hardships. His trial. His imprisonment and death. Inquiry into the traditions concerning his imprisonment and death, and the imprisonment and crucifixion of St. Peter at Rome. The tradition of St. Peter's Episcopate, at Rome, not a true tradition. The absence of proof of the fact; and the presumptions against the fact. Conclusion........................ 237

XII.

The Claim of the Church of Rome to Sanctity, Infallibility, and Unity considered.

The relation of the Church and the Word of God. Sanctity asserted to be found only in the Church of Rome. Confutation of this claim. The claim of infallibility based upon its necessity. The necessity denied, and the infallibility of the Church of Rome confuted. The unity of the Church of Rome shown to be less real than that of Protestantism. Concluding observations.. 268

ST. PAUL IN ROME.

LECTURE I.

ST. PAUL'S RELATION TO THE CHURCH OF ROME AS EXHIBITED IN HIS EPISTLE TO THE ROMANS.

To all that be in Rome, beloved of God, called to be saints; grace be to you and peace from God our Father and the Lord Jesus Christ.—ROMANS, i. 7.

I PROPOSE to deliver a series of discourses on St. Paul in the relations which he sustained to Rome and the church in Rome; and I commence the series with the consideration of his Epistle to the Romans.

If the Papacy had not been a gradual growth, rather than a manufacture or an invention, it would seem as if St. Paul and not St. Peter would have been designated as the Prince of the Apostles and head of the church, with his see at Rome. A far more powerful argument, independent of Romish tradition, could certainly be constructed for the claims of the former than of the latter.

It is certain that St. Paul was long at Rome. It is probable that he visited it a second time, and underwent martyrdom in Rome during the persecution of the church by Nero. That St. Peter was ever there is more than doubtful. The learned Dr.

Barrow has demonstrated that there is no proof that St. Peter ever went to Rome.

It was to St. Paul that the Apostleship of the Gentiles was distinctly assigned, and to St. Peter that of the circumcision.

The qualifications of St. Paul, no less than his express designation to the Apostleship of the Gentiles, fitted him far better for this office, if such an office were to be established, than St. Peter. St. Paul was not only learned as a Jew, but was also largely imbued with Gentile learning. St. Peter was an uncultured fisherman. St. Paul was a man of large and balanced powers, set in constant and energetic motion by a fervor which never destroyed his judgment. St. Peter was fervid indeed, but rash and inconstant. In all that constitutes qualification for headship, and the administration of a large body, composed of Jews and Gentiles, Greeks and Barbarians, newly united in the profession of a religion which was the opprobrium of the world, St. Paul was immeasurably the superior. Nor is it an answer to this suggestion to say that God hath chosen the folly of the world, and the weakness of the world to overthrow its wisdom and its strength, for of that which was all equal folly and weakness in the eye of the world, he made choices and special adaptations; and it was under divine guidance that he became "to the Greeks as a Greek."

On the ground of probability, we can scarcely suppose that he alone of all the twelve who had denied his Master, would have been designated as the Prince of the Apostles, rather than the ever-loyal and devoted Paul.

If we search for Scripture proof to countenance

this claim for one or other of the Apostles, how much more to the purpose than the strained interpretations of the expressions, "thou art Peter," and "feed my sheep," is the direct assertion of St. Paul, "that which cometh upon me daily, *the care of all the churches?*"

In such an argument, the fact that St. Paul was miraculously called by the ascended Christ, the glorified head of the church, and set apart for an Apostleship peculiar in its extent and its sufferings, in connection with the fact that he actually traversed a large portion of the Roman world, and addressed the churches in a tone of authority, might be adduced with much plausibility.

Nor would it be a less remarkable fact, in this connection, that in accordance with what might have been reasonably expected from the head of the church, there are in the sacred canon fourteen Epistles of St. Paul, some of them the most elaborate and best adapted to the wants of the church universal; while there are but two from St. Peter, which, though glowing and glorious, are addressed to the strangers, or the dispersed Jewish Christians.

And lastly, the fact that the most elaborate of all these Epistles is addressed to the *Roman Christians*, and adopts toward them the tone of one who feels that he has over them a divinely commissioned superintendence, while nothing of this kind remains of St. Peter, confirms the conviction that if the Papacy had been not an historical development, but a theological invention, to St. Paul and not to St. Peter would have been assigned the headship of the Apostles, and the Vicarate of Christ.

It is to the relation of St. Paul to the Church of

Rome, previous to his personal presence in it, and as seen in his Epistle to the Romans, that I now direct my argument.

I. The *tone* and *purport* of the Epistle to the Romans preclude the supposition that St. Peter had superintendence and charge of the Church of Rome, because he makes no allusion to the presence of St. Peter, or any other Apostle at Rome, and seems in it distinctly to assume authority over it for himself.

1. The omission to mention the presence and authority of St. Peter, and to enjoin upon the Roman Church spiritual obedience to him, is incredible upon the supposition that he was then, and had been for fifteen years, the recognized Bishop of that see. The claim of the Church of Rome is that St. Peter became Bishop of Rome in the year of our Lord 43, and held the episcopate for twenty-three years. His Epistle was written in the year 58. Now nothing could be more unbecoming, intrusive, discourteous, and less like St. Paul, than an epistle to the Romans without a single allusion to their Bishop of fifteen years' standing, and as if he himself possessed a rightful authority to admonish and teach and guide them. Even on the supposition that St. Paul had been the divinely constituted head of all the churches upon earth, it is impossible to conceive him guilty of such an omission. Even if in his administration of that see St. Peter was to be blamed, St. Paul would not have hesitated, as upon another occasion, to have blamed him. It is perfectly incredible, on the supposition that St. Peter was then Bishop of Rome, and head of all the churches, that St. Paul should not have recognized him in either of these

characters, nor alluded to him either for praise or censure.

2. But he distinctly *claims for himself the office of Apostle of the Gentiles.* Three times he calls himself such: "For I speak unto you Gentiles, inasmuch as *I am the Apostle of the Gentiles,* I magnify my office."* Here he declares that he speaks to them, *Gentiles,* because he is the Apostle of the Gentiles; because he has been set apart for that very office, and hence has a right to speak; and in view of this designation he magnifies his office. In the opening words of the Epistle, he declares that he has received from the risen Saviour, "grace and Apostleship for obedience to the faith, *among all nations,* for his name;" and then adds, "among whom *are ye also,* the called of Jesus Christ;" and then he pronounces upon them the Apostolic blessing of "grace and peace." Here his claims cannot be misunderstood. It is an Apostleship in order to the obedience of faith among all nations, and of them were the Roman Christians. And then, assuming that relation, he introduces his Epistle with the customary Apostolic benediction.

Still more directly to this purpose is his language in another place:† "Nevertheless, brethren, I have written unto you the more boldly, in some sort, as putting you in mind, because of the grace that is given to me of God, that I should be the minister of Jesus Christ to the Gentiles, ministering the gospel of God, that the offering up of the Gentiles might be acceptable, being sanctified of the Holy Ghost. I have, therefore, whereof I may glory, through Christ Jesus, in those things which pertain to God." What

---

* Rom. xii. 13.　　† Rom. xv. 15, 16, 17.

could be more explicit? He writes to them, reminding them that, through the grace of God, he has been made the minister of God to them, the Gentiles. Hence it is that he speaks to them boldly. Hence he has whereof he may glory. As the Apostle of the Gentiles, he here claims the right and the duty to address to them the Epistle which contains the fullest exposition of Christian doctrine and duty which is contained in the sacred canon.

3. Besides this explicit claim of the right to address them as the Apostle of the Gentiles, *the whole tenor of the Epistle implies that sense of right, of obligation, and of authority*. It is true that in some other Epistles may be found more distinct assertions of his Apostolic authority, but it is in cases where he feels called upon to minister rebuke to churches which he had planted, or had ministered to, in person. When he wrote to the Romans it was to a church which he had not founded, and for which he had not words of rebuke but commendation. "Their faith was spoken of throughout the world." Hence he had no "need to use sharpness according to the power which the Lord had given him,"* and to vindicate his Apostolic authority as in the second Epistle to the Corinthians; but was at liberty to speak to them as a father, with the affection and the Christian courtesy which was one of the most pleasing traits of his varied and balanced character. It was because the Church of Rome originated without Apostolic agency that St. Paul felt the more urgently the obligation, as the Apostle of the Gentiles, to visit them; and in the inability to do that as

---

* 2 Corin. xiii. 10.

soon as he desired, to explain the causes of his delay; and, in the mean time, to address to them such teaching and exhortation as their case required. That such is the tone of his Epistle throughout, must be recognized by every attentive reader. I adduce but two passages in illustration of the remark.

After a declaration of his divinely commissioned Apostleship, St. Paul proceeds to address the Christians at Rome. "For I thank my God, through Jesus Christ, for you all, that your faith is spoken of throughout the whole world. For God is my witness, whom I serve with my spirit in the Gospel of his Son, that without ceasing I make mention of you always in my prayers; making request, if by any means now at length I might have a prosperous journey, by the will of God, to come to you; for I long to see you, that I may impart unto you some spiritual gift, to the end ye may be established; that is, that I may be comforted with you by the mutual faith both of you and me. Now, I would not have you ignorant, brethren, how that oftentimes I purposed to come unto you, (but was let hitherto,) that I might have some fruit among you also, as among other Gentiles."* It is all the language of a spiritual father, who feels that those to whom he writes have no other father, and that he has a duty toward them of oversight and ministration; who would convince those to whom he is thus related that he has not willingly neglected them; that he longed to see them, and that he constantly remembered them in his prayers. He purposed oftentimes to go to them,—he longed to see them,—he desired both to

---

* Rom. i. 8–14.

impart and to receive spiritual gifts. It is incredible that St. Paul should have written in this strain if St. Peter had been Bishop of Rome and Vicar of Christ.

Similar in its tone and purport to this introduction is St. Paul's language toward the close of the Epistle. "But as it is written to whom he was not spoken of they shall see, and they that have not heard shall understand. From which cause also I have been much hindered in coming to you; but now, having no more place in these parts, and having a great desire these many years to come unto you, whensoever I take my journey into Spain I will come to you, for I trust to see you in my journey, and to be brought on my way thitherward by you, if first I be somewhat filled with your company. But now I go unto Jerusalem to minister unto the saints; when therefore I have performed this, and have sealed to them this fruit, I will come unto you by Spain. And I am sure that when I come unto you I shall come in the fullness of the blessing of the Gospel of Christ. Now, I beseech you, brethren, for the Lord Jesus Christ's sake, and for the love of the Spirit, that ye strive together with me in your prayers to God for me, that I may be delivered from them that do not believe in Judea, and that my service which I have for Jerusalem may be accepted of the saints; that I may come unto you with joy by the will of God, and may with you be refreshed. Now the God of peace be with you all. Amen."

Here the Apostle declares that he has had a great desire these many years to go to Rome, but had been many ways hindered. But now he trusts to see them on his way, in his purposed visit to Spain. He expresses the hope that after he shall have some time enjoyed their company, they (some of them, we may suppose) will accompany him on his way thither. He repeats the assurance that he will visit them on his way to Spain; he feels sure that he will come in the fullness of the blessing of the Gospel of Christ. He asks their prayers that he may be delivered from his enemies in Judea, and reach them, and be refreshed by them. What is this but the courteous Christian language of one who feels that he has alike duties and prerogatives among those to whom he writes, and expects the welcome and the attention which is appropriate from those by whom they are recognized?

Such was the relation of St. Paul to the infant Church of Rome. As Rome was mistress of the nations, and the radiating center of influence and power throughout the world, St. Paul could not but see how supremely important to the future interests of the church it was that the Church of Rome should be rightly constituted; that it should hold fast to the truth as it is in Jesus; and should exhibit holiness, consistency, and zeal. Hence, in the midst of his overwhelming labors, which had long hindered his earnest desire to visit the church at Rome, he addressed to them his most elaborate Epistle. He wished to mould that church to such a form and animate it with such a spirit as that its commanding influence should be exerted in behalf of the pure Gospel of Christ, unmixed with Pagan or Jewish errors. With the then condition of the Church of Rome, with its practical holiness of zeal, he seems to have been entirely satisfied. He thanks God that their faith is spoken of throughout the world. He not only wishes to impart unto them some spiritual gift, but he expects to be comforted by their mutual faith. Even his painstaking confutation of Judaizing errors seems to be made with no special reference to the peculiar prevalence of such errors at Rome, but rather in view of their general dissemination among Jewish converts, and for purposes of warning and instruction. It will be interesting to examine what were the great truths which St. Paul was so earnest in impressing upon the Church of Rome, just as it was assuming an organized existence, in order that the pure and unchangeable Gospel of Christ might, through all the world and all the ages, radiate from that central seat its clear and steady light. Let us briefly examine the purport of the Epistle.

II. It treats of many topics, but its main argument is not difficult to be discerned. The points which he most wishes to impress and the errors which he is most anxious to confute are clear enough.

He opens the Epistle with salutations and blessings. He then proceeds to show what was the condition of mankind, and begins with the pagan world. It is a dark, awful, but unexaggerated picture which he draws of the pagan character, the justice of which must have been abundantly evident to the Christian residents at Rome. That such wickedness cannot escape the justice of God, is his first conclusion. Then he turns to the Jews. He warns them not to boast because of their superior privileges over the Gentiles. Their circumcision cannot save them if they obey not the law. But they neither do nor can keep the law. What follows? "By the deeds of the law shall no flesh be justified." Of what use was the law then if it could not be kept? His answer is, "By the law is the knowledge of sin." When sin is both known and felt, then there is *preparation* for salvation.

From this point, toward the conclusion of the third chapter, opens his grand argumentation, chiefly with the Jew, and yet incidentally sometimes, and always by implication, with the Gentile. THE great point and argument of the Epistle is this: Neither the Gentile by observing the law of his natural conscience, nor the Jew by observing the divine law, can obtain salvation. They can only attain to the knowledge that it is unattainable, and that they are lost. But for the salvation of the lost, Christ Jesus is revealed. Because all have sinned he assumed the sins of all, and died to atone for all. God accepts the atonement, and pardons all who by believing can receive the Holy Ghost, and become holy. The Gentile and the Jew alike may believe and live. The Jew is taught that all the sacrifices of the law, which atoned for ceremonial sins, for the temporal punishment of some violations of the moral law, were intended to point his faith to the one great sacrifice, which was to come and has come, Christ, the Lamb of God who taketh away the sins of the world.

Now it results from this statement that man cannot be saved by works of any kind. It was just because he could not be, that Christ came and laid down his life. Now that he has come and presented that which was a substitute for impossible obedience, it is of course still impossible that the still impossible obedience should secure salvation. No means remains but to accept the salvation which Christ has wrought. To accept it is to believe. To believe, in the Gospel sense of that expression, is to accept. It is an act which involves conviction of the mind, followed by the acquiescence of the will and a conformity of the conduct. By faith only is a man justified. By faith without works. Not even by the working of the faith, but yet by the faith which works, and not by a faith which does not work. "Works are excluded." And this is the point, salvation by faith, faith without works, simple acceptance with no merit, and with a deep sense of demerit,—it is this point which St. Paul strenuously argues with the Jew. He could, with great difficulty, believe that his being a Jew, and having the custody of the oracles of God, and having been circumcised, counted nothing in the way of merit toward his acceptance. It seemed to irk him that all these historical and divine treasures, and all his good works must be cast down when he came up to the cross; and that he and the hated Gentile should stand there on an absolute equality, both with nothing but their sins, and that both should smite upon their breasts in penitence, and cry, "God be merciful to us, sinners," and both obtain salvation by the faith that merely *accepts* with the consciousness of dying need, and not that one, the favored Jew, should obtain it by the privileges and works which *buy* and *barter* life.

Now it is easy to see that it is this doctrine which St. Paul is supremely anxious to clear up, and to impress upon the minds and hearts of the Roman Christians, both Jew and Gentile. He gives to its illustration and enforcement a large space. He puts his whole heart into the argument. His soul seems to ache with anxiety to lodge this truth in the innermost conviction of the reluctant Jew. He patiently follows him into every subterfuge. His heart breaks out in tender concern lest he should fail to receive that simple truth upon which his salvation depends. He yearns over his countrymen with inexpressible affection. He admits and glories in the privileges of the Jew, but shows that they were only privileges of superior *preparation* for the reception of this great truth, this supreme essential blessing of salvation by simple faith. Seldom do we find so much heart in an argument as in this. He guards it on all sides, that their prejudices may be as little as possible offended. He shows that salvation is not license to omit obedience, but on the contrary, the one spring and motive and life of all holy obedience. And thus, when at the eighth chapter he feels warranted to announce it as a demonstrated truth that "there is no condemnation to them that are in Christ Jesus, who walk not after the flesh but after the Spirit," he expatiates upon the glory and blessedness of that great salvation, and upon the holiness, zeal, and love which it awakens in the penitent and believing heart. And then his kindled soul breaks forth into one of the sublimest utterances in the Word of God, which is but an eulogy and an amplification, and a personal and loving grasp of the great truth of salvation by faith in Christ Jesus. "It is God that justifieth. Who is it that condemneth? It is Christ that died, yea, rather that has risen again, who is even at the right hand of God, who also maketh intercession for us. Who shall separate us from the love of Christ? Shall tribulation or distress, or persecution or famine, or nakedness, or peril or sword?" "For I am persuaded that neither death nor life, nor angels, nor principalities, nor powers, nor things present, nor things to come, nor height, nor depth, nor any other creature shall be able to separate us from the love of God *who is in Christ Jesus our Lord.*"

Such was the great central truth which St. Paul addressed to the Christians of Rome, as that which was essential, upon which all other truths were dependent, by which all errors were to be destroyed, and all doctrines tested.

III. There are two points upon which St. Paul was particularly careful to correct Jewish misapprehension. One would lead them to reject the doctrine of justification by faith only; and the other to draw from it a mistaken inference.

1. The Jews of his generation had become fixed in the doctrine of merit as the purchase of salvation. The Pharisees especially were arrogantly self-righteous. They relied upon their alms, and fasts, and long prayers, and tithes of mint, anise, and cummin, for acceptance with God, even while living in neglect of truth, judgment, and mercy. They had misinterpreted that principle of the Jewish administration which had affixed temporal blessings to obedience, and punishment to rebellion. It had been designed to teach them the divine law of rewards and punishments, only in part and in advance ministered upon earth, and to be perfectly administered hereafter. They learned from it only the error that merit was to purchase the favor of God in the future world. Nor had they less grossly misunderstood the institution of sacrifice. It was designed to throw their minds forward to the world-atoning sacrifice of Christ. While the institution was yet in existence they had

failed to see its meaning, and its long disuse had unfitted them to welcome the atonement which furnished salvation, as a full and free expiation to the penitent and believing. Hence, when told that this was all; that they were not to merit and work out salvation; that on that side there was no hope; that neither by the works of the abrogated Jewish law, nor by their own obedience to the moral law, could they find life, they were vexed, perplexed, confounded. It seemed to them like sending kings out to beg. And this is the point which St. Paul persistently labors. "A man is justified by faith without the deeds of the law." "By the works of the law shall no flesh be justified." These two propositions St. Paul reiterates in every variety of form—in argument and exhortation, for comfort to faith, and for the rebuke of self-righteousness.

2. Nor did the Jews fail to insist that if we were justified by faith only, without works, licentiousness would follow, obedience would be unnecessary, and holiness superfluous. Against this misapprehension St. Paul is peculiarly emphatic. "Shall we continue in sin that grace may abound? God forbid!" He labors to show that obedience is wrapped up in faith; that its very manifestation implies death to sin, and life to righteousness; that it is the condition of the reception of the Spirit's aid, whereby alone good works are wrought, and holiness obtained.

Such are the teachings of St. Paul, divinely commissioned and inspired, to the Church of Rome, over whose faith it became him sedulously to watch. Such were the doctrines received and accepted by the early Church of Rome.

IV. It is most interesting to stand in the very city

to which this great Epistle was directed, and to think of its reception. "Here," we say to ourselves, "eighteen hundred years ago, the first Christians of Rome conversed of the words of Paul as they walked together, (where we are now assembled,) in this, then *Campus Martius,* in the groves, and walks, and porticoes that surrounded the mausoleum of Augustus; and here their hearts burned within them as they unfolded to each other this newly developed scripture. Here the Epistle was read to the church which was wont to gather in the house of Aquila and Priscilla. Here the hearts of the beloved and faithful disciples and fellow-helpers in the Gospel, converts and friends of St. Paul, whom he had known, and loved, and labored with in different portions of his wide missionary field, were refreshed by his loving messages, and animated by his faithful exhortations. As the Epistle drew toward its close, and weighty doctrine and earnest exhortations were followed by affectionate salutations, we can imagine how, with dim eyes and parted lips and eager expectation, they listened for the paternal and fraternal messages of the beloved and loving Apostle. Priscilla and Aquila, his hospitable hosts in Corinth, helpers in Christ; well-beloved Epænetus, the first fruits of Achaia; Mary, who devoted much labor upon him; Andronicus and Junia, kinsmen, and fellow-prisoners; beloved Amplias; Urbane, his helper in the Lord; Stachys, his beloved; Appelles, well approved; Aristobulus, and his household; Herodian, his kinsman; the household of Narcissus; Tryphena and Tryphosa, laborers in the Lord; beloved Persis, who labored much; Rufus, chosen in the Lord, and his mother—and, says the affectionate Apostle, *mine;*

Asyncritus, Phlegon, Hermas, Patrobas, Hermes, Philologus, Julia, Nereas, and his sister, and Olympas, and all the saints, that are with them." What a goodly company is this, and how highly favored! St. Paul loves them, blesses them, commands them! They were chief saints of a church whose faith and obedience were known throughout the world. Scarcely anything is known of any of them, except what is here recorded, that they were faithful and laborious disciples of the Saviour, and beloved brethren of St. Paul.

How profoundly affecting it is to think of this group, and their fellow-disciples; a holy seed of many nations and many stations in life, in the midst of this then vast, magnificent, and awfully wicked city, enjoying temporary peace and toleration, at the beginning of the reign of Nero, soon to be followed by persecution, when he should have surrendered himself to debauchery, cruelty, wild extravagance, and frenzied dissipation! Doubtless, many of them were subsequently enrolled in the noble army of martyrs. As St. Paul contemplated them in their insecure position, living and walking under the shadow of that imperial palace from which at any moment of capricious passion the mandate might issue for their extermination; and living near the amphitheaters and circuses in which the clamors of a brutal and blood-fed populace might soon demand that they should be given to the lions; when he remembered that they were set for a light in that dark place, it is not surprising that he put so much heart into his salutations, and so tenderly names his beloved brethren one by one. No wonder that his earnestness is so fervent, when he guards them from error, and leads them into truth, and exhorts them to duty. He would have them strong in the Lord; he would have their light shine; he would have them fitted for the high position assigned them of soon becoming the most conspicuous of the churches. They would need to put on the whole armor of God. They would need the most vigorous and heroic spiritual development. Christian athletes, they required to be fed with strong meats, and to be girded with power. They must learn to comprehend, and live upon, and cling to the most essential and vital truths; and they must be taught to shun the errors which would corrupt their faith, or chill their love, or misguide their zeal. Such was the task before the Apostle. It was accomplished in his great Epistle. We have reason to believe that it was accepted and did its work. We know that its truths were reiterated by St. Clement, called, in the Roman succession, the third Bishop of Rome. We know what faithful testimony was given by the Roman martyrs. The Roman Church adopted and lived upon and disseminated the truths so earnestly inculcated by St. Paul.

The Church of Rome still exists. A Bishop of Rome occupies the see which seems not to have been constituted, or at least occupied, at the time in which St. Paul wrote his Epistle. A few months since he proclaimed the sorrow which he felt at the palpable decay of faith, the spread of practical irreligion and of speculative infidelity, throughout Italy and the world. He addressed to the faithful animated exhortations to second his efforts to win back the favor of God, and to revive faith and sanctity in the minds of men. We know, from St. Paul's Epistle, what exhortations he would have addressed to the saints in Rome at such a crisis. He would have exhorted them to earnest prayer to the Father through the Son, for the converting, reviving, and sanctifying power of the Holy Ghost to be poured out upon priests and people. He would have reminded them of their high privileges as the freely forgiven children of God, by faith in Christ Jesus; and of the obligation, through the constraining love of Christ, to live holily and unblamably, and in a spirit of true consecration to God, and love to man. Were these, or similar exhortations, addressed by the Bishop of Rome to the saints that are in Rome? Not these, but other exhortations were employed. They were enjoined with their presence and faith and prayer to attend a spectacle, for healing the evils of the times and propitiating the favor of Heaven. A picture of the Saviour would be carried by Pope and cardinals, priests and monks, with banner and music and incense and the pomp of gilded vestments, from the Basilica of St. John Lateran to that of Santa Maria Maggiore. It was this picture in which the hope of the restoration of faith and holiness seemed to be reposed. It was said to have been outlined by St. Luke for the Virgin Mary, three days after Christ's ascension; to have been miraculously colored in the night; to have been carried during the siege of Titus to Pella and subsequently to Constantinople; to have been taken away in the seventh century by the persecuted Bishop of Constantinople, and consigned to the sea, over which it passed, in a perpendicular position, to Ostia, in twenty-four hours, when, seeing the Pope ready to receive it upon shore, it rose and placed itself in his hands. The Bishop of Rome's method of reviving faith and religion was the transfer of this picture from the Basilica of St. John Lateran to that of Santa Maria Maggiore. It evidently differs from the method which would have been adopted by St. Paul. He knew of no such means of grace.*

And the *tokens of divine favor* which have followed this act of faith are also of such a kind as would not have been appreciated by St. Paul. In the little town of Vico Varo, in the Sabine Mountains, in a miniature chapel, I saw, last spring, a picture of the Virgin Mary. It seems that this picture has for some months been in the habit of rolling up its eyes, and changing perceptibly its color.† This is received as evidence that the Virgin Mary has heard the supplications of the faithful, and that she will intercede with her Son to intercede with the Father to avert the evils which threaten the Church of Rome and the world, and to bestow upon them anew his blessing. Another picture in the same region makes the same miraculous manifestations. Homage to a pic-

---

* All the statements above mentioned, elaborately and diffusely narrated, are found in a printed document, scattered all over Rome at the time of the exposition of the picture, entitled "Origine della S. Imagine," and concluding with the words, "Con permesso." The crowds who attended its transfer and its exposition were immense. During the last days the press of people toward the picture, with rosaries, crosses, jewels, handkerchiefs, books, and other articles, kept two priests constantly employed in touching them to the glass in front, by which a miraculous virtue was supposed to be imparted to them; and the Swiss guard could with difficulty keep the crowd back from the altar. The exposition continued from the 6th to the 13th of September. (1862.)

† The eyes are not only rolled up and down, but sometimes move sideways, and occasionally the eyelashes also move.

ture of the Saviour, painted by St. Luke, to act as the effectual prayer; and pictures of the Madonna, that roll their eyes up and down, and occasionally sideways, with a movement of the eyelids, as answers to the prayer,—this is the method of seeking and proclaiming spiritual blessing adopted by the present Church of Rome. It was a method evidently unknown to St. Paul.*

In view of these new methods of the Church of Rome, it is scarcely necessary to ask if the *truths* which St. Paul so earnestly labored to implant have lived and thriven and borne holy fruits where they were so early introduced? Alas! there is not one of them which the Church of Rome accepts. There is not one of them which she does not reject. Justification by faith only, over which holy Paul lifted a glowing anthem, Rome visits with anathema. How is it with the errors against which St. Paul so strenuously labored? Rome adopts them. She preaches the merit which Paul denounced. And what in the place of Paul's fundamentals are hers? Dogmas of which there is not the shadow of a trace in his Epistle. The supremacy of St. Peter and his Vicarate of Christ, Transubstantiation, the Immaculate Conception of the Virgin, and—but why should I name them? Of all these fundamental dogmas, we find in the Epistle of St. Paul, intended to be the chart and guide of the Church of Rome through all time, that there is not a word—not a word! Simply to state such a fact is more impressive than

---

* It is a significant comment on this miracle, that the vicar of the parish at Vico Varo, who wrote glowing accounts of this miraculous manifestation, has since absconded with all the offerings of the faithful.

it could be made by the most mournful and impassioned declamation.

There has recently been found beneath the Church of San Clemente, a larger and nobler edifice, upon which the present edifice, much less homogeneous and complete than the former, has been erected. That original church, itself founded on the ruins of pagan structures, was filled up with rubbish, and so completely hidden from view, that its existence was unknown for ages. The descriptions of the original edifice have been misappropriated to the second and meaner structure. It is now in the process of excavation, and as one pillar after another of precious and polished marble is disclosed, its superiority has become more and more apparent. And so under the present Church of Rome, there lies buried and filled with superstitious rubbish and forgotten for ages, a nobler and purer church, the church of St. Paul and of Clement. But instead of uncovering to the light its walls, which are salvation, and its gates, which are praise, instead of disclosing its pure altars and its polished pillars, Rome piles new rubbish on, and packs it down, and does not permit her children even to know of its existence.

But these blessed truths, repudiated by the false Church of Rome, are still the heritage of the churches; and because she, to whom was committed the precious deposit, was faithless to her trust, it becomes them to cling with warmer loyalty and love to that which, while it is Gospel, is to fallen man the most effective law. "Being justified by faith, we have peace with God." "Faith *worketh* by love."

In these scenes and with these memories we will cling to them and love them as we have never done before. We pass over the intervening ages. We gather with the disciples who are assembled to hear St. Paul's Epistle. Its precious truths sink into our hearts; and, oh! how we need its divine conclusion, in the midst of this groaning and travailing creation, in the midst of the tumults of the world and the sorrows of the churches! "Being justified by faith, we have *peace with God.*"

LECTURE II.

THE CIRCUMSTANCES WHICH PRECEDED ST. PAUL'S JOURNEY TO ROME.

And the night following, the Lord stood by him, and said: Be of good cheer, Paul, for as thou hast testified of me at Jerusalem, so must thou bear witness also at Rome. —ACTS, xxiii. 11.

WHEN the devout Christian visits Rome, his first thought is not of Romulus, Cæsar, or Augustus, of Gregory, or of Leo, but of Paul. Here he was brought in bonds. Here he lived two years. Here he conferred with Jews and Gentiles. Here he wrote some of his most precious epistles. Here devoted Christian brethren and friends gathered about him; and in his hired house, (near where we now worship,) what luminous expositions of the truth as it is in Jesus; what fitting in of fact with prophecy; what demonstrated correspondence between the type and the reality; what earnest prayer; what joyful praise; what loving intercession; what affectionate fellowship; what peaceable wisdom; what heroic zeal!

How the Church of Rome originated does not appear. The Apostolic history does not designate its founder. Had it been an Apostle, we can scarcely doubt that the fact would have been recorded. It probably originated with some of the disciples scattered abroad, after the martyrdom of St. Stephen. "They went *everywhere* preaching the word." (Acts, vii. 4.) Though originating with Jewish converts, it had already acquired a preponderance of the Gentile element when St. Paul wrote his Epistle to the Romans. He claims the right to address them on the ground that he was the Apostle of the Gentiles. The names of the Christian friends and brethren whom St. Paul salutes at the end of his Epistle are largely Greek and Roman.

St. Paul's Epistle to the Romans was written at Corinth, and sent by Phœbe, a deaconess of the church at Cenchrea, adjoining that city. In it he assures them that after he shall have gone up to Jerusalem, to distribute to the poor saints there the contributions of their wealthier brethren in Macedonia and Achaia, he would visit the disciples at Rome. Anxious as he was to see the brethren at Rome, and confer with, and properly to constitute and regulate a church, whose influence at the political center of the world would be immense, he must yet first see his poor disciples at Jerusalem; he must himself present to them the gifts of their brethren, and increase their grateful joy; he must tell them how fully and freely Christian love poured forth those gifts; he must be a partaker of their holy joy; he must endeavor to correct their growing errors of doctrine and misapprehension concerning his own character, purposes, and views.

We have spoken of St. Paul's purposed journey to Rome. He went at length, not as a free apostle, but as a chained captive. The story, as recorded in the latter chapter of the Acts of the Apostles, is one of exceeding interest.

The church in Jerusalem was in a transition state. The Jewish rites and ceremonies were continued at the Temple at the same time that the church, which was to supersede them, was established by its side. Christ had declared that he came not to destroy the law but to fulfill. The true meaning of this declaration many of the Jewish Christians failed to apprehend. They did not see that in fulfilling, Christianity superseded Judaism; that it completed it by merging it into itself; that it was the plant which of necessity absorbed the seed from which it sprung. They supposed that Judaism was to remain entire, and that as Moses inaugurated it, and David strengthened it, and Isaiah, and Jeremiah, and Ezekiel, and all the prophets illustrated and explained it, and foretold its glories, so Christ was to complete it, and place it on immovable foundations, and fill out the types of Moses, and the glowing delineations of the prophets. Consolidated and completed Judaism, seated upon a throne, and crowned with power by a conquering Messiah,—that was their faith and hope. Slowly and reluctantly were their minds drawn from these carnal views. Many of them still clung to Jewish customs. They would retain circumcision, and many of the ceremonies of the law.

Now St. Paul, in his large and loving wisdom, dealt gently with these half emancipated minds. While he proclaimed the utter freedom of the disciples of Christ, and the necessity of reliance only on his work for pardon, grace, and life, he would yet not rudely tear away the tendrils of affection and association from the Jewish institutes, but would wait until, of their own spiritual affinity, they should all be untwined and disengaged, and gently swayed toward the cross. Yet St. Paul was disliked by the less advanced of the Jewish converts, because he only tolerated for the present, and did not enjoin permanent adhesion to some of the ceremonies of the law; and they falsely represented him as an enemy who reviled customs which were at least venerable, even if they had ceased to be obligatory.

St. Paul came to Jerusalem in part to refute these accusations. He was well received. "When we came to Jerusalem, the brethren received us gladly." (Acts, xxi. 17.) The next day the elders of the church, called together by James and Paul, "declared particularly what things God had wrought among the Gentiles by his ministry" (Acts, xxi. 19) since he parted from Jerusalem four years before. When they heard it, "they glorified the Lord." (v. 20.) And, as we may suppose, after such a reception, from *kindness* to him, they reminded him that thousands of the Jews who believed were still zealous of the law, (v. 20;) that they had been made to believe that he went about teaching the Jews to forsake Moses, and abandon circumcision and the customs. (v. 21.) They told him that his coming would soon be known, and intimated that crowds would gather and violent excitements would arise. (v. 22.) Hence, as there were with them at that time four Jewish Christians who were under the Nazaritic vow, they advised St. Paul to go with them to the Temple, and pay the expenses attendant upon the completion of the ceremonies and the vow. (v. 23, 24.)

The regulations of the Nazaritic vow are found in the Book of Numbers. (Num. vi. 2–5.) A Jew delivered from peril, or desiring to testify in public a peculiarly solemn consecration to God, took upon himself this vow. During the period which it embraced, which was sometimes for life and sometimes for a few months only, he was to drink no wine, and to leave his hair uncut. At the termination of the period, he was to resort to the Temple with offerings, and the hair of his head and beard was there shorn, and cast upon the altar. This was one of the "customs" which the Jews, who were zealous for the law, retained. While, however, St. Paul's friends advised him to go with these men, and to pay their charges, they assured him that they did not intend to impose these customs upon the Gentiles, "for," they added, "as touching the Gentiles who believed, we have written that they observe no such thing, save only that they keep themselves from things offered unto idols, and from blood, and from strangled, and from fornication." (Acts, xxi. 25.)

St. Paul readily consented. Was it from fear or for favor? Was it against his principles? Not at all! It was in precise harmony with those principles of broad and loving toleration which he had so beautifully unfolded in the closing chapters of his Epistle to the Romans. *Charity* was the supreme law. For its sake, and in matters indifferent, he would be a Jew with Jews, and a Greek with Greeks. For peace and love he circumcised Timothy, because he was the son of a Jewess. He was free alike from superstitious repugnance to ceremonies, and superstitious adherence to them. His doctrine left him equally at liberty to practice or forsake those that were innocent, and not of present divine obligation. If one enjoined them on him as *essential*, he would not admit them for a moment; if one clung to them in doubt, or from old affection, or from a conviction that they were edifying if not obligatory, he allowed them, and joined in them. Nay, if one still practiced them because he believed them to be essential, he would even then tolerate them, while he endeavored to extricate him from bondage to ordinances. "Neither circumcision availeth anything nor uncircumcision, but a *new creature.*" (Gal. vi. 15.) This was his great principle.

How wise, how grand, how sublimely simple it is! Yet how many persons utterly fail to comprehend it! How slowly have Christians worked their way out of the spirit of Judaism into the self-restraining freedom wherewith Christ has made his people free! How soon did they again lapse into essential Judaism! We should not wonder that Christianity should have first appeared at Jerusalem with this Jewish stamp upon it. The lines and marks of the grub are impressed upon the back of the butterfly when he breaks from it and spreads his wings and flies! Let us wonder rather that the freed and bright child of the sunshine should fold his wings and crowd himself back into the dry shell from which he had broken! Let us wonder that Christianity, once emancipated from bondage, should submit to it again! Let us wonder that the Roman Church, which St. Paul praised, should be the church of to-day! But why wonder at all, when we remember that the spirit of all delusion is not yet locked up in the pit, but is at large, and that man is ever spiritually stupid? Only "great grace," and simple faith, and ardent love can retain churches and individuals in this high temper. It can be reached by the lowliest through the enlightenment of love. It will be missed by the loftiest without it. In our day we will still hear one denomination of Christians, or one style of Christian character among all denominations, saying: "This observance is essential, and without it the foundation will be overthrown, and then what will the righteous do?" Another replies: "Nay, without the overthrow of that form, and adherence to this essential dogma, there can be no spiritual life." Even now, the rarest of all styles of Christian character is that so beautifully portrayed by holy, lofty Paul. We often find high devotional fervor—and not this! We hear seraphic preaching—and not this! We meet with burning zeal—and not this! It is the last lesson which the ripest Christian learns; which many holy men never learn, and the fierce denial of which constitutes the first dogma of churches, which include more than half the Christians of the world!

St. Paul's ready compliance with the advice of the council must have silenced those who were opposed to him on the ground of his hostility to the national worship. But some Jews from Ephesus, enraged because in that city he had defeated their arguments in the Synagogue, and had built up there a powerful church of converted Jews, seized this unexpected opportunity of revenge. When they saw him in the Temple, "they laid hands on him, crying out, Men of Israel, help! This is the man that teacheth all men everywhere, against the people and the law, and this place; and further, brought Greeks also into the Temple, and hath polluted this holy place." (Acts, xxi. 27, 28.) A violent tumult arose. A vast multitude hurried to the Temple. They were filled with horror at the alleged profanation of the holy place. They dragged him from the inner court into the court of the Gentiles, and closed the gates, and were about to kill him.

But the design was suddenly arrested. The Roman garrison in the neighboring tower of Antonia, whose sentinels could overlook the open court of the Gentiles, was at once roused. Claudius Lysias, the commandant of the garrison, hearing that all Jerusalem was in an uproar, hastened to the scene with centurions and soldiers. As the veterans marched into the court with flashing arms and steady tramp, the fanatical mob recognized their masters, and "left off beating of Paul." Lysias took him and bound him with two chains, and inquired who he was, and what he had done. "Some cried one thing and some another." Unable to ascertain the truth, because of the tumult and confusion, he took him into the tower of Antonia. So violent was the crowd that St. Paul was borne up the stairs by the pressure of the multitude, amid the cries, "Away with him!"

Then St. Paul, with great presence of mind, turned to the commanding officer and said in Greek, "May I speak with thee?" Lysias, who had hitherto supposed that he was an Egyptian ringleader of a late rebellion, was startled to hear him speak Greek, and yielded to his request that he might address the people. Strange, that by a gesture of the hand he should have secured at first "great silence" in that wild, heaving, tumultuous crowd. Less strange that the silence should have continued when they perceived that he spoke in the Hebrew tongue. (Acts, xxi. 31–40.)

His speech was as conciliatory as fidelity to his Master would permit. (Acts, xxii. 1–21.) He told them that he was a Jew and a scholar of the famous Gamaliel. But Christ had appeared to him in a miraculous manifestation. He was struck down when he was on his way to Damascus to persecute the followers of Christ. He arose convinced and converted; and was subsequently bidden to go and preach to the Gentiles.

Then Jewish fanaticism flashed forth. A child of Abraham degrading himself by becoming a messenger to uncircumcised Gentiles, and blasphemously professing to call them to higher privileges than those of God's chosen people! This touched them to the quick. It was a provocation and an insult not to be borne. They were wrought up to a frenzy of indignation, and cried, "Away with this fellow from the earth, for it is not fit that he should live." (Acts, xxii. 22.) They rent their clothes, and in their wild Eastern way threw dust into the air. The spell of Paul's speech was broken. The chief captain, not understanding their clamors, would have had him examined by scourging, and his body was even stretched out to receive the lashes, (v. 25,) but when he claimed exemption as a Roman citizen, Lysias became alarmed that he had even bound him. (v. 29.)

On the morrow the scene was changed. Lysias summoned the Jewish Sanhedrim with the High Priest, that he might learn from them the nature of Paul's offense. Paul arraigned before the Sanhedrim of which he had been a member when St. Stephen was condemned! How that hour and scene must have returned to him as he stood arraigned before those with whom he had once sat as judge! Now he understood St. Stephen's holy calm; his unflinching yet humble fortitude; for it was in his own soul. "Earnestly beholding" the council, looking steadily, sorrowfully, and yearningly, we may well suppose, at brethren, many of whom had been personal friends, whose false and fiery zeal he had so lately shared, he began by declaring: "Men and brethren, I have lived in all good conscience before God unto this day." (Acts, xxiii. 1.) The High Priest, Ananias, enraged that he should claim this honest conscience, ordered those who stood by him to smite him upon the mouth. "God shall smite thee, thou whited wall!" was the Apostle's indignant rejoinder to the unprovoked brutality. He expressed his regret, however, when he ascertained that the insult came from the High Priest; "Seeing it is written, thou shalt not speak evil of the ruler of thy people." (Acts, xxiii. 5.) The incident shows the singular balance of St. Paul's character and conduct even in such a trying scene. As a man the author of such an outrage deserved rebuke. As God's High Priest the law enjoined reverence and submission to him. In that moment of high excitement, Paul could remember the injunction and was so far removed from the impulse of mere human indignation that he could make the apology, which, if he had yielded to pride alone, would have been withheld. But the words which had thus escaped from him in indignation proved to be a prophecy. God did smite Ananias. He was murdered by Jews more fiercely fanatical than himself—the Sicarrii, or dagger assassins of the Jewish war.

The Apostle from the commencement saw that there was as little hope for him as there had been for St. Stephen, in the justice or moderation of his judges. He therefore sought safety by enlisting on his side one of the parties into which the Sanhedrim was divided. He adroitly proclaimed himself a Pharisee, and the son of a Pharisee. "For the hope of the resurrection from the dead," he cried, "am I to be judged this day." (Acts, xxiii. 6.) In this one doctrine he knew that he should have the Pharisees on his side. A dissension arose among them. There was a temporary diversion in his favor. "The Pharisees arose and strove, saying, We find no evil in this man; but if a spirit or an angel have spoken unto him, let us not fight against God." (v. 9.) A great dissension arose. Lysias feared that St. Paul would be torn to pieces by the doctors as he had before feared that he would be killed by the mob. Fanaticism is a mighty leveler. The doctors of the Sanhedrim became as savage under its sway as the rabble of the streets. The learned and eloquent Legislative Assembly of France, howling like demons, and the tumultuous Jacobin Club, and the sanguinary Club of the Cordeliers, and the ferocious human wolves of St. Antoine,—what was there to choose between them? As loving zeal lifts the lowly to the high plane of angelic life, so does malignant zeal sink the lofty to the level of the fiend.

But night and silence came. A prisoner in the Roman barracks, with no human sympathy near, and conscious that he was surrounded by the fanatical and infuriated hate of the population of a great city who thirsted for his blood, what were the thoughts and feelings of St. Paul? We know not; but from our knowledge of his susceptibility to affection, we infer a corresponding sensibility to hate; from his ardent love to his countrymen we cannot but conclude that their bitter malignity pierced his heart with the keenest anguish. We know, moreover, that when an angel came to comfort Jesus it was in the hour of his extremest agony in the garden. And now the gracious Master, who then needed an angel to strengthen him,—a compassionate High Priest, touched with a feeling of the infirmities of his faithful apostle,—stood by him in the visions of the night, and said to him, "Be of good cheer, Paul, for as thou hast testified of me at Jerusalem, so also must thou testify of me at Rome." (v. 11.) It was enough; the Lord stood by him. Then must he have remembered that he who was for him was greater than all who could be against him. To one who should have looked upon him, as exhausted with excitement and fatigue, he stretched himself on the cold stone floor of the barracks, with a soldier guarding him, with frenzied fanatical wrath waiting only for the dawn for his destruction, after a day in which he had been rescued from the wrath of the mob only to be exposed to the equally deadly wrath of the Sanhedrim,—to one who should have perceived only these circumstances of his position, how pitiable would the fate of the Apostle have seemed! But who among all the then inhabitants or sojourners in Jerusalem was so truly to be envied as St. Paul? The Lord, the Creator of the worlds, the redeemer of sinners, the ascended and crowned Saviour, the Lord stood by him and said, "Paul, be of good cheer." It was the Master's approval, after a faithful, and because faithful, triumphant struggle against the powers of darkness.

But how singular the grounds on which the Lord bade Paul be of good cheer! He gave him no assurance that his troubles would come to a speedy end. He did not promise that he should overcome his enemies. He simply assured him that as he had been faithful at Jerusalem, he should have the privilege of testifying of him at Rome. He did not even foretell large results from his testimony. And for this he was to be of good cheer! To have the privilege of testifying for the Master is then one of the high privileges of the ministers and people of God, whether men will hear or whether they will forbear. And this is indeed the great vocation of the church. It is a light in a dark place. It is a voice crying in the wilderness. Even unto the end this is to be its essential character; for the Gospel is to be preached for a witness to all nations before the end shall come. And it is even to rejoice in giving testimony to Christ and his Gospel. To speak, in a world of hates, of so much love; in a world of sins, of so much purity; in a world of sorrows, of so much consolation; in a world of falsehood, of one so true; in a world of the condemned, of one who is so great a redeemer; in a world that vanishes with all its poor joys, of one who opens a world that is eternal, and joys that never fade! Oh! let us ever, with full hearts and faithful speech and holy living, give testimony to the Saviour. In society, in the family, in the world of business, let us all testify of Jesus that he is the Son of God; that life, and grace, and pardon, and salvation, and peace, and power,—all that is good in the life that is, and all that gives sure hope for the life that is to come,—are to be found nowhere but in *Him*. Simply to *testify* for him is the highest privilege, even though it be in peril and persecution; for this was the consolation which Jesus gave to Paul in his sorest need. Let us not doubt that he felt the joy of it when, a few days after, before Festus and Agrippa, he uttered his noble testimony for his Master, and experienced a loftier pleasure than Cæsar ever knew.

The consolation was needed, for Jewish malignity was awake with the early dawn; and forty of his enemies had bound themselves with a curse that they would neither eat nor drink till they had slain him. Such an extraordinary vow, so suddenly taken by such a number, measured the wide-spread and dreadful fanaticism of hatred to which Paul was exposed. It was in vain to think of turning it aside. Their plan was to induce the council to have Paul remanded for further examination, and then to spring upon him suddenly and kill him before the guard could rally in his defense.

The plan was defeated. Paul's sister's son heard of the conspiracy, and immediately resorted to the castle to advise him of the fact. Paul sent him to Lysias. Lysias listened, enjoined silence on Paul's nephew, and immediately sent Paul, at the third hour of the night, to Cæsarea, under a guard of two hundred soldiers, seventy horsemen, and two hundred spearmen. The rage against St. Paul must have risen to a great height to have made such a guard necessary. Lysias sent a letter to Felix, referring the case to him. The whole party escorted Paul as far as Antipatris, from whence he proceeded to Cæsarea, under the guard of horsemen. (Acts, xxiii. 12–35.)

After five days, the High Priest Ananias went to Cæsarea with the elders, and an orator named Tertullus. The charges brought against him were of the vaguest character. Even before the Sanhedrim, Paul could not have been lawfully condemned upon them; for they could not be proved. Paul stated truly that he had done nothing contrary to the Jewish law. Before a Roman tribunal they could not have been even properly entertained. They were not offenses which came within its cognizance. The Jews evidently expected by clamor to carry their point. They believed that for the purpose of conciliating them, Felix, without law, or against law, would not hesitate to sacrifice an obnoxious Jew to their violent and unanimous hatred. As in the case of the Saviour, they wished to make the Roman Government the instrument of shedding blood, which they were not permitted by the law to do. A pestilent fellow, a mover of sedition among the Jews throughout the world, a ringleader of the Nazarenes, and a profaner of the Temple,—these were the charges. Felix evaded them. His reply was: "When Lysias, the chief captain, shall come down, I will know the uttermost of your matter." (Acts, xxiv. 22.) He showed some interest or curiosity at least in Paul's views, for after some days he came with his wife Drusilla, who was a Jewess, and heard him concerning the faith of Christ. "And as he reasoned of temperance, of righteousness, and of judgment to come," Felix trembled, and answered: "Go thy way for this time; when I have a convenient season I will call for thee." (Acts, xxiv. 25.) Temperance, or continence, and righteousness, and judgment to come, were topics well calculated to terrify one who was a gross libertine, living in adulterous union with a profligate Jewish princess, and who was in all respects pre-eminently vicious in an age of vice. But this trembling was only the temporary effects of fear, produced on one who, in the graphic language of Tacitus, "exercised the power of a king with the temper of a slave." We are told that he retained Paul in custody in the hope that his friends and disciples would raise a ransom for him. (Acts, xxiv. 26.)

Again the scene changes. Festus succeeds Felix in the government of the province. Proceeding immediately to Jerusalem, he was importuned by the Jews to send Paul there for trial. Their object was to have him waylaid and killed. Festus, a better man than Felix, at first refused. He decreed that St. Paul's accuser should appear before his tribunal at Cæsarea. On his return they went down, and laid many and grievous things to his charge, "which," adds the sacred writer, "they could not prove." Festus at length, in order to please the Jews, proposed to Paul to proceed to Jerusalem under his protection, and there be tried in his presence. The Apostle no doubt knew that a proconsul's proposal to his prisoner was equivalent to a command; and anticipating from this compliance with Jewish injustice but little firmness in an emergency, and knowing by experience the deadly hatred of his enemy, he uttered the memorable words which resulted in his voyage as a prisoner to Rome: "I APPEAL TO CÆSAR." The appeal could not be refused; it was the right of every Roman citizen, and it could not be disregarded with impunity. (Acts, xxv. 1–11.)

A few days after, Herod Agrippa II. King of Calchis, and his sister Bernice, came on a complimentary visit to the new governor of the province. Festus described to him the peculiar case of Paul.

Agrippa expressed a desire to hear from Paul himself an account of his doctrine. (Acts, xxv. 13–22.)

On the morrow, with great pomp, Agrippa and Bernice, and the chief captains and principal men of the city assembled in the audience chamber of the palace, and Paul was permitted to speak for himself. It was a most interesting audience, and a speech of singular felicity and power. He defended himself against the charge of heresy; described his own former fiery zeal against the Christians; his conversion and divine commission, and the consequent hatred of the Jews. Festus believed that long and enthusiastic study, on mysterious themes, had turned Paul's brain. Agrippa, a Jew, who could at least accept the premises which Paul laid down, either sincerely or in the way of compliment, declared that he felt almost constrained to yield to the Apostle's conclusion. "Almost thou persuadest me to be a Christian," was his declaration. He subsequently declared that St. Paul might have been set at liberty if he had not appealed unto Cæsar. (Acts, xxvi.)

The voyage of Paul the prisoner to Italy was replete with striking incidents. My plan constrains me to omit all notice of this memorable voyage, and to resume in the next lecture the history of St. Paul on his arrival at Puteoli.

In the incidents which we have so rapidly surveyed, we have a remarkable exhibition in the Jews of malignant, fanatical, persecuting zeal; and an equally striking exemplification in St. Paul of the manner in which it should be met. It is vindictive and wicked persecution encountering holy and loving zeal.

This spirit of fanatical and vindictive persecution

is a fearful and monstrous manifestation of our fallen nature. At the first view it seems simply an insane, absurd, illogical depravity. Men say to us, "We have the truth of God. You are in error. You hold and propagate wrong views of God and right and duty. They will ruin your soul and other souls." What in this state of things should be their feeling toward us? It should, evidently, be affectionate interest. What should be their conduct? A loving effort to win us to the truth. What should be their conduct and their feeling if they fail? Profound pity, continued kindness, and still hopeful prayer. This is the legitimate and ordinary working of holiness in possession of the truth. It was the spirit and conduct manifested by St. Paul.

But instead of this loving spirit, false, fiery, fanatical, persecuting zeal exhibits perhaps the most deadly and awful hatred that ever takes possession, or can take possession, of a being who has not yet become a fiend.

It is a strange and hideous manifestation of human depravity. We shudder as we hear it howling about St. Paul in the daytime, as he stands in the midst of the infuriated rabble in the court of the Gentiles, and among the vindictive doctors of the Sanhedrim, or as we see it in the midnight conclave of forty Jews, who bind themselves by awful imprecations not to eat or drink until they shall have slain the Apostle. As this spirit is hideous in its full development, so it is repulsive in every form and degree of its manifestation.

Yet we must not forget that it arises from the perversion of the highest part of our nature, conscience. The true work of conscience is to reprove personal sins. Its right action is within. It is not to be wounded by the sins of others. Love may suffer because of them, and conscience prompt love to work for their removal and their forgiveness. Conscience, guided by love, takes truth and goes forth to win others by it away from sin, and its companion sorrow, and its doom, death. If it fails, it is not turned into hatred. If it withdraws, it is because it has ceased to hope. It does not scowl, but it weeps when it retires.

But in the case of fanatical and persecuting zeal, conscience performs a different function. Not being an enlightened and sanctified conscience, it does not perform its appropriate work. It does not act on personal sins. It is wounded by the sins and unbeliefs of others. It works itself out from under the mountain load of its own iniquities, by which it might be crushed into humility, and be made to bleed in contrition, and it rushes against the sins of others, and is thus maddened into pride and resentment and fierce self-assertion, which it sanctifies with the holy name of zeal. In this misdirection of a perverted conscience, it does not abandon love, for love was never with it; but it takes with it the whole dread sisterhood of the malignant passions, and it is these which it drives on to the work of converting, coercing, persecuting, and destroying. The true definition of fanatical persecution then seems to be that it is *a perverted conscience employing hatred to do the work which love alone can do.* Then it is a Jehu in his chariot, from whom not alone the enemies, but the friends of God must flee if they would live. And that which is most awful in this portentous wickedness is that it considers itself eminently righteous. Never are the malignant passions so horrible as when driven on by conscience. When men persuade themselves that it is their duty to be vindictive, to let loose their evil passions, to hate, and persecute, and torture, then will there be such fiendish developments of humanity as are never elsewhere witnessed.

It is to be observed that it is not often the truth which is thus used in the service of persecuting zeal; but it is some perversion of truth, or half truth, or single truths separated from those, without which they are errors; or it is simple error and falsehood which are thus employed. Holy truth refuses to be used except by holy love. The spear of Gabriel cannot be fitted to the hand of Lucifer. This persecuting fanaticism is Phariseeism, destroying the spirit of the law by the letter, and imposing upon men human traditions in the place of divine laws. It is Judaism, ignorant of the spirit and yet clinging to the forms of an abrogated economy. It is Mohammedanism, with its false prophet, its flaming sword, and its impure heaven. It is the zeal of the Jews that assailed Paul in the Temple, and raged around him in the Sanhedrim. It is the zeal of the Inquisition, the zeal of Alva, the zeal of Philip of Spain and Louis XIV. of France, the zeal of those who followed the saints of Savoy with fire and sword to their mountain fastnesses, and drove the Huguenots, noble martyrs and confessors, into the wild glens of the Cevennes.

"Oh, my soul, come not into their secret: unto their assembly mine honor be not thou united." It is an utterly hateful and horrible spirit. Let us be far from it. There is no danger that Protestant Christians should exhibit it in its full development. But it has its beginnings and its partial manifestations in all hearts and in all churches. It is to be found in its germ in all those manifestations of zeal in which the consciences of the righteous are more troubled by the sins of others than by their own. It is seen wherever there is excessive zeal in imposing particular dogmas upon others, and in making individual convictions of duty the standard for the churches, rather than by a loving effort to develop holiness of heart and life in others, chiefly by the beautiful and winning exhibition of it in themselves. Man is capable of such singular contradictions and inconsistencies, that we may not, perhaps, say that he who has most of truth will manifest the most of love; but we may say that he ought to do so, and may add, that he who has the most of love will be *likely* to learn the most truth; and that when he shows himself not lovingly zealous, but fanatically intolerant and persecuting in behalf of any doctrine, it is likely to prove either a complete error or but a partial truth.

St. Paul's conduct when exposed to this fiery fanaticism teaches us in what spirit and with what holy prudence it should be met. Nothing can be more calculated to stir up a spirit of resentment and indignation. However these may have been excited, and however just they might have been, they were overcome by love and holy zeal for his deluded brethren in the flesh. Very touching is the declaration which he made to his brethren whom he called together at Rome: "Not that I have aught to accuse my nation of." To us it seems as if there were much cause to accuse them; but *he*, remembering his journey to

Damascus, and how recently he had shared their views and feelings, felt that it was not for *him* to accuse his nation, although they had thirsted for his blood, and driven him to Rome in chains. In all his speeches there are no words of denunciation. He vindicates himself. He endeavors to convince and propitiate his enemies, in order that he may present to them the hope of Israel, and persuade them to accept the great salvation. And when it becomes evident that his words will be unavailing, he bows to the storm, and remembering the Master's assurance that he must testify of him at Rome, avails himself of the facilities which providence supplied to enable him to escape from their hands.

How beautiful in contrast to the persecuting zeal of the Jews is the loving zeal of Paul for his persecutors!

We shall miss the moral of this instructive history if we learn only to abhor the one, and do not learn to love and imitate the other.

LECTURE III.

ST. PAUL'S JOURNEY TO ROME FROM PUTEOLI.

And from thence we fetched a compass, and came to Rhegium: and after one day the south wind blew, and we came to Puteoli:
Where we found brethren, and were desired to tarry with them seven days; and so we went toward Rome.
And from thence, when the brethren heard of us, they came to meet us as far as Appii Forum, and the Three Taverns; whom, when Paul saw, he thanked God and took courage.
And when we came to Rome, the centurion delivered the prisoners to the captain of the guard; but Paul was suffered to dwell by himself with a soldier that kept him.—ACTS, xxviii. 13-16.

RESCUED from shipwreck, and beaten by storms, Paul at length reached Italy. At no part of that stormy voyage could he have doubted that he would be saved; for the Lord had appeared to him when a prisoner in the castle of Antonia, with the assurance that he should testify of him at Rome; and again, at the height of the storm, before his shipwreck upon the island of Melita, (now Malta,) he had repeated the assurance: "Fear not; thou must stand before Cæsar."

The ship called Castor and Pollux, the names of the saviors of Rome, and the patrons of sailors, anchored at Puteoli, (now Pozzuoli, near Baii.) Puteoli divided, at that time, with Ostia the commerce of the sea, between Rome and the provinces. It was the chief port of the corn vessels of Alexandria. The amount of corn transmitted from Egypt to Italy at this period was immense. The commerce of Puteoli was then so large that an English writer calls it "the Liverpool of Italy."

When St. Paul rounded the promontory of Minerva, at the southeastern limit of the Bay of Naples, a scene of unparalleled loveliness must have burst upon his view. The admiration of the world, in our day, for its natural charms and its picturesque ruins, its shores were then everywhere alive with prosperous cities and villages; and imperial and patrician magnificence had covered the whole of the adjoining beautiful landscape of the bay, from the promontory of Minerva to that of Misenum, with villas, gardens, and vineyards. Opposite the promontory, as he entered the bay, slept the Isle of Capri, so softly peaceful and lovely under its veil of blue, that it would seem as if the imperial monster, Tiberius, must have started back with remorse as he approached it with the view of making it the scene of his hideous vices. Vesuvius, not then furrowed and scarred with lava, but green and laughing with vineyards, rose in perfect symmetry from a sea and against a sky whose pure and brilliant tints are all that time and desolation have not stained or dimmed, and formed an appropriate background to the matchless scene. Herculaneum and Pompeii slept, unconscious of danger, nestled as for protection at his giant feet. Little could St. Paul then imagine that Drusilla, who, with Felix, had heard him reason of righteousness, and continence, and judgment to come, at Cæsarea, would, in a few years, perish with the child born from her adulterous marriage with Felix, under a fire-storm like that which overwhelmed Sodom and Gomorrah, and whose coming perhaps awakened with horror the memory of the solemn warnings of the Apostle!

As the ship proceeded up the bay to Misenum, St. Paul might have discerned the imperial fleet, which was habitually stationed in that harbor, and which the younger Pliny commanded at the period of the eruption of Vesuvius. Nearing the lovely and quiet cove at the recess of the bay, between Baii and Puteoli, he obtained a closer view of that portion of the coast which was the summer resort of patricians of the higher rank, and hence was most magnificent and gay. A lettered man, Paul was familiar no doubt with some of the incidents of which this region had been the scene. As they approached the harbor, it might be told to him how that here the aged and invalid Augustus, cruising in the bay for health, was recognized by the sailors of an Alexandrian cornship, like that in which he sailed, and how they brought out garlands and incense, paying to him divine honors, and attributing to him their prosperous voyage; and how the dying mortal, pleased to be called a god, distributed to them profuse gold for their impious flattery. Another might point out to him the remains upon the shore of that useless and wondrous floating bridge, nearly a league in length, with its pavements, and fountains, and works of art, which the mad Caligula constructed across the bay, over which he rode in the chariot rifled from the tomb of Alexander, in the character of a conquering imperator; and from which, when he returned at night— night converted into day by innumerable torches— drunk with cruelty and wine, he remorselessly consigned a multitude of his attendants, guiltless victims of his drunken frenzy, to the sea. Another, with bated breath, might point out to him Bauli, where the then reigning Nero, only two years before, had laid the plot for the murder of his mother Agrippina. As he entered the mole, massive ruins of which still remain, the gay yachts of the patricians would multiply around him; and there upon the seashore he would learn that the vast pile which hung over the sea, and whose ruins still remain, once belonged to Julius Cæsar; and that on the slope of the hill above was the villa of Cicero, where, as he might remember or be told, the Dictator paid a visit of state, accompanied with six thousand soldiers, in order to intimidate or seduce the vain and vacillating statesman, who was too patriotic to approve, and too timid or politic to resist his guilty ambition. There also, in the city, he would discern the conspicuous temple of the Egyptian deity Serapis, some of whose columns the tourist still sees standing in the midst of the surrounding desolation.

What were the emotions of the solitary prisoner Paul, as he prepared to set his foot upon the Italian shore, in the midst of the rude crowds that throng the quays of a seaport city? It is no disparagement to him, or to the grace that was with him, to suppose that they may have been sad. He was approaching the city which dominated over the nations. He saw thus far off evidences of its unparalleled magnificence and power. He knew that heathenism occupied at Rome a more stable throne than that of the Cæsars. Its sway was over the soul. It held Cæsars and subjects in subjection alike by their consciences and their fears, and by appeals to their passions and their lusts. It was tolerant of all idolatries, but vindictive toward true religion. It admitted the sensual divinities of Egypt and the abominable idolatries of Syria, while it denounced

Judaism as a malignant superstition, the spirit of which was hatred to man and disloyalty to the empire. It defamed Christianity as impure, while it multiplied temples to Venus, and presented such "gods as guilt makes welcome," whose chief attributes were lust, selfishness, hatred, and cruelty. And the work of Paul was—what? To carry into such a scene the simple, holy, self-denying religion of the Lord Jesus Christ. That religion could not take its place by the side of the thousand idolatries that prevailed at Rome. By its very nature it claimed all men, and excluded as false, impious, degrading, and ruinous, all idolatries. Its promulgation would involve at once bitter wrath and scorn, and at length persecution, torture, death. And the agency by which it was to be accomplished was—the foolishness of preaching! The story of the cross and resurrection, as supplying the antidote and atonement for sin, and the triumph over death—this story with the promised presence of the Holy Spirit—this was his instrument. Men without position, influence, or power,—lowly men for the most part and unlearned,—were thus to propagate a religion, against which all the passions, vices, associations, and present interests of the world would be arrayed. These were their arts and these their arms,—no other and no more! Well might it seem to mere human judgment, weighing human forces, a wild and impracticable scheme!

It would not have been surprising, therefore, if at such a moment, in contemplating his journey to Rome, however unshaken his faith and fidelity and resolutions, a deep depression had settled upon his soul. We infer that there had been something of this feeling previous to his meeting of the brethren at the Appii Forum and the Three Taverns, from the fact that when he saw them he thanked God and *took courage.* The expression would seem to imply a previous sinking of his heart. All that we know of the quick, sensitive, affectionate, all-alive, and impressible character of Paul, leads us to the inference that his heart must have been heavy. He was affectionate and craved affection, and he had been long alone, in scenes of peril and suffering, without Christian sympathy or aid. He longed for and loved his brethren according to the flesh; and yet only as an outcast, and a prisoner in chains, could he escape assassination at their hands. He had passed through toils, imprisonments, persecutions, defamations, scourgings, and perils without number. He was bound with a chain to a soldier that kept him. We must suppose him almost more than human, if, at that moment, he did not wish at least that it had been the Master's will to release him and send him to his rest. But he did not, like Moses, beg to be released. His heroic faith and patience, his unfailing love and unfaltering zeal appear all the more remarkable when we consider the position in which he was placed, and take the measure of the obstacles which they overcame. And this is precisely the work of grace—the triumph of God's strength in the midst of human weakness, and the emergence of God's joy from the midst of human sorrow. The contemplation of Paul, a slight, worn, and weary man in chains, stepping from the ship Castor and Pollux on the crowded quay of Puteoli, testifies in the most striking way, that not by power nor might, but by the Spirit of the Lord, does God confound the mighty. We walk amid the ruins of that mighty empire; but the kingdom which Paul planted is spreading over the world, and will at last become the everlasting kingdom of righteousness and peace which shall cover all the earth. No event in the annals of Rome at that period, whether it were the march of armies, or the wild, gigantic crimes of Nero, are to be compared in significance and importance to the landing of that chained and tempest-tossed captive at the port of Puteoli.

But whatever may have been his feelings before landing, doubtless his heart was reassured when the brethren met him and urged him to remain seven days. Julius acceded to their request. The news of Paul's arrival was sent to the brethren at Rome. They must have been to him days of bodily and spiritual refreshment, which fitted him for his journey and his work.

St. Paul's journey to Rome is in part indicated in the Acts of the Apostles, and can with great probability be conjectured as a whole. He probably struck the great Appian Way, which reached from Rome to Brundusium—the queen of roads, as a Roman poet calls it,—at Capua. There his eye rested on that colossal amphitheater, which must have been to him an overwhelming demonstration of the truth of his representations of the cruelty and brutality of man, which he had appropriately addressed to the Romans. The first part of the journey to Cumæ, the modern traveler visits with great interest, as the scene of the early mythology of Italy and of Virgil's poetical conceptions of the other world. Capua was then a magnificent city, basking in the sunshine of imperial favor. From Capua to Terracina, a distance of seventy miles, the way was strewn with historic memories, the localities of which were no doubt pointed out to Paul by the courteous Julius. As the road skirted the Bay of Formiæ, with its villas on the sloping hills, that of Cicero would be pointed out, and the scene depicted in which the bewildered statesman, agitated by conflicting purposes, borne in his lectica, or coach, was met and murdered by assassins, the emissaries of Mark Antony. From Terracina, the great Campagna, with the Pontine Marshes immediately below, spread out to the blue Alban hills. Whether the transit from this point across the unwholesome marsh to the Appii Forum was made upon the road or upon the canal which was cut by Augustus with a view to drain it, does not appear. But on his arrival at the latter place, an incident occurred which is one of the most touching in the eventful life of Paul.

In the itineries which remain, we find enumerated as post stations on the Appian Way from Rome, Aricia, the Three Taverns, and the Appii Forum. The Appii Forum was the northern termination of the canal, and 43 miles from Rome. Horace describes it as a low place filled with bargemen and tavern-keepers. It was at this distance from Rome that Christian brethren and friends, who had heard of his arrival at Puteoli, came out to meet him. No doubt some of those whom the Apostle names in the closing chapter of the Epistle to the Romans, as his fellow-helpers, his well-beloved and honored disciples and friends, were among the number. We can scarcely suppose Aquila and Priscilla to have been absent. Behold how these Christians love one another! We seem to recall the meeting and the greeting in that rude scene. The weary Apostle, forgetting the heavy chain and the soldier to whom he was perpetually bound, as to a body of death; the sorrow of the brethren to see their beloved and holy teacher, worthy of all honor, as a prisoner on his way to trial; the warm expressions and the animated gestures of sympathy and affection which belong to the inhabitants of these Southern lands; the gratitude and animation of the Apostle; the rapid and eager question and reply concerning mutual Christian friends and the interests of their loved Master's kingdom; Paul's prayer with the brethren, in the open air, as before at Miletus, where he parted with the elders, in which he could now, indeed, lift up his free heart, but not his manacled hand, to Heaven; and the wonder, not perhaps unmixed with scorn and jeer of the attendants and of the soldier to whom Paul was chained, and of the rude, staring multitude around them,—we see it all. Oh! when Christian brethren were so few, in the midst of a world lying in wickedness, how precious to both parties must have been that meeting on the confines of the Pontine Marshes! It is only in foreign missionary fields of labor, where the disciples of Christ are as a handful of corn upon the top of the mountains, that the affection, the joy, the sorrow, the elevation, the consolation, the fervent prayers and the tearful praises of that meeting can be realized.

At a distance of ten miles farther, at the "Three Taverns," St. Paul was welcomed by another group of brethren. Three roads met at this point, and hence perhaps the name and thing—"The Three Taverns." The place subsequently became, in consequence of the celebrity acquired by the incident here mentioned, a flourishing city and the seat of an Episcopate, the records of which reach to the ninth century. When Paul saw the brethren, he thanked God and took courage.

From that point the interest of the journey must have increased, and his mind must have been kept upon the alert by converse with his friends, and by the indications everywhere multiplying that he was approaching the capital of the world. The beautiful blue Alban range of hills, with its then conspicuous Temple of Jupiter upon Monte Cavo, in the spot now disfigured by the hideous monastery of the Passionists, rose before him, as the road wound around its southern slope, which was covered with villas, to the point now called Albano. From that position, not too high or distant for the view to be intelligible, he gazed upon a scene of beauty rarely surpassed, and upon the signs and evidences of power concentrated at its imperial seat, never before or since, in the history of nations, equaled. The vast Campagna, even now singularly and mysteriously lovely in its desolation, was then bright and fresh in all the charms which cultivation, luxury, and art could add to those of nature. It was a scene of solid, palatial villas, of slighter "houses of pleasure," as they were called, of temples and converging roads, and stately, far-stretching aqueducts, in the midst of meadows and vineyards and gardens. It must have been then an era in any man's life when he first saw Rome in her glory, as it is now when he first sees her in her desolation.

The first distinct point at which the city would plainly appear, and at which a traveler would naturally pause, was that at which the lofty monument of Pompey, erected by his widow, stood, as its stripped and desolate shaft now stands. At his left he would see the villa of the great triumvir, whose ruins can still be traced, transformed into an imperial summer residence. Before him the road would be seen to lie straight as an arrow,—as the same road recently opened can still be seen,—to its entrance into the city at the Porta Capena. But how changed its aspect from then to now! Now a street of scattered, broken tombs; then the most thronged and splendid avenue to a city of probably two millions of inhabitants, through fifteen miles of intervening villas and gardens, which were themselves almost a continuous city, in the midst of groves and vineyards. The custom of lining the main avenues to their city with tombs, which was adopted by the Romans, did not, in their external aspect at least, render them gloomy and repulsive. The tombs were structures of the utmost elegance and beauty. The ingenuity of architects was taxed to make them graceful and pleasing. They were adorned with busts and statues of the departed. Upon the slopes of those tombs which were fashioned after the Etruscan manner, trees and parterres of flowers were planted. As a mere method of giving beauty to an avenue which constituted the approach to a great city, nothing so effective could have been devised. As they are reproduced in the engravings of Canina, it is evident that the intermixture of the vast Etruscan mound-like tombs, the graceful Grecian miniature temples, the round Roman sepulchers, like that of Cecilia Metella, the square altars, the massive simple sarcophagi, like that of Scipio,

ST. PAUL IN ROME.

interspersed with innumerable columns and niches for busts and statues, must have presented an avenue of architectural variety and beauty never elsewhere equaled. Between the tombs, as they passed, the travelers must have been constantly regaled with the view of the villas and gardens that were placed behind them. The city, from the slope of the Alban hills, might have been distinctly seen; and though wanting in those picturesque spires and campaniles and those impressive domes which give so much effect to modern cities, it must have had more than a compensation in the gleaming roofs of bronze, which covered many of the loftier edifices, and in those numerous and splendid colonnades and porticoes, than which nothing gives greater architectural pomp and majesty to a city. The uplifted Palatine hill, with its far-stretching line of palaces, its white gleaming temple of Apollo, and its innumerable porticoes and colonnades, the theater and portico of Pompey, the portico of Octavia, the mausoleum of Augustus with its gardens, and high eminent over all the city the arx of the steep Capitol hill, and the resplendent temple of Jupiter Capitolinus. What a scene of unequaled magnificence it must have been! The one dome of the Pantheon could scarcely have been overlooked, and the eyes of Paul no doubt rested upon that shining heathen bronze, which has since been converted into the sacred baldachino of St. Peter's and the orthodox cannon of St. Angelo.

In the representation of our Lord's temptation by Satan, in the Paradise Regained, He is made to gaze in vision upon imperial Rome. We may well conceive that Milton had this point of view in mind as that from which the magnificent spectacle was seen. If we except the poetical license of "turrets and glittering spires," the description is as literally accurate as it is gorgeously beautiful.

> "The city which thou seest, no other deem
> Than great and glorious Rome, Queen of the Earth,
> So far renowned, and with the spoils enriched
> Of nations; there the Capitol thou seest
> Above the rest lifting his stately head
> On the Tarpeian rock, her citadel
> Impregnable; and there Mount Palatine
> The imperial palace, compass huge and high
> The structure, skill of noblest architects,
> With gilded battlements, conspicuous far,
> Turrets, and terraces, and glittering spires;
> Many a fair edifice besides, more like
> Houses of gods, so well I have disposed
> My aery microscope, thou may'st behold
> Outside and inside both, pillars and roofs,
> Carved work, the hand of famed artificers,
> In cedar, marble, ivory, and gold.
> Thence to the gates cast round thine eye, and see
> What conflux issuing forth, or entering in;
> Prætors, Proconsuls to their provinces
> Hasting, or on return, in robes of state,
> Lictors and rods, the ensigns of their power,
> Legions and cohorts, turms of horse and wings;
> Or embassies from regions far remote,
> In various habits, on the Appian road,
> Or on the Emilian; some from farthest south,
> Syene, and where the shadow both way falls.
> Meroe, Nilotic isle; and, more to west,
> The realm of Bocchus to the Black-moor sea,
> From the Asian kings, and Parthian, among these;
> From India, and the Golden Chersonese,
> And utmost Indian isle, Taprobane,
> Dark faces with white silken turbans wreathed;
> From Gallia, Gades, and the British west;
> Germans, and Scythians, and Sarmatians, north,
> Beyond Danubius to the Tauric pool.

> All nations now to Rome obedience pay;
> To Rome's great emperor, whose wide domain,
> In ample territory, wealth, and power,
> Civility of manners, arts, and arms,
> And long renown, thou justly may prefer."

This custom of placing tombs upon a gay and crowded avenue, and of making them *riant* and graceful, rather than solemn and impressive, seems strange and repulsive to our Christian sentiment. We seek to bury the dead apart from the living, in scenes which human noises do not reach, and where only the voices of falling waters, and rustling leaves, and singing birds are heard. And this difference of sentiment and feeling has its sufficient reason in the far different views of the other world entertained by the pagan and the Christian. To the Roman, death was simply gloomy. In this life only was the good and the joyful certainly to be found. To the multitude the future world was a dim, chill land of restless ghosts, in the torture of Tartarus, or the dull peace of Elysium. To the cultivated mind it was, as to Cæsar, nothingness; or, as to Cicero, a thing of hope and yet of doubt. Hence prayers and offerings to the gods were only supplications and bribes, as to beings moved by human motives, for long life, and health, and wealth, and pleasure. To live here on earth, in the midst of earthly good, secure from want and care, was their highest idea of well-being. Their loftiest philosophy had no better consolation than the mocking lie: "The sorrows and pains of life are nothing if you will only think so!" Hence they clung to life. They could not bear to be torn away from their human haunts, and be forgotten. They would still live in memory by their presence in busts and statues in their olden homes. Hence these were placed, together with their family records, in the "*tabulinum,*" one of the most conspicuous portions of their dwellings. Hence also their tombs must be upon the public ways, that old friends might see and remember them every day; and that they might have a feeling before they died, that their life was in this way, in some sort, protracted among them. These great pompous sepulchers then,—what were they all to Paul but gigantic characters stretching over the Campagna, and writing the sad record, which in its defacement we still can trace, "*No joy and no sure hope beyond the tomb!*" But the children of the resurrection, whose bodies rest, not in despair but hope, desire not that their flesh should be laid in cold marble, or their ashes gathered in unperishable urns, amid the noise and tumult of our poor earthly life, but, remembering the sublime declaration, "the seed is not quickened except it die," they desire to place the immortal body safely in the earth, the mother of its second glorious birth, apart from the noise of cities, in a peaceful *campo santo,* circled by silence, and calm and sweet with sober beauty. It is only a true Christian sentiment which thus honors and reverences the body, which, "sown in weakness," is to be "raised in power." Only a false system, which gives up the bodies of the saved to ages of purgatorial torment, could produce that horror and shrinking from the dear dead, which leads wives and husbands, parents and children, to allow their departed loved ones to be carried to the tomb, not with joyful resurrection anthems, but with most mournful dirges, in which there is no undertone of hope, and to be borne away from them by black-robed officials and hired Cappucini, under grim death's-head effigies, to the church, thence to be carried out at midnight, without a friend, and to be thrust naked into a common receptacle of the decaying dead, to be consumed by lime more rapidly than by nature's process of decay. In that stately street of tombs, Paul could see the Roman's joyless heathenism, as in these misnamed "*Campi Santi,*"—bare stone holes,—we read the perverted Christianity of the Romanist.

It is an interesting thought to us, that Paul's eye must have rapidly glanced, as he passed by, at some of those epitaphs which we now read in the Hall of Inscriptions, in the Vatican. How exceeding sad they sometimes are! How affectingly they portray the "sorrow without hope" of heathen bereavement! Two of these epitaphs which I recently saw in the Roman burial-ground at Arles, in France, will express the two feelings that generally pervade them all. The one, in its cold and sharp conciseness, sounds like hard despair; the other is the wail of inconsolable maternal grief. The one reads thus: "*Fui. Non sum. Estis. Non eritis. Nemo immortalis.*" "I was. I am not. Thou art. Thou wilt not be. No one is immortal." The other exclaims: "Oh grief! what bitter tears have watered the sepulcher where the ashes of Lucina lie,—Lucina, the joy of her mother, and the sweet flower of her old age. Would that the gods might permit her to return to life, that she might know how great is my affliction. She lived 27 years, 10 months, and 13 days. I, Parthenoppe, her unhappy mother, have erected to her this monument." In view of the spiritual darkness and destitution of the souls of the Romans, thus exhibited in their pompous monuments, we may well suppose that the magnificence of Rome impressed Paul more with pity than with awe. To them were applicable the words of the Master: "Thou sayest that thou art rich and increased in goods and have need of nothing; and knowest not that thou art wretched, and miserable, and poor, and blind, and naked." The pomp of their sepulchers was a symbol of their entire condition. It was splendor shrouding death!

If St. Paul approached the Porta Capena at the close of the day, he would find it a scene of gayety and bustle. It was the hour, as that was the locality, in which the patricians and fashionables of Rome—as now upon the Pincian hill—took their walk or drive. As he passed under the arch, the Apostle could scarcely have avoided meditating upon the streams of human life that had for centuries been flowing through it, to and from the most distant regions of the earth. Victorious generals and emperors with their legions, and captives, and spoils, pacing in stately and slow magnificence, from morning until evening; ambassadors, and kings, the guests of the empire, from beyond the Euphrates, on the east, to Gaul and Britain, on the west; the representatives of every nationality from every class of life; the funereal pomps of Cæsars and patricians,—what sorrows, what hopes, what pride, what despair, what passion, what vice, what glory, and what shame had poured for centuries through that avenue as through a channel, a noisy, foaming, rapid tide of life, rushing on to the great sea of death!

And now within the city, and leaving the crowded Aventine hill on the left, and passing between the Cælian and the southern portion of the Palatine hill, he emerges on the ridge *Velia,* where the arch of Titus was subsequently built; and the famous Forum, the very beating heart of Rome, with all its architectural magnificence is before him! On the left, the Palatine hill, with its connected imperial palaces and temples around its entire circuit, and covering with their dependent gardens and areas all its surface. In the Forum itself, the immense basilica Julia, commenced by Cæsar and completed by Augustus, and the opposite, almost equal basilica Æmilia, and between them, and above and below them, temples, porticoes, altars, and rostra; and above, dominating over all, on the abrupt high hill of the Capitol, the resplendent temple of Jupiter Capitolinus—all in its unparalleled magnificence, burst upon the view of Paul the prisoner!

But he was not permitted long to gaze. Julius transferred his prisoner to the charge of the Prætorian prefect. It has been a question whether the captain of the guard, as the Prætorian prefect is called in the Acts of the Apostles, when Paul was delivered to him, transferred him to the Prætorian camp without the walls, or to the *Prætorium* connected with the palace. The latter appears to me the much more probable opinion. The Prætorian cohort was originally the personal guard, the body guard in modern phrase, of the emperor; and the quarters were within the palace, or at the entrance of the palace, in a barrack called the Prætorium. Under Tiberius, the Prætorian soldiers were much more numerous than under Augustus, and became, instead of a body guard to the emperor, rather for state than for defense, the instrument of the tyrant for holding the city in subjection, and preserving him from their violence and revenge. It was then that the camp of the Prætorians was placed beyond the walls, by the advice and under the direction of Sejanus, then the Prætorian prefect, and the detestable minister of all the cruelties of the suspicious despot. But his headquarters were still at the palace, and a sufficient number of soldiers were retained there for the imperial dignity and protection.

The office of Prætorian prefect at the date of Paul's entrance into Rome was held by the celebrated Burrus. He was one of the few characters in whom, during this period, we can find anything to praise. It was due to him and the philosopher Seneca, who had been Nero's tutor, who were his chief ministers and advisers, that the early part of the reign of Nero was as mild and just as his private life was contemptible and atrocious. We may account for the kind treatment which St. Paul received, and for the privilege which he enjoyed of living in his own hired house, to the personal character of Burrus.

If then St. Paul was transferred to the *Prætorium* of the palace, as we can scarcely doubt, then we are able, with great probability, to fix its precise position. At the foot of the hill, directly beneath the site of the palaces of Augustus and Tiberius, and connected with them, there has been uncovered within a few years a portion of what antiquarians generally agree in considering the quarters of the *Prætorium* of the palace. One of its porticoes has been reconstructed in part, from the fragments of the former portico, in order to show its original form. Everything connected with it is similar to the Prætorium disclosed at Pompeii, and at other places, and seems to have been constructed with the magnificence appropriate to its imperial use. That which gives it a peculiar interest, and enables us, as it were, to reproduce the scene of Paul's introduction to these quarters, is the fact that on the plaster of the walls there remain the names of several soldiers, some rudely scratched as by an illiterate hand, and others more carefully cut out in larger letters. We fancy that we can see one of these idle soldiers while on guard thus whiling away his time, turning to look, and placing himself suddenly in position in the soldier's attitude, with his arms in hand, as the centurion arrives with his prisoner and his little squad of military attendants, and his group of Christian friends, and the message was sent up to Burrus for direction as to the disposition to be made of the prisoner. Who knows, I said to myself, as I visited the scene, but that as he sat upon the stone benches of the barracks, waiting to hear whether he was to be cast into prison, or whether his friends might be permitted to receive him with the Roman soldier to whom he was chained,—who knows but St. Paul's eye may have wandered vaguely over these very scrawls which we now see!

"Paul was permitted to dwell by himself with a soldier that kept him!" "A soldier that kept him!" How suggestive is this record! It was in chains that St. Paul preached the free and emancipating Gospel. It was a captive at Rome that proclaimed liberty to those that bound him. At his subsequent visit to Rome, he writes to Timothy that he suffers as an evil-doer even unto bonds; but he adds, by a sublime and unselfish turn of thought, "the word of God is not bound." In the subterranean of the Church of Santa Maria via Lata, which is said to have been Paul's hired house, on the pillar to which St. Paul is said to have been chained, these words *"the word of God is not bound"* are engraved. If Paul had been chained to that pillar, it would have been an apt and most expressive thing to have placed upon it the words, "the word of God is not bound;" but even then it would have been a singular record for that church to make, which so carefully and jealously strives to bind that Word. Yet if these words are to be set up anywhere by the Church of Rome, it is certainly in keeping that they should be engraved in a dark crypt of a church, which is open but once a year, and seen only by a few. To have placed these words in large gilt capitals upon the forefront of St. Peter's and St. Paul's, and over the few pulpits from which the year's accumulated dust is swept away on Passion Week, would not have been so appropriate.

And yet with St. Paul preaching it in bonds, the Word of God was not bound. Its sound has gone into all the world. It is thus through, and in connection with, the sufferings of the preachers and the churches, that the Word from the beginning has gone forth with the most penetrating and holy power. And this is after the manner of the Master. He was bound to the accursed tree, but the words which he then uttered have gone forth through the world and through all ages; and that dying testimony has been the world's life and salvation. St. Paul's bonds turned out to the furtherance of the Gospel; for they were known in all the Prætorium, and in all other places. And when St. Paul reminds the Thessalonians that they received the Word in much affliction, and with joy of the Holy Ghost, (a divine and singular conjunction!) then he adds, "from you *sounded out the Word of the Lord*, in Macedonia and Achaia and in every place!" The Word of God is not bound, but set free by the sufferings of its teachers and preachers. In all straits and afflictions they feel anew its power, and give it forth more fully, and their faith and prayer wins to it the demonstration of the Spirit. That Word, once in the world, like light, its emblem, cannot be bound. It is our joy and comfort to believe that it will reach souls in many places whence the effort is made to keep it out. Into the dark caverns of unbelief a single ray will often penetrate, and reveal to the soul its gloom and loss, at the same time that it tells of the radiant source from which it comes. Even in churches that keep out this pure light, or admit it only through stained mediæval glass, it will still come in; and however the name and the work of Christ whom Paul preached, is covered and muffled and subordinated, there is in that all-saving name such an omnipotence of love, that it will be to thousands, even thus in its hindered power, the light of life. The Word of God is not and cannot be bound.

Paul's manacled hand pointing to the crucified and bleeding Jesus! What an affecting demonstration is this, that it is *liberty and joy and peace of soul*, which it is the great gift of the Gospel to bestow, and not outward happiness and prosperity and gain! This is the Gospel, the good news to those who need it. It is joy in sorrow. It is comfort in affliction. It is liberty in bonds. It is peace in tumult. It is rejoicing in tribulation. Hence it has been best proclaimed from the midst of the sufferings which it overcomes. The Saviour announces it in sorrow and humiliation, and seals it with his blood upon the cross. The church testifies of it in the wilderness. The witnesses prophesy it in sackcloth. And it is best that we should be in such a world, while with a nature only sanctified in part, we are struggling for spiritual purity and peace. Prosperity and joy uninterrupted would foster all our earthliness and draw our hearts from heaven and the holiness without which it cannot be entered. Hence our state is mixed, and though God gives us many joys, and would give us more but for his love, it is in the fullness of his love that he himself died upon the cross, and often sends his ministering servants forth to sow in sorrow, that they who sow and they who reap may rejoice together with exceeding joy. Then is Paul far above our pity when he enters Rome in bonds, and points, with a manacled hand, to his crucified Redeemer!

LECTURE IV.

ST. PAUL AND THE JEWS IN ROME.

And it came to pass, that after three days Paul called the chief of the Jews together: and when they were come together, he said unto them, Men and brethren, though I have committed nothing against the people, or customs of our fathers, yet was I delivered prisoner from Jerusalem into the hands of the Romans.

Who, when they had examined me, would have let me go, because there was no cause of death in me.

But when the Jews spake against it, I was constrained to appeal unto Cæsar; not that I had aught to accuse my nation of.

For this cause therefore have I called for you, to see you, and to speak with you: because that for the hope of Israel I am bound with this chain.

And they said unto him, We neither received letters out of Judea concerning thee, neither any of the brethren that came showed or spake any harm of thee.

But we desire to hear of thee what thou thinkest: for as concerning this sect, we know that everywhere it is spoken against.

And when they had appointed him a day, there came many to him into his lodging; to whom he expounded and testified the kingdom of God, persuading them concerning Jesus, both out of the law of Moses, and out of the prophets, from morning till evening.

And some believed the things which were spoken, and some believed not.

And when they agreed not among themselves, they departed, after that Paul had spoken one word, Well spake the Holy Ghost by Esaias the prophet unto our fathers,

Saying, Go unto this people, and say, Hearing ye shall hear, and shall not understand; and seeing ye shall see, and not perceive:

For the heart of this people is waxed gross, and their ears are dull of hearing, and their eyes have they closed; lest they should see with

their eyes, and hear with their ears, and understand with their heart, and should be converted, and I should heal them.
Be it known therefore unto you, that the salvation of God is sent unto the Gentiles, and that they will hear it.—ACTS, xxviii. 17–28.

THE profound interest of St. Paul in his countrymen is seen in the fact, that after he had been in Rome but three days, he sent for the chief of the Jews, to speak to them and explain to them the circumstances of his arrest. Abstaining from all crimination of his brethren at Jerusalem, he declared: "For the hope of Israel I am bound with this chain." "*This chain,*"—doubtless the Apostle lifted it as he spake.

His brethren declared that they had received no letters from Judea concerning him; and that no Jews coming from there had showed or spoken any harm of him. But they desired to hear somewhat of his doctrine; which they candidly declared to him was everywhere "spoken against."

A day was appointed for this purpose, and many came to his lodging; to whom he expounded and testified the kingdom of God, persuading them concerning Jesus, both out of the law of Moses and out of the prophets, from morning until evening.

It would be an interesting thing to us if we knew where this lodging of St. Paul was, at which he received the Jews, and spent the day in this exposition and testimony. We should visit it with profound emotion. It seems a little singular that there should be at Rome no authentic tradition concerning the fact of St. Paul's residence in it,—a fact which is mentioned in sacred Scripture,—and yet that the traditions concerning him, which are not mentioned in Scripture, should be superfluously and incredibly numerous and minute; while concerning saints with-, out number, some of whom never lived, we have details which are exceedingly unimportant, even if true.

That which is certain is, that St. Paul was not retained in the Prætorium, nor sent to a prison by the captain of the guard; for it is stated that he "was suffered to dwell by himself with a soldier that kept him." (Acts, xxviii. 16.) The soldier who kept him was responsible with his own life for that of his captive; and had his own left hand chained to the prisoner's right. Burrus, the then captain of the guard, or Prætorian prefect, was one of that better class of officials, with which Nero, perhaps under the influence of Seneca, was surrounded in the earlier years of his reign; and he seems to have treated Paul with all the indulgence that his position as a prisoner would permit. We learn from Josephus, that when Agrippa's imprisonment at Rome was relaxed, he was permitted to have his chain unloosed at meals. The incident shows what was the kind of alleviation which it was in the power of Burrus to allow.

Though Paul dwelt by himself when he addressed the Jews, it does not appear that he was yet in his own hired house, in which he lived two whole years. The Romish tradition indeed makes him to have had but one place of sojourn in Rome. But, apart from the probability that some of his Christian friends, such as his former hosts, Aquila and Priscilla, might have received him or obtained a temporary lodging for him until a permanent home could be secured, the phrases employed in the two cases have a signification which countenances the impression that he occupied a temporary lodging before he removed to his own hired house. One expression is that he dwelt *by himself;* and the other, that the Jews came to *his lodging.* These are general expressions which might agree with the supposition of a temporary resting-place; whereas the other is specific—"his own hired house." Moreover, the Italian translation renders the word "*lodging*" "*albergo*," or inn. Wherever therefore it might have been—and there is no testimony or tradition concerning this point—it probably was not at his own hired house that St. Paul preached Jesus to the Jews.

I. State of the Jews.

We have already seen what was the state of the Jewish mind at Jerusalem. It was probably somewhat less virulent and fanatical at Rome. Yet everything in their recent history had conspired to arouse an intense nationality of spirit, and a bigoted and fierce adherence to the distinctive doctrines and practices of their religion. This feeling, awakened at first against the Romans, by whom they were subjugated and oppressed, was ready to flame out against the Christians, as a sect springing from themselves and disloyal to their divinely-descended institutes, at a crisis when fidelity was most required. Hence they were ready to regard Christianity with peculiar abhorrence and contempt.

We shall not be able to comprehend the state of Jewish feeling at this period, unless we contemplate the indignities and cruelties to which they had been subjected since the days of Pompey. It was made up of the disappointment of glowing hopes of national glory; of a bewilderment of mind because of the failure of divine prophecies, which they were sure they understood, and sure would be accomplished, and which were yet, in contradiction to these seeming certainties, delayed; of an intense longing to be revenged; and of the smothered rage of perfect powerlessness under the giant grasp of Rome. The judgments of God began to gather darkly around them. The blood of the Crucified, which they had invoked upon themselves and upon their children, cried from Calvary; and retribution was now answering the cry! And yet even previous to the capture of Jerusalem, so cruelly outraged had they been in all their most sacred feelings, that we do not wonder that they were subsequently driven to madness; and we forget their guilt as we think of their unparalleled provocation and their unequaled woes.

When Pompey returned from the conquest of Jerusalem, he brought with him many Jewish captives. They came with the recollection burning at their heart, that the impious conqueror had profaned the holy of holies by his presence. This was the beginning of the Jewish community at Rome. Many of them became freedmen and wealthy merchants; and their numbers rapidly increased. Cæsar treated them with his accustomed magnanimity; and they regarded him with enthusiastic gratitude. Augustus followed his example. Tiberius, in the beginning of his reign, showed them special kindness. But in the popular apprehension they were confounded with the Egyptians, whose secret rites of worship were the object of peculiar obloquy and suspicion. In the fifth year of the reign of Tiberius, when this feeling ran high, four thousand Jewish freedmen were impressed into the army and sent to extirpate brigandage in Sardinia. Tacitus shows the prevailing Roman feeling toward them, when he coldly remarks, that if they had all perished by the rigor of the winter, it would have been *vile damnum*, a small damage. The incident shows that their numbers at Rome must have been, at that time, large.

The causes of mutual hatred, which culminated in the capture of Jerusalem ten years later, were already in violent activity. Caligula's conduct was calculated to lash them into ungovernable rage. He proclaimed himself a god, and required that his statue should be everywhere worshiped. To the Pagans it could have been no great grief; for between Caligula and most of their gods, there was not much to choose as to character and as to the benefits which were looked for at their hands. But the demand was intolerable to the Jews. Dead to the spirit of true religion, as holiness and love, they were fanatical for rites and dogmas. The unity of God and hatred of images,—the one was their creed, and the other their passion. Their faith and zeal were concentrated on these two points; hence it was inevitable that animosities and tumults should arise.

They began at Alexandria, where the Jews were very numerous, and very cordially hated. The Egyptians, who worshiped crocodiles and serpents, had no difficulty in adding Caligula to the number of their gods. They demanded that the statue of the Emperor should be placed in the synagogues of the Jews. Resistance was made to the demand. Tumults and seditions arose. They were declared to be no longer citizens of Alexandria, but strangers and aliens. They were crowded into one of the two quarters which they had before occupied. The houses from which they were driven were sacked. Horrible cruelties were exercised against them, and multitudes perished. All this cruelty was connived at and fostered by Flaccus, the governor at Alexandria, who had the basest reasons for propitiating the favor of Caligula.

His example was followed by Capito, the prefect at Jerusalem, who erected there a large altar to the "god Caius." The Jews arose and demolished the altar. Capito wrote an account of the affair to the Emperor, which inflamed his already excited mind still more against the Jews. The madman determined that a colossal statue of himself, in the character of Jupiter Olympus, should be erected in the Temple consecrated to the one Jehovah. Conscious of the opposition which it would meet with from the whole nation, he ordered an army to be ready to accompany the statue, and to carry the edict into effect. Capito called the principal Jews together, and endeavored to secure their peaceable acquiescence in this outrage against their faith and feelings. It was in vain. They answered him only with the most passionate expressions of grief and horror.

It is a most painful page of history. The whole nation was roused to the wildest excitement. Thousands of men, women, and children abandoned the cities and villages and the cultivation of the fields, in order to throw themselves at the feet of the Proconsul Petronius, to supplicate his mercy and his intervention in their behalf with the Emperor. The narrative of the historian is most affecting.

Their troop was so numerous that it spread over all the country like a cloud. They prostrated themselves before him, and when he ordered them to arise, they stood with their hands behind their backs, their heads covered with dust, their eyes bathed in tears, and one of their old men spoke in these terms: "We are as you see without arms, and we are most unjustly accused of rebellion. We hold our hands in a position which proves that we place ourselves defenseless in your hands. We have also brought with us our wives and children that we may be saved or may perish together. Petronius, we are peaceful by inclination, and our religion breathes only peace. When Caius became Emperor, we were the first in Syria to congratulate him on his auspicious accession to the throne. Our Temple was the first in which sacrifices were offered for his prosperity. Why then is it the first to have its religious rites abolished? We will abandon our houses, our cities, our goods: we are ready to place at your feet all that we possess, and we shall not feel that we have purchased at too dear a price the preservation of the purity of our worship. But, oh! if we cannot obtain our demands, then nothing remains for us but that we should die, or see an evil more terrible to us than death. We hear that troops of infantry and cavalry are to be led against us if we resist the consecration of the statue. Slaves are not so senseless as to resist the will of their master. We present our neck to the sword. Kill us, immolate us, cut us to pieces; we will suffer everything without resistance and without lamentation."

Petronius was moved by this remarkable national demonstration. He determined to ascertain if this was the general feeling of the Jews. Going to Tiberias he found that the same scene was repeated. The pressure of prayer and importunity on the part of the Jews was irresistible. He delayed the execution of the order, and cast the blame of the delay upon the artists, who needed time for a statue which was to be at the same time colossal and highly wrought. He expressed his apprehension that despair and frenzy would drive the Jews into unanimous rebellion, and announced to Caius the danger of his contemplated presence at its inauguration. The Emperor was furious, and wrote back more stringent orders than before. After a temporary modification of the order through the intercession of Agrippa, the playmate of his boyhood, the capricious Emperor again determined that the statue should be erected, and that he himself would be present at its inauguration. The assassination of Caligula alone prevented the execution of this hideous purpose.

The Jews at Rome must have fully shared with their brethren at Jerusalem the immense relief of the riddance of this monster from the earth. Yet they were still occasionally subject to popular violence and clamor. During the reign of Claudius many were banished from the city. The reign of Nero, up to the period of Paul's entrance into Rome, had been mild and just. The Jews and Christians, who were confounded in the popular apprehension, had been treated with lenity. Although the personal character of Nero from the beginning had been base and abandoned in the extreme, yet the first five years of his reign, under the influence of Seneca and Burrus, had been marked by none of the atrocities which have made it supremely infamous in history, when having murdered his faithful ministers, he gave himself up to the guidance of eunuchs and freedmen, and the licentious and atrocious Poppea.

These details are given for the purpose of showing how little the Jews at that period were prepared, as a body, to receive a Messiah, who should only release them from the bondage of sin and not from Roman bondage.

II. Testimony of St. Paul, and its Reception by the Jews.

When the day which was fixed for the meeting with the Jews arrived, they came in great numbers to Paul's lodgings; and earnestly and long did he plead with them. He expounded and testified the Kingdom of God, persuading them concerning Jesus, both out of the law of Moses and out of the prophets, from morning till evening. Some believed the things which were spoken, and some believed not.

In view of the woes that were gathering over them, and soon fell upon them, we cannot but repeat the Saviour's tender lamentation: "If thou hadst known in this thy day the things that belong unto thy peace!" A despised and oppressed people, with no hope of national restoration, how blessed it would have been for them in their sorrow if they could have realized their spiritual privileges as God's chosen people; as the keepers of his oracles; as the favored nation from whom Christ, according to the flesh, came; and could have rejoiced in thus giving to Rome and to the world a greater boon than she took from them, when she robbed them of national liberty and life!

III. Their Judicial Blindness.

But these things were hidden from their eyes. A few individuals believed, but as a nation they rejected their Redeemer. A judicial blindness, the result of long rebellion and resistance to miraculous testimony and miraculous mercy, at length fell upon them. Seeing that they would not believe what Moses and the prophets had written, St. Paul, after a day's exposition and exhortation, closed the interview with the solemn application to them of one of the most fearful of the prophecies. "And when they agreed not among themselves, they departed, after that Paul had spoken one word, well spake the Holy Ghost by Esaias the prophet, unto our fathers, saying, Go unto this people and say, Hearing ye shall hear and not understand; and seeing ye shall see and not perceive; for the heart of this people is waxed gross, and their ears are dull of hearing, and their eyes have they closed; lest they should see with their eyes, and hear with their ears, and understand with their heart, and should be converted and I should heal them. Be it known unto you that the salvation of God is sent unto the Gentiles and that they will hear it." Here their self-induced continued blindness and insensibility to the Gospel is foretold, repeated in the long ago previous language of Isaiah, in contrast to the Gentiles who would accept it, and from whom the Kingdom of God would henceforth be chiefly recruited and composed.

IV. This Blindness in Connection with their Dispersion and Persecution.

Now it is to be observed how closely this unbelief of the Jews is connected in the prophecies with their continued dispersion and oppression by the nations. In the verses immediately succeeding the prophesy of Isaiah quoted by St. Paul, (Is. vi. 11, 12,) the prophet continues: "Then said I, Lord, how long? How long is this judgment of impenitence and disbelief to continue?" "And he answered, Until the cities be wasted without inhabitant, and the houses without man, and the land be utterly desolate; and the Lord have removed man far away and there be a great forsaking in the midst of the land." Here the impenitence, it is declared, will be of the same duration as the dispersion of the Jews and the desolation of Judea; as elsewhere it is announced that the restoration of the Jews to their own land, and their conversion to Christ, will be simultaneous. So that the presence of the Jews in the Ghetto, in wretchedness and degradation and oppression, and in an obstinate clinging to the faith of their fathers, which no suffering and no persecution can overcome, is not only a fulfillment on the very spot where the words were uttered by St. Paul, of the solemn declaration of their continued disbelief, but also of the connected prophecies of their dispersed, trampled, peeled, stripped, and wretched state, during the period of their resistance to the Gospel, with which these prophecies of disbelief are inseparably associated. The poor Jews of the Ghetto are more than a wretched and pitiable population. They are a fulfilled prophecy.

They are a proof of the divine oracles. They are witnesses to the fidelity of God to his threatened judgments. They are solemn warnings to all who disbelieve and reject the testimony of God.

We have been accustomed to refer to the destruction of Jerusalem by Titus, and the judgments that fell upon the nation in their native land, and in Babylon, during the captivity, and to their condition among the Eastern nations, as the most striking illustration of the fulfillment of the prophecies. And so no doubt they are. These demonstrations are large and conspicuous. But there is something so peculiar in the tenacity with which a few Jews have retained their position and life and faith in the City of Rome, amid poverty and persecution and degradation, in all ages, and against the first law and the otherwise unvarying policy of the Papacy,— there is something so evidently supernatural in their preservation in the midst of hostilities of government and society and nature herself, which it seems certain would have crushed out the nationality of any other people, that we are made to feel that though not so appalling and awful a demonstration of prophecy as that of Jerusalem, compassed with armies, and trodden down of the Gentiles, it is yet as convincing to the mind, as affecting to the heart, and as admonitory to the conscience. The Coliseum, the labor of captive Jews, and the Ghetto, their wretched abode, speak to us as impressively of the truth and judgment of God toward his disobedient and gainsaying people, as do Jerusalem in her desolation, and the mosque upon the hill of Zion.

V. Condition of the Jews since the Days of Paul.

We have seen something of the state of the Jews at Jerusalem, in Judea, and at Rome, up to the period when Paul addressed them. Let us give some indications of their subsequent condition in Rome.

That it became constantly worse at Rome as the rebellion in Judea became more fierce and fanatical, may well be supposed. They seem already to have been driven out into the valley of Egeria, where they were confined for several centuries. When Juvenal wrote, he refers to them as a poor and beggarly race, who swarmed under the old trees, with hay and mats as the only substance in which they trafficked. Ten years after Paul addressed them they were compelled to witness the triumphal procession of Vespasian and Titus into the city, with the captives and spoils of their conquered and desecrated city and Temple. It is thus described by Josephus:

"The day of this proud pomp having arrived, no one of the vast multitude of Rome was willing to be absent from it. The legions did not wait for the dawn to commence their march. They resorted in magnificent array to the doors of the Temple of Isis, where the Emperor Vespasian and his son Titus had passed the night; and the sun had but begun to brighten the horizon when the two Emperors issued forth crowned with laurels and clothed with purple. The senate, the knights, and the principal men of the republic awaited them near the portico of Octavia. A stage had been erected there with two thrones of ivory. When the emperors were seated, the soldiers began to celebrate their exploits, of which they had been witnesses, and to acknowledge how much they owed to their bravery. Vespasian modestly silenced them, and then arose, and covering his head in part with his mantle, as did Titus also, offered the usual prayers and vows. Then they marched to the Triumphal Gate, so called because it is the only one through which the triumphal processions pass.

"It is impossible to describe the magnificence of this august pomp. The captives themselves had been clothed with so much care, and in such a variety of modes, that the sadness imprinted upon their countenance was scarcely observed. But nothing excited so much admiration in the spectators as those structures, sometimes three or four stories high, on which were painted, with marvelous fidelity, the most important incidents of the war. There were seen the most beautiful provinces ravaged, entire troops of soldiers cut to peices, cities carried by assault, and the population given up to slaughter, even those who had no other weapons than stones. There were seen the temples burning; the owners of habitations crushed beneath them, and horrible cruelties by fire and sword. All these things the Jews had suffered.

"Then followed several ships, and amid many other spoils, those which had been taken from the Temple in Jerusalem; the table of gold, whose weight was many talents, and the golden candlestick, a masterpiece of art. From its base rose a column, and from this column issued, like the branches of a tree, seven hollow tubes, at the end of each of which there was a lamp; and last a copy of the Jewish law, which, more than anything else in the world the Jews reverence, closed this magnificent exposition of all the rich spoils conquered by the Romans.

"The triumph closed at the Temple of Jupiter Capitolinus, where they paused according to custom, until the moment when the death of the chief of their enemies had been announced. This chief was Simon, the son of Gioras. After having appeared in the triumph, with the other captives, he had been drawn with a cord about his neck, beaten with rods, and executed in the Forum. After his death had been announced, and the people testified their joy by loud applause, sacrifices, accompanied by prayers and vows, were offered. The emperors returned to their palace, where a great feast was provided. Other feasts were held all over the city."

Since that period the condition of the Jews in Rome has been one of extreme contempt, degradation, persecution, and wretchedness, both under Pagan and Christian rule. The classic writers allude to them only to express abhorrence and disdain.* To hate the race that murdered our blessed Lord—though he died for them as well as by them—was considered by Christians rather a duty than a sin. When the church, escaping from persecution, had learned no better lesson than to persecute in turn all heresy and unbelief, it visited the obstinate infidelity of the Jews with relentless cruelty. They were looked upon as a race accursed of God, because of

---

* Juvenal speaks of them, as English writers of three centuries ago speak of the gypsies. Seneca calls them "*scelleratissima gens*,"—a most wicked race, scattered over all the world. Tacitus, compelled to testify to the spiritual purity of their religion, denounces their exclusiveness as hatred to all other nations.

the crucifixion of the Saviour. They were believed to be reserved by miracle as a witness of the judgments of God upon them. While no other form of unbelief or dissent was tolerated in Rome for ages, they have been permitted to remain, because, as it is stated in a bull of one of the Popes, they gave Christ to the world; and because they were believed to be reserved to live and suffer in the world, as an instance of judgment for having crucified him who was both their Saviour and their brother. To have exterminated or banished them would have been in their view to have interfered with God's plans of judgment. To have allowed them to live otherwise than in wretchedness and persecution, a by-word and a hissing, to be mocked, and spit upon, and trampled, would have been an equal resistance of the purposes of God. Hence those fearful descriptions in the prophets, of their peeled, and stripped, and despised, and wretched condition, when dispersed among the nations, have received in Rome perhaps their most striking exemplification.

As the Jews are not citizens of Rome, they have had no rights to be protected; and hence have always been subjected not only to the most vexatious and cruel oppression from the government, but to every species of unredressed outrage on the part of the people. This license to wound their feelings, and insult and wrong them without redress, has been the most constant and bitter portion of their misery. Social persecution, and personal indignities and contempts are hotter, and sharper, and more poisoned swords for the soul than legal disabilities. The great Master of human passion has expressed the horribly bitter and revengeful spirit which this persecution must of necessity have engendered in those Jewish hearts, out of which all manhood had not been crushed. Only one Shylock has spoken; but thousands of them have lived, not only in Venice, but as well doubtless in the Ghetto; and he has spoken for them all.

> "Seignior Antonio, many a time and oft,
> In the Rialto, you have rated me
> About my moneys and my usances.
> Still have I borne it with a patient shrug;
> For sufferance is the badge of all my tribe.
> You call me misbeliever, cut-throat dog!
> And spit upon my Jewish gabardine,
> And all for use of that which is mine own.
> Well then, it now appears you need my help.
> Go to, then; you come to me and you say:
> Shylock, we would have moneys; you say so;
> You, that did void your rheum upon my beard,
> And foot me, as you spurn a stranger cur
> Over your threshold; moneys is your suit.
> What shall I say to you? Should I not say,
> Hath a dog money? Is it possible
> A cur can lend three thousand ducats? or
> Shall I bend low, and in a bondman's key,
> With bated breath, and whispering humbleness,
> Say this:—
> 'Fair sir, you spit on me on Wednesday last;
> You spurned me such a day; another time
> You called me dog! and for these courtesies
> I'll lend you thus much moneys?'"

No doubt this is a true picture of the treatment to which Jews in all Italy, and especially in Rome, were for ages subjected; and of the feelings of smothered bitterness and rage which sometimes found expression when their moneys were needed to extricate bankrupt merchants, or spendthrift patricians, from embarrassment or ruin.

The persecutions and outrages suffered by the Jews were so extreme that the Popes sometimes felt constrained to intervene for their protection. The Constitutions of Martin V. in the middle of the fifteenth century, a bull of Pius IV. toward the close of the sixteenth century, and a brief of Sixtus V. still later, considerably mitigate the hardships to which they were exposed. But they were effectually neutralized by the edicts of other Pontiffs. The bull of Pius V., in 1566, is full of degrading and vexatious restrictions and regulations. It prescribes articles of dress which mark them as a proscribed race; it puts a limit to the amount of property which they may be permitted to hold; and forbids them to receive Christians into their families. The bulls of Clement VIII., in 1593, which have never been repealed, are cruel in the extreme. One drives them from all the cities of the States of the Church, except Rome, Ancona, and Aunione. In this bull, they are accused of grievous crimes, and especially of usury. If within a certain period a Jew was found in any other than the three designated places, all his possessions were to revert to the government. A sweeping clause revokes positively and absolutely every provision made by previous Popes in their favor. The whole tone of the document is savage and relentless. It was followed in a few days by another which prohibited the Jews from retaining the Talmud, or any other of their sacred books except the Bible. And this provision, I understand, has never been repealed. The Jews here have no records even of their own history. They are not permitted to possess vindications or expositions of Judaism; for those would be considered attacks upon Christianity and Catholicism.

From this reference to some of the severe enactments of the Papacy, it will be seen that the condition of the Jews in Rome is wretched indeed. The Popes have constantly, in all the ages past, enforced pecuniary exactions and loans. The Jews have been subjected to acts of the most degrading servility. They have been compressed into close and unwholesome quarters. Their industry has been crippled in every direction. They have been driven from many towns in the Papal States. They have been forbidden to apply for aid or protection to the constituted authorities. They have been forced to attend sermons composed to convert them, and filled with the most dreadful denunciations against them. They have not been permitted to exercise any trade or art, but only traffic; nor to live, nor to have shops outside of the Ghetto; nor to have the benefit of any of the institutions of the city for the relief of suffering; their children were not permitted to be taught with Christians, nor could a Jew teach Christians. They could not be servants to Christians, nor employ them as servants. When all these disabilities, indignities, and oppressions were explained to me in detail by an intelligent Jew, I felt the full force of his remark, and at the same time sadly felt that he did not perceive his unconscious testimony to the truth of the sacred oracles, when he declared that the preservation of the Jews in Rome *was a miracle.*

The humiliations to which they have been subjected have been unspeakable. Not until the reign of the present Pope, who has kindly mitigated many of the sufferings and removed some of the indignities to which they have been subjected, were they relieved from defraying the expenses of the Carnival.

And worse than this were the Jewish races in the Corso, at the Carnival, for the amusement of the people. Not only the fleet and young, but decrepit old men and women, after being made to drink to intoxication, were compelled to furnish brutal pastime to a degraded and scoffing population. Pope Benedict XIV., in the middle of the last century, substituted horses without riders; but the Jews were compelled to pay eight hundred crowns for the substitution. The sum was carried with great parade to the senator, who dismissed them with indignity; and then it was taken by them to one of the city commissioners, with the humble request that they might be permitted to reside in Rome one year longer. This humiliation is now spared them. From another, however, they have not been exempted. At the accession of a new Pope, the deputies of the Jews place themselves in the path of the holy father, near the arch of Titus, and present to him the Jewish scriptures, saying, "We beg permission to offer to your Holiness a copy of our law." The Pope accepts it, saying, "Excellent law! Detestable race!" A little church is planted at the entrance of the Ghetto, on which is inscribed the text of Isaiah—"All the day long have I stretched forth my hand to a disobedient and gainsaying people." In this church, and in the Church of St. Angelo, in Pescheria, three hundred Jewish men and fifty Jewish women were compelled to assemble every Sunday, to hear a sermon which was intended for their conversion. The number was usually complete, because the Jewish community was compelled to pay three pauls for every absentee.

Although some of the Popes have shown themselves mild and tolerant, yet no changes for the better have been made in the existing laws. Pius VII. treated the Jews with unusual kindness, but he never revoked the pontifical constitution which imposed severe restrictions and disabilities upon the Jews. They might at any moment be put in force. They had no security therefore that their comparatively happy state under this pontiff would continue. Their temporary toleration was largely due to French influence. Indeed, during the French occupation, from 1809 to 1814, they were placed on the same footing as other citizens. Subsequent to this period, under the same Pope, they were permitted to have shops outside of the Ghetto; and in some cases their families lived where their business was conducted. They were allowed to traffic in towns and boroughs of the States of the Church without being obliged as formerly to provide themselves with a license from the Inquisition. Many of them were permitted to purchase real estate. They were not forced to attend preachings until near the time of the death of Pius VII., in 1823, when this was again made obligatory by an edict of Cardinal della Genza, afterward his successor under the name of Leo XII. He restored most of the severe regulations of Paul IV., of Pius V., and of Clement VIII. Then followed the pauperization and ruin of the Jews. From that period they have suffered evils of every kind; privations and impediments in business; losses in trade; greatly diminished numbers; depression, hopelessness, and inability to struggle against the fatal accumulation of difficulties under which they groan. Gregory XVI. softened some of the regulations of his predecessor. The kindness of the present Pope—who has removed the gates that shut them within the Ghetto at night, remitted the expense of the Carnival, and ceased to compel their attendance on preachings—has come too late to afford them true relief. They seem to the eye of sense to be wasting away in hopeless poverty and wretchedness; and yet still survive with a tenacious dying life which tells us at once how much they suffer for the past, and how surely they are reserved for a glorious future.

Their present condition is indeed deplorable, and well calculated to awaken profound pity in their behalf. Since 1842 the Jewish population has diminished from 12,700 to a little more than 4000. This diminution arises chiefly from emigration. It commenced in 1814, when many who enjoyed a good position during the French occupation, left the city on the re-establishment of the Pontifical Government. Others followed on the publication of the rigorous orders by Leo XII., in 1824 and 1825. Others left in 1850, after the return of the present pontiff from Gæta, when it was feared that all their old unrepealed disabilities were about to be enforced. These emigrations still continue, and are very disastrous to the population that remain. Those who emigrate are generally the most prosperous portion of the community. About 3000 of the 4000 that now remain in Rome are described to me, by a competent authority, as excessively poor.* The proportion of the poor increases as the number of those who can aid them diminishes. Thus the forced contributions, (some of which still continue,) the expenses of their five synagogues, the

---

* A collection was made for the Jews when this discourse was preached.

aid required for the infirm and sick, now fall on a few persons of limited means. It would seem as if, but for occasional contributions from their wealthy brethren in other cities, some of them would perish. When we remember that they are permitted to exercise no trade but that of tailoring; that they have no relief from public institutions; that immense impediments in the way of trade place them at every disadvantage; that they are not accepted as servants; that their wretched quarter is most uninviting as a place to which to resort for making purchases, and that it is damp and unwholesome, and liable to inundations from the overflow of the Tiber, it will readily be seen that their condition must indeed be wretched. I am sure that I do but give you an opportunity to exercise the charity to which you are already prompted, when I ask you to-day to contribute to the relief of the sufferings of poor and infirm Jews during this rigorous winter.

It is creditable to a people whose position is one of so many disabilities,—one calculated to stir up so much evil in the heart,—that there is very little crime among them. The number of those who are imprisoned is small. It is generally for very slight offenses that they are committed. The crimes of murder, assassination, forgery, and felony are unknown among them.

That the efforts which are made to convert them to Romanism are not successful, is not surprising. We know that love, and not persecution, is the great means to draw men to Him who is incarnate love. Moreover, the one sin which the Jews believe to transcend all other sins is idolatry. They believe that Romanism is a system of idolatry; and hence ages of attendance on the preachings intended for their conversion have been utterly without effect. When the present pontiff dispensed the Jews from attending the services, and sent a converted Jew to preach to them, the experiment failed. The church was empty.

It is a melancholy picture which we have sketched. It is part of that doom, the view of which through the vista of centuries called forth melodious lamentations from the tender spirit of Jeremiah. "All her people sigh, they seek bread; they have given their pleasant things for meat to relieve their soul; see, oh Lord, and consider, for I have become vile. Is it nothing to you all ye that pass by? Behold and see if there be any sorrow like unto my sorrow, which is done unto me, wherewith the Lord hath afflicted me in the day of his fierce anger. The yoke of my transgressions is bound by his hand; they are wreathed and come up upon my neck. He hath made my strength to fail. The Lord hath delivered me into their hands, from whom I am not able to look up. For these things I weep. Mine eye, mine eye runneth down with water because the comforter that should relieve my soul is far from me."

1. But this is not always to be their doom. They are never to cease their existence as a nation,—for God has said that only "when the ordinances of day and night fail shall the seed of Israel cease to be a nation before him,"—but their humiliation has an appointed end. The preserved remnant of the Jews shall be restored to the Holy Land, and accept their long rejected Messiah, and again live and thrive under the smile of God. "The remnant that is escaped of the house of Judah shall again take root

downward and bear fruit upward." (Is. xxxvii. 31.) "Behold, I will gather them out of all countries;"—"And I will cause the captivity of Israel and the captivity of Judah to return, and will build them as at the first." (Jer. xxxii. 37, xxxiii. 7.) "But fear not thou, oh my servant Jacob, and be not thou dismayed, oh Israel, for behold I will save thee from far off, and thy seed from the land of thy captivity; and Jacob shall return and be at rest and ease, and none shall make him afraid." So speaks God through Isaiah and Jeremiah. And that this restoration to their own land, and this blessing from God will be connected with their conversion to Christ, is evident from the fact that they are under a judgment only so long as they disbelieve. When they shall be blessed it will be because they shall have ceased to be unbelieving and disobedient. St. Paul's eleventh chapter to the Romans unfolds not only their restoration to God's favor, but the pre-eminent privileges which will belong to them as God's first kingdom. They are the original olive tree; we, a wild olive tree, have been "graffed in among them;" the root of the original tree survives alive. The life of the engrafted tree will again be received through it; for, says the Apostle, after having used this illustration—"For I would not, brethren, that ye should be ignorant of this mystery, (lest ye should be wise in your own conceits,) that blindness in part has happened unto Israel, until the fullness of the Gentiles be come in. *And so all Israel shall be saved.* As it is written, there shall come out of Zion the deliverer, and shall turn away ungodliness from Jacob." For, as he had said above, "If the casting away of them be the reconciling of the world—that is, the bringing in of the

Gentiles—what shall the receiving of them be but life from the dead?"

2. Hence, although the dispersion and persecution and misery of the Jews is God's judgment on their obstinate impenitency and unbelief, we must not feel that we are called upon to be the agents of that judgment, and either to oppress them or to leave them to suffer in cold indifference, as if to relieve them and to strive to do them good would be a presumptuous attempt to turn aside or thwart God's awful retribution. On the contrary, God denounces his wrath on those who afflict his people. Mark how emphatic is His language in Zephaniah: "Behold at that time"—the time of her restoration—"*I will undo all that afflict thee;* and I will save her that halteth, and gather her that was driven out; and I will give them praise and fame in every land where they have been put to shame." (Zeph. iii. 19.) We should share the tender spirit of St. Paul toward them. We should see in now wretched Israel a discrowned queen, who is again to resume her scepter and her throne. We should treat her with pitying honor. We should aid her with a sense of privilege. We should remember her glorious past, and her more glorious future. We should not forget that of them, according to the flesh, our Saviour and their Saviour came. If they are the children of those who invoked and called down the guilt of the blood of the Son of God upon themselves and upon their children, we must not forget that that blood cleanseth from all sin, even that unspeakable sin, and was shed *for them* in love, though *by them* in hatred, and that it cries from the ground, not to invoke upon them a vengeance which shall be inexorable, but to

plead with them to yield and live. Its language is, "though your sins be as scarlet, they shall be as white as snow; though they be red like crimson, yet they shall be as wool." Those judgments are themselves a part of that instrumentality of mercy by which at last they shall hail Jesus as their Messiah, and go up to restored Zion with everlasting joy upon their heads.

God's already executed judgments upon sinning Israel solemnly warn us that all his threatenings will be fulfilled, and that unrepented sin must incur its eternal penalty. His promised restoration of *penitent Israel* tenderly assures us that his mercy and patience are infinite, and that Christ is able to save unto the uttermost, and that his blood cleanseth from all sin. Let us heed both these lessons, and turn to Him and live!

LECTURE V.

ST. PAUL IN HIS OWN HIRED HOUSE.

And Paul dwelt two whole years in his own hired house, and received all that came in unto him;
Preaching the Kingdom of God, and teaching those things which concern the Lord Jesus Christ, with all confidence, no man forbidding him.—ACTS, xxviii. 30, 31.

A TRADITION preserved in the Roman Church points out the site of St. Paul's hired house. It is a tradition which one would wish to be able to believe. It belongs to that kind of tradition which is the least likely to be untrue. As St. Paul certainly resided in Rome, it would not have been strange if Christian affection and respect had faithfully transmitted from age to age the memory of the place of his abode.

The subterranean chapel of the Church *St. Maria Via Lata* is indicated as the site of Paul's hired house, on the authority of a tradition which is traced no higher than to St. Jerome. He, however, only mentions that his house was on the *Via Lata*. Later tradition fixes it at the site of *St. Maria*. The *Via Lata* started from the Capitol, and issuing from the then wall of Rome, near the present piazza Venezia, traversed the Campus Martius on the line of the modern Corso. If tradition had pointed out some site within the walls, near the Capitol, it would have been readily accepted. But the Church *St. Maria Via Lata* is in the then *Campus Martius*, in which there were baths, porticoes, sepulchers, colonnades, and other structures, but in which, if there could have been any private dwellings, they must have been very few, and those near the walls. Canina refers the remains of an ancient structure under St. Maria, too massive evidently for a private dwelling, to one of the three arches that adorned the Via Lata, the new arch of Diocletian, and to a colonnade, constructed by Agrippa, in the site of the *Septi*,—an inclosure where the people of Rome assembled to vote on questions submitted to their decision. Cardinal Wiseman, in his tale of Fabiola, forgetful apparently of the decision of his church, makes the same statement as to the character of these remains. Thus where the tradition of the Roman Church locates the house of St. Paul, the learned antiquarian and scholar, and the illustrious cardinal, place an arch and a colonnade. We are compelled, therefore, to discredit the tradition which fixes St. Paul's house under St. Maria Via Lata, and to conclude that it must have been near to the wall, and immediately under the shadow of the temple of Jupiter Capitolinus.

The text gives us a general description of the mode in which St. Paul employed the two whole years which he passed in Rome in his own hired house. It was in "preaching the Kingdom of God, and teaching those things which concern the Lord Jesus." He remembered, no doubt constantly, that solemn night in the tower of Antonia, when his Master stood by him and said, "Be of good cheer, Paul, for as thou hast testified of me at Jerusalem, so must thou bear witness also at Rome." Hence, when as free, so in bonds, he determined to know nothing among those to whom he ministered but Christ and Him crucified.

I. When we remember how soon after this period Nero persecuted the church, it seems strange to read that Paul was permitted at that time so openly to preach and to testify, "with all confidence, no man forbidding him."

In order to understand this, it will be necessary to refer briefly to the then condition and spirit of the Roman government.

Nero had succeeded to the empire, in the year A.D. 54, nearly seven years before the arrival of St. Paul in Rome. His character from his earliest youth gave fearful promise of its development into those portentous vices which have made his name pre-eminent in infamy. It was the policy of his evil mother, Agrippina, to foster all his private vices, in order that she might withdraw him from the cares of state, and rule the empire through him as she had through her dull husband, the Emperor Claudius. She indulged all his tastes for the circus and theater, and association with players and charioteers and pantomimists; and surrounded him with a host of polluting parasites, freedmen, and teachers in all the luxuriant vices of that most degenerate age. It may readily be supposed how rapidly a youth of seventeen, with bad blood in him, and prone to all the vices, would ripen in iniquity in such a school, when put in possession of the vast and irresponsible imperial power,—the greatest power ever enjoyed by man.

1. Against these powerful influences of evil, in

the beginning of his reign, Seneca and Burrus, his chief advisers and ministers, struggled not altogether in vain. Seneca had been Nero's tutor. His fame for wisdom and probity were so high that he had been talked of as the successor of Claudius to the empire. He retained, for a time, his ascendency over the mind of the Emperor, restraining somewhat at least, the outward manifestations of his private vices, and giving a mild, popular, and just character to his public administration. Burrus, the Prætorian prefect, the constant friend and helper of Seneca, and having more of the spirit of the old and virtuous Roman in him, was less afraid of Agrippina, and more peremptory with Nero, than the timid and politic philosopher. Nero, having full sweep to all his will in the direction of his youthful tastes and vices, was rather amused than offended to see the struggle between his astute mother on the one hand, and the philosopher and soldier on the other, for that control of the public administration which he knew that he himself could at any time assume. Under the guidance of these two wise and prudent statesmen, the public administration continued to be beneficent and just, long after Nero had emancipated his private life from the control of them and of Agrippina, and had given himself up to utter license, self-will, and evil passion, and had become the deliberate murderer of his brother and his mother. The contrast between his private life and his public administration was indeed remarkable. It may be doubted whether there had been any period since the reign of Augustus in which the empire had been so wisely, justly, and beneficently administered, as during the first six or seven years of Nero's reign. Trajan, an emperor so just that Gregory the Great is said to have prayed God to make an exception in his case and admit him into Paradise, expressed the wish that the best years of his reign might resemble the first years of Nero's administration.

The Roman people must indeed have greatly enjoyed that bright and peaceful lull in the long, dark storm of tyranny under which they had timidly cowered or recklessly reveled. Instead of the suspicion, espionage, banishments and beheadings, the dull void created by the absence of the Emperor and court from Rome, the comparative rarity of games and shows, which were the characteristics of the reign of the morose, suspicious, and gloomy Tiberius, there was a sudden disappearance of spies and informers; a revival of literature, poetry, and art; the Palatine hill became alive and gay with imperial pomp and activity; games and shows were profusely multiplied, and largess and bread were freely scattered among the people. In place of the capricious tyranny of the mad Caligula, whose fantastic atrocities kept the whole city and empire in a state of nervous apprehension, there was an assurance, on the part of the citizens, that the strong hand of Burrus would direct the Prætorian cohorts for their protection and not for their destruction, and that the civil administration under Seneca would assure and not rob them of their rights. Instead of the degrading rule of freedmen and of Messalina and Agrippina, a mixed anarch reign, as it were, of satyrs and of furies, in which all the old Roman dignity disappeared, and in which the lives and property of citizens were at the mercy of their spies and poisoners, there was a government whose chief officials were men of the highest rank and character, and under which imperial crimes were confined to the imperial circle. The people at that time were ready to consider an emperor eminently good who confined his murders within his palace, and who always, at this period of his reign, followed up a private atrocity by some reform in the public administration, or some new benefaction to the public. It is this peculiarity of Nero's reign, this recollection of its bright beginning, which accounts for the fact that among the populace of Rome the popularity of Nero was never wholly effaced, even by his subsequent public atrocities; and that it was through the influence of this feeling chiefly that Otho was subsequently elevated to the empire.

As St. Paul resided in Rome during the latter part of the good portion of Nero's reign, we can perceive, in the then policy of the government, the reason why he was permitted to teach and preach "with all confidence, no man forbidding." During this period, neither the Jews nor the Christians were molested.

2. At this period, moreover, the essential antagonism of Christianity to all pagan systems had not become fully apparent. Rome, the capital of the world, was accustomed, when she incorporated a nation into the empire, to receive its gods also into her mythology. When indeed some foreign superstition gave freer play to licentiousness than even licentious Rome approved, laws were passed for the prohibition of its rites. But in such cases the trivial open sore became by suppression a secret poison in the blood. Judaism had long been de-

nounced as an unsocial and malignant superstition, because it refused alike to admit and to be admitted into the system of thousandfold Polytheism that prevailed at Rome. But its nature was not aggressive. It sought, with intense exclusiveness, self-preservation, but not extension. It could not be extended without pollution; it could not be mixed with other worships without blasphemy. It had been placed in a position of antagonism to Rome, not because it had attempted Proselytism, but because it had resisted the impious effort of Caligula to usurp in the Temple of Jerusalem the place of the Most High God. Christianity was at that time regarded as but a form of Judaism. It was hated simply because it refused to coalesce with the prevailing idolatry. But it was not then denounced as impiety, and as dangerous to the state. Later, indeed, when the persistent defamation of Christians as guilty of all crimes and enormities in their worship was universally received, they were persecuted simply because they bore the name of Christians. We find, from the correspondence of Pliny with the Emperor Trajan, that this was the policy of the government at that period. A confession of Christianity was considered equivalent to a proof of the practice of enormities subversive of the existence of society. Yet the real motive of this malignant misrepresentation and this persecuting hate was to be found in the fact that Christianity denounced the idolatry of the Romans, and demanded their entire allegiance, and their holy consecration to the Lord Jesus Christ, the crucified man of Calvary and the ascended God of Olivet. It was not to be borne by the haughty masters of the world, that they who ought humbly to seek mere toleration, should come with rebukes and warnings, and inexorable claims, and awful denunciations of wrath and woe to the unbelieving and disobedient. They hated the light, and persecuted the children of light, because their deeds were evil.

3. The favor also of the infamous Poppea is believed at this time to have protected both the Jews and Christians. Josephus states that she had become a proselyte to Judaism. At this period her power was in the ascendant. No one possessed equal influence over Nero. A little later, on the birth of her daughter, temples were erected to her and her infant, and divine honors were paid to both. Her Judaism must have been of a very lax kind to have permitted her to receive these divine honors. Yet Josephus calls her a religious woman. There was in Rome at that period a Judaism which had become very loose, having been corrupted by the surrounding paganism. In the position of suspicion and obloquy which the Jews occupied at Rome, those who were not made by it more rigid in their faith, would become more compliant with pagan sentiments and customs. The Pharisee would become more sternly bigoted, and the Sadducee more accommodatingly loose. The luxurious, the rich, the timid, would seek to propitiate the favor of the Romans, by bringing their systems as nearly as possible into line with all other tolerated worships. Josephus himself is an illustration of this remark. We may find a *symbol* at least, even if it shall not prove to be an historical illustration, of this style of Judaism, in what are called the Jewish Catacombs, recently opened, in which are found mixed Jewish and classic emblems, the golden candlestick and ark of the

covenant, in connection with some of the usual representations of heathen mythology. The prevalence of an easy and fashionable style of Judaism may account for Poppea's adhesion. She was not one who would have adopted a stern and rigid rule of faith or practice. A system, adherence to which enabled Josephus to call Poppea "a religious woman," could not have been very strict. No doubt, if at Rome as at Jerusalem a bitter persecution of the Christians by the Jews had arisen, she might have lent herself as the instrument of their hatred. But directly under the imperial influence, as it were, the Judaism of Rome could scarcely have been the bitter, malignant, and persecuting thing it was at Jerusalem. Hence the comparatively kind personal reception which Paul met with at the hands of his countrymen in Rome. They may have thought that, obnoxious as they were to the Romans, and apt to be confounded as they were with the Christians in the popular apprehension, their own safety might be involved in that of the hated Nazarenes, and they may have rejoiced, therefore, that the protection of their imperial patroness shielded those whom many of them would otherwise gladly have seen given to the lions. It is a confirmation of this remark that the persecution of the Christians was soon followed by that of the Jews.

4. There is another reason for the change in the imperial policy from careless toleration to the most cruel persecution. After the conflagration of Rome, Nero became so obnoxious to the citizens, in consequence of the suspicion that it was his work, that it became necessary to divert the public hatred. It was directed upon the heads of the Christians. They

were accused of the crime of having burned the city. They were denounced as guilty of impiety to the gods and disloyalty to the empire. The most atrocious falsehoods were circulated with regard to them. They were accused of sacrificing children, and feeding upon their flesh, and of joining to their worship rites more obscene and abominable than those of Venus and of Isis. In the gardens of Nero on the Vatican hill, Christians were tortured and martyred with many circumstances of indignity and cruelty worse than death. At night, tied up in sacks and smeared with pitch and wax to serve as torches, they were made a spectacle for the populace; and amid the illuminated scene the imperial wretch drove his chariot with the joy of a gratified, malignant demon. It was because that, previous to this period, the sacrifice and persecution of the Christians could have served no purpose of the tyrant, and might have done him harm, that St. Paul was permitted for two whole years, in his own hired house, "to teach and preach with all confidence, no man forbidding him."

II. St. Paul received "all that came in unto him." The words seem to imply that his house had become a place of much resort. We have seen that tradition has assigned it to the *Via Lata*. If it were there, St. Paul was in precisely that part of the city where he would be most likely to be known, and his history and his doctrine to be discussed. It was on the great thoroughfare which led from the Forum and the Capitol to the *Campus Martius*. The tide of life which flowed through it was that of persons at leisure and in search of recreation. The crowds which perpetually passed Paul's house were going and coming to and from the baths, or games, or drives, or strolls, in the *Campus Martius*. It would not be singular if such a peculiar case as that of Paul's should, from such vast and mixed multitudes, have drawn daily a concourse to listen to his expositions sufficient to have filled his probably narrow *atrium* and adjoining chambers. Some of his own beloved Christian friends and disciples would be always there. They would bring others with them, in the hope that they would be convicted and convinced by the Apostle's faithful rebukes, luminous expositions, and earnest appeals. We cannot doubt that each day believers thus came, bringing with them Jewish or heathen friends; for it is to be observed in the salutations of St. Paul to the Roman Christians, how much he commends them as "helpers," "work-fellows," and "laborers in the Lord." The soldiers, who on successive days kept him and listened to his words, might have been so struck and won by his heroism and his love, as to have frequently returned. It must have been through them that the Apostle's bonds were known in all the Prætorium; and through that knowledge in Cæsar's house, and in all other places. What singular sensations of wonder, and sometimes of admiration and of sympathy, must have thrilled through those rude men, when St. Paul, in the ardor of his prayer or speech, lifted up the short and heavy chain which bound him to his guard, and made him as it were a partaker and helper of his solemn warnings and affectionate persuasions! The clank of that common chain may, to their startled minds, have ominously seconded his vivid reasonings of righteousness and of judgment to come. Brethren and children of the

Apostle, his converts, from Ephesus, Corinth, Philippi, and many other places, would hasten to the scene, and St. Paul's eye might first discern them in his over-shifting audience, in the midst of some exposition or appeal. How often may the sight of some brand plucked from the burning have added fervor to his representations of the fullness and sufficiency of redeeming grace, or the sudden view of some dear Christian brother, who had tenderly ministered to his necessities or sorrows, have added to the divine beauty of his representations of the blessedness of Christian love!

And there, shrinking in the corner, is the poor, tattered, and guilty slave Onesimus. Perhaps in his extremity he has come to Paul, whom he had known at his master's house, for human help, and has found a heavenly treasure. There, mixed with the crowd, are slaves and servitors and freedmen, whose badges proclaim them to be of Cæsar's household. That proud senator that sweeps by with a troop of clients and attendants,—will he enter? No. A sycophant, as he pauses a moment before the door, gives him a ludicrous account of the bold and enthusiastic prisoner, and the haughty Roman laughs and passes on. That young patrician candidate for the honors of the Forum,—will he step in? Yes; he will turn back a moment, for one of his friends has given him assurance that this man has a certain sort of natural eloquence, which, though careless of the rules of art, is not coarse or common. That grave and sad man, whom the atrocities and sorrows of the time have driven into the only system of that era which has anything of strength or dignity,—the system of the Stoics, which is beginning to prevail, and will soon have one of its best disciples on the throne,—will he gather up his robe and join that motley crowd? Almost ashamed, and looking around to see that no friend is near, he will indulge his curiosity; for his mind is tortured with the problems and enigmas of this dark world, and he has heard that this Jew is a joyful man, and speaks of the immortality of the soul and its glorious development in the future, in a strain of eloquence worthy of the divine Plato, and with a certainty of conviction which Plato never reached, though strangely mixed with fables and with abject representations of the moral condition of the soul of majestic man. Such are Paul's audiences. Nor are his words in vain. His bonds turn out rather to the furtherance of the Gospel. Onesimus is begotten on his bonds. Saints are found in Cæsar's household. The gay and busy crowd pass by. But few of those who passed in pomp and splendor have done anything for man or have lived in history; while that poor prisoner, whose case might have been the subject of a moment's wondering or contemptuous comment, as they saw the crowd before his door, has been, and is, and will be remembered with gratitude by millions of regenerated souls on earth and in heaven.

III. We know St. Paul's one theme,—*Christ*. It was "Jesus and the resurrection;" "Christ, and him crucified." In the text, however, we are told that he remained at Rome "preaching the *Kingdom of God.*" To preach the kingdom of God and to preach only Christ are not inconsistent things. Christ came to establish God's Kingdom. To believe in Christ, to profess faith in him, to be converted and sanctified, was to belong to God's Kingdom in heart, and to be ready to be enrolled among his disciples in that visible kingdom of which Christ was head, which had its own appropriate rites, and its own duties to its members and to the world.

It is a deplorable mistake when the Church or Kingdom of God is preached, as if it, and not the truth which it should hold and dispense, is that which is supremely important; and as if its sacraments and rites were, of themselves, salutary and saving, without the truth or against the truth, for the soul of man. It is an error scarcely less fatal in its final effects upon the world, to represent the truth as so alone important as to speak slightingly and irreverently of the Church of God, and its divinely instituted rites; and to feel no duty in reference to its extension and support. It is true that it is not the cup but the water of life that refreshes and saves the soul; but the water is presented in the cup. Who will drink the water and then dash the cup contemptuously to the earth? The truth is that which is to convince, convict, and save the soul, or rather it is Christ that saves the soul through the Word administered by the Spirit; but it is the church that presents the Word. It is the Bible that is the soul's treasure; but the casket in which it is laid up, and from which it is brought forth, is the church. The truth is for the soul and the church is for the truth, and both are so connected in the divine purpose, because so important to each other, that St. Paul, in the same breath, is said to have preached the *Kingdom of God*, and to have taught *those things which concern the Lord Jesus*.

Suppose that there were no church, no sacraments, no ministry, no visible union of believers, no organization for united duty, helpfulness, and prayer; conceive the Gospel to have been proclaimed by the Saviour and committed to writing, and faith in the Saviour to have been as it is now, the one only way of life. Then the Gospel, or truth of God, would be in the world precisely as different moral theories are in it; and would be adopted by individuals who would not be associated in any visible organizations. Now as this Gospel is light from heaven which men hate, which they do not love to see by when it is in a candlestick, which they hold behind them when it is placed in their hands, we may be sure they would not be likely to find it and be guided by it when it was placed under a bushel. With how few souls would it come in contact! How soon it would die out in the world! Instead of taking its course through this dry and barren land, the world, as an abounding and beautiful river, sparkling in the sun, and diffusing fertility, it would sink under ground and creep through sunless caverns. Men will not go after a Gospel which condemns them. Rather they will strive to flee from it when it comes to them. If it holds them it will be by grasping their conscience first, while it repels their heart. The mercy which is to save them must be aggressive mercy. The orb of truth which is to enlighten them must be above the horizon. The truth privately proclaimed, merely announced, with no provision made for its conservation and diffusion by a permanent organization, would be as the commission of God to Moses, when it was shut up in his unwilling heart, when he cried, "Oh, Lord! send whom thou wilt send!" But when it is committed to an organization, it is like the same commission as it came down on wings of fire from Sinai to the assembled thousands that trembled at its base. It would be like the dim light that struggled with the dark chaos of the world's first day, if it were left to diffuse itself of its own spontaneous power from heart to heart. But committed to an organization, it is like light compacted into the orb of day and diffusing its radiance over all the earth. The church, deriving its light from Christ, is the light of the world. Its office, like that of each individual of which it is composed, is that of holding forth the Word of Life.

In preaching the Kingdom of God at Rome, in proclaiming a new, heavenly, earth-embracing *Institution* in which there was truth, and life, and happiness, and the beginning of a bright immortality for man, St. Paul no doubt adapted himself to what he knew was among the most deeply felt of the moral wants of those whom he addressed. The philosophy of the ages past had utterly failed to furnish a refuge and give peace to the heart. There had been a flitting succession of schools and theories, which had left only one deep conviction behind them, and that was that truth was nowhere to be found. They had neither succeeded in establishing truth on which the soul could rest, nor in imposing upon the human mind a plausible falsehood in the place of truth. The hopefulness which inspired the earlier thinkers had been changed into despondency or despair. The brilliant lights of the Platonic philosophy, which played upon the horizon and seemed to be the dawning brightness of the coming day, proved to be the ushers of a gloomy night. All attempts to explain man's present state, or forecast his future doom, had failed. The foaming and sparkling philosophies of the past had left but this one poor residuum,— the inexplicable *fact* of human ignorance and wretchedness. All that remained to man was to make the best of it. The only two systems, called philosophy, which remained at this period, attempted to do no more than practically to make the best that could be made of this lamentable fact. The Epicurean adopted one mode and the Stoic another. The one said, "Our ignorance we will not lament, and our sorrow we will drive away; let us eat, drink, and be merry!" The other stoutly denied that what were called pain and sorrow were real, or if real, that they should disturb a good man's peace. The latter was the nobler system; but in their results the only difference between the two was that the one was a gay and frivolous, and the other was a dignified and mournful wretchedness.

Now it is evident that such minds must have profoundly felt that theories, however subtle and brilliant, could be of no avail. If St. Paul had come to them with a mere new system of truth, which explained evil, and the soul, and God, and the future, it could not have met their needs. They would have been in no mood to listen to its proofs. The world had already had more than enough of theories and systems. But that which St. Paul announced was a practical remedy to felt and incumbent ills. Its truth could be even better learned by being *tested* than by being examined. He came with facts and not theories. The facts made all theories and systems superfluous. The understanding of the system followed the acceptance of the well-attested facts. Paul said to them, "You have groped after God.

Behold, he has revealed himself through his Son! That Son, in the form and nature of man, has come to tell us the truth, remove our sin and sorrow, and take us to a perfectly holy and happy and eternal home. He died for our sin, and God forgives it. He has gone back to heaven, and there awaits us, and thence sends down holy power into our souls to prepare us for it. See the proofs of it in the life, death, and resurrection of the God-man Saviour. See them here, in the Kingdom of God which he established. See! here are its laws, its rites, its privileges, its purifications, and its joys! Christ now in heaven is at the head of it. His life is in it. Its work in the soul is a matter of fact and of experience. Try it and you will have the experience. Look, and you will see the fact. The Kingdom of God has come unto you. Enter it and live. All the past, present, and future of man and earth and heaven are here explained, and here all that is sorrowful and evil begins the process of restoration to purity and joy." Oh! how to many hearts torn with sorrow, to consciences pierced with the sense of sin, to minds bewildered by doubt; how to souls so consciously alone, and desolate and helpless, must the *proclamation of the Kingdom of God*—a heaven-descended reality in which there was divine life and love and power, and sweet and mutually sustaining fellowship and present peace, and the sure hope of future rest and glory,—how must it have come with power and with self-evidencing light to snatch them from despair!

It should be remembered, too, that the proclamation of "the Kingdom of God," of the actual presence of God's government in the world, must have been a most comforting truth to those who lived under the Kingdom of the Cæsars. Under their awful domination it must have seemed as if the gods had abandoned the earth, and that it had been given up to the rule of irresistible, crushing, evil power. It must have seemed as if all the principles of morality and honor and mercy, which had hitherto at least struggled to maintain a place in human affairs, had at length given way, and resigned the world to the single sway of power employed as the instrument of luxury, rapacity, lust, cruelty, and the varied crimes whose evil brotherhood is never broken. The government of the Cæsars had become almost an earthly omnipotence and omniscience in the regard of the Romans and the subject nations. It had destroyed all the old Roman virtues, which if stern and even savage, were at least bold and manly and often magnanimous and heroic. Cringing, flattery, falsehood, treachery, and a wild pursuit of pleasure, all the more keen because it was upon the edge of death, became the prevailing characteristics of the time. Learning and philosophy, which had formerly aimed to lift men above luxury and pleasure, were now employed as the instruments to give them new and richer zest. The citizens looked alone to Cæsar and the government for all their good, and from it alone they feared their chiefest evil. It had become to them their providence or their fate. Nothing astonishes the reader of the Roman annals of this period more than the tameness with which proud and powerful men gave themselves up to the evil will of the government, as to a fate which it would be madness to attempt either to escape or to resist. They seemed to feel that there was no desert, cave, nor mountain height, nor lonely isle, where the Argus-eyed and million-handed Roman power could not track and grasp and strangle them. Even generals at the head of mighty armies, when they heard of the displeasure or suspicion of Cæsar, hastened to open their veins, and for the sake of their children died confessing crimes they had not committed, and praising and invoking the clemency of the master of the world. This awful weight of evil power upon Rome and upon the nations reached its maximum under Nero. Of the latter years of his hideous tyranny it might have been said, in the wonderful words of Shakspeare:—

> Everything includes itself in *power*,
> Power into *will*, will into *appetite*,
> And appetite, an universal wolf,
> So doubly seconded by will and power,
> Must make perforce an universal prey,
> And last eat up himself!

Now to be assured that there was a good and righteous God, that he was not dead nor sleeping, that he had not abdicated the government of the world, that earth was not and was not to be given up to the sole sway of the Cæsars, that there was a Kingdom of God set up on earth, which was to extend until it should embrace all nations—we may well suppose that this would be a message to arrest the attention of those who were reveling or crouching or wondering or weeping under the fearful kingdom of the Cæsars. St. Paul, under the shadow of the Palatine hill, preaching the Kingdom of God and demonstrating in his own person its mighty and superior power, in the midst of what seemed his absolute subjection to the power of the Cæsars, and rejoicing in its glorious liberty as he shook the chains that bound him,—St. Paul, thus demonstrating freedom in servitude, and power in weakness, must have spoken thrilling words to many who paused to hear him on the *Via Lata*.

It is comforting as we walk up and down the Corso, by the spot where Paul preached, to remember that the free Kingdom of God was then here in the midst of the servitudes of Pagan Rome. It will be well if the thought shall increase our own rejoicing liberty in Christ, in the midst of the Christian bondage which has taken the place of the Pagan, and has been wrought out of the very freedom which Paul preached and enjoyed in the midst of his imprisonment and bonds.

Paul enjoyed and gave freedom in the midst of servitude. The Church of Rome has taken the instruments by which Paul broke the bonds of Pagan servitude, and out of them has forged new chains of so-called *Christian* bondage.

IV. St. Paul was not only occupied in "preaching the Kingdom of God," but also in "teaching those things that concern the Lord Jesus." They are different functions—preaching and teaching—of the same office. His great and primary work was to "preach the Kingdom." This was his more public, formal, official heralding of salvation through Christ, and his invitation to accept it and to be enrolled in the Kingdom of God. It is to be followed up by teaching those things that concern the Lord Jesus. While each function is to be discharged both to the world and the church, yet the preaching had more reference to the former and the teaching to the latter. After salvation and the Kingdom of God are announced as facts, present, saving, and available to all, there remain many things to be taught concerning the Lord Jesus, the founder and the head of this glorious kingdom. After St. Paul had stood up and preached the Gospel, inviting sinners to accept it, and unfolding to saints its privileges and duties, we can imagine a group remaining when the crowd had dispersed, to whose questions concerning the Lord Jesus he would answer at length; we can see the children of the saints come in and sit at his feet while he unfolds the histories and types and prophecies which refer to Him, and tells the story of the Saviour's life, and his miracles of love and power. How much there would be to teach concerning the Lord Jesus to both Jew and Gentile! The teaching would make the preaching more precious to the heart, and the preaching would animate it with holy curiosity and thirst for fuller teaching. Only they who, like Paul, teach concerning Jesus, can like him successfully preach the kingdom.

We are assembled, it is probable, very near the place where St. Paul preached the Kingdom of God and taught concerning Jesus. Now, alas! there is little other preaching in Rome than that of the kingdom, temporal and spiritual, of the Pope, and the things that concern Mary! The name and the work of the Saviour are becoming here an appendage, and an appendage increasingly insignificant, to that of Mary. The dogmatic theology of Rome, which always follows and systematizes and elevates into articles of faith the superstitions of the people and the exaggerations of the clergy, not long ago decreed, through the Pope, the Immaculate Conception of the Virgin. This has given a prodigious popular impulse to an enlargement of her power and glory; and soon the church must come forward and express in dogma what priests and people now so freely express in devotion, viz., the proper deification of the Virgin, and her supreme and exclusive administration of the Kingdom of God on earth. Another divine person is practically added to the Trinity, and to her is practically consigned the government of the Kingdom of God. I quote a few words of a little work commemorating a miraculous picture of the Virgin at Spolato, purchased close by the place where Paul preached the Kingdom of God and taught concerning Jesus.

"Who is there that does not need the *mediation* deservedly *omnipotent* of the celestial Mother of God and *of men?* He only who has no need of anything in time or in eternity. Every one without distinction, sovereign or subject, wise or ignorant, rich or poor, good or bad, sick or well, in life or in death, in need whether of body or of mind, all must have the maternal, pitiful, and most efficacious protection of the Virgin Mother of God and of us *her* children. This is because Mary *has been made by the thrice Holy Trinity the dispenser of all graces, temporal and spiritual,* and has decreed that the children of Eve the sinner, should obtain them through the mediation of the *first-born,* immaculate, and ever-virgin Mother and ever-holy Spouse of God. It [*i.e.* the Trinity] has decreed that we should receive all things through Mary."

It is impossible for language to be used which shall more absolutely take away all the attributes and powers, and all the works of Christ, and consign them to the Virgin.

It is very sad, after 1800 years, to find this other Gospel and other Kingdom and other Saviour and other God preached where Paul preached Jesus and his Kingdom. It makes us long for the coming of the day when our poor sinful hearts and darkened minds shall no longer corrupt the truth as it is in Jesus, and when that millennium Kingdom of God shall be established over all the earth, which shall never again lapse backward into error, but shall go forward and at length be merged into the perfect kingdom into which nothing that defileth or deceiveth shall ever enter.

LECTURE VI.

CÆSAR'S HOUSEHOLD, AND THE SAINTS.

All the saints salute you, chiefly they that are of Cæsar's household.—PHIL. iv. 22.

THESE words not only show that there were saints in Cæsar's household, but they seem to imply, in the word *chiefly*, a peculiar predominance of these saints over others in Rome, or a peculiarly close relation of St. Paul with them, or of them with the Christians of Philippi.

No contrast could be greater than that which is presented by the first Christianity of Rome, and its then prevailing Paganism. It is suggested by the text, which points out on the one hand, the house and household of Cæsar, and on the other, the saints that were there, and the other saints of Rome.

When Paul lived in his own hired house, the Golden House of Nero was not yet built. Yet Cæsar's house when Paul wrote—as the ruins of the Palatine hill abundantly testify—must have been exceedingly magnificent.

I. The labors of the learned, and especially of Canina, enable us to obtain an impressive conception of Cæsar's house at the time when Paul wrote. If they cannot be sure of all the details which they suggest, and if they differ among themselves, they yet agree in many main particulars, and do not fail to convey to us—that which is most important for our present purpose—the same impressions of the grandeur and luxury of Cæsar's house.

In the time of Nero, the Palatine hill had become one vast congeries of imperial piles for the private residence of the emperors and the officials of the court, and for some public purposes. It included palaces, temples, libraries, baths, and fountains, the gardens of Adonis, and an area for athletic games. Previous to the empire it had been occupied chiefly by patrician residences. Augustus had purchased the house of the orator Hortensius, lying midway on the southeastern crest of the hill opposite the Circus Maximus. It was described as a modest mansion, compared to the sumptuous palaces that were subsequently constructed. One of the columns of the portico, however, preserved in the Church *Ara Cœli*, suggests that it must have been massive if not gorgeous. Behind it, on the central portion of the hill, he constructed, of pure white Carrara marble, the exquisite Temple of Apollo. Its surrounding porticoes were adorned with fifty equestrian statues of the sons of Danaus, and with fifty statues of his daughters; and within its *atrium* there was a statue of Apollo fifty feet high. Beyond this he constructed the celebrated Greek and Latin libraries. Tiberius added a still more sumptuous palace, which was connected with that of Augustus, and stretched toward the north, though still overlooking the Circus Maximus. A large temple intervened between these palaces and that still more magnificent which Caligula constructed on the hill which overlooks the Forum, and the exceedingly massive remains and foundations of which are now in process of being opened by the Emperor of the French. Beyond this palace began the extensive additions of Nero, the first of which was the new or renewed ground entrance to the palace near that which the visitor now enters, and which led to the imperial residences through the courts of the libraries and the corridors of the portico of the Temple of Apollo. Thence, occupying the portion of the hill which overlooked the *Via Sacra* and the *Velia*, with the famous gardens of Adonis, he stretched a pile of palaces, some of whose enormous arches can still be seen, around the southern portion of the hill, until they touched, on the southwestern side, the original palace of Augustus. In addition to this complete occupancy of the Palatine hill, he constructed another palace, the *Domus Transitoria*, across the space now occupied by the Coliseum, which ascended the slope of the Esquiline to the borders of the gardens of Mecænas. Such was even then, before the insane extravagance of the Golden House, the enormous extent, the vast splendor, and the immense variety of magnificence included under the name of "Cæsar's house." And all this pile of palaces was rich beyond all modern luxury, in marbles, and gilding, and frescoes, and bronzes, and mosaics, and statuary, and paintings. There the luxury of life, the extravagance of expenditure in furniture, and feasts, and wines; the employment of troops of players, mimics, musicians, athletes, gladiators, charioteers, and nameless ministers of nameless vices, were such as Christian civilization in its most splendid and vicious periods has never known.

II. *The Household of Cæsar.* We cannot describe it so as at the same time to convey a just impression of its character and retain the reserve which propriety demands. When we enter it in thought, what dreadful memories of guilt start up from every corridor and hall! If one should seek the most striking demonstration of the unfitness of man to be put in the possession of unlimited power, and the awfully degrading and polluting effects of it on the character of those who come under its immediate influence, as well as the general demoralization of a whole age and empire which it involves, he could find nowhere such ample proofs of his position as in the house of Cæsar, from the reign of Augustus to that of Vespasian.

Before we look in upon its inmates, of the period of St. Paul's sojourn at Rome, let us glance at some who have preceded them. What a tangle of intrigues, crimes, and woes does the family history of the Cæsars present! It is a revolting medley of adoptions, divorces, remarryings, adulteries, incests, betrayals, and murders. Augustus, mourning the untimely death of his destined heir and successor, the young Marcellus, over whom Virgil poured such melodious lamentations, begins this deplorable history, which deepens in tragic horrors to the end of Nero's reign. That death was soon followed by that of his two nephews, Caius and Lucius, who are believed to have fallen victims to his own wife's ambition for her son Tiberius. His reluctant consent to the succession of Tiberius, whose horrible temper and veiled vices the sagacious Emperor discerned; his repudiation of his third wife because of her depraved manners; the banishment of his daughter

Julia, and again of *her* daughter Julia, to desolate islands, because of their intolerable and shameless licentiousness; himself perhaps the victim of his wife's impatience to see her son Tiberius upon the throne,—all this exhibits the great Augustus as wretched in his private as he was fortunate in his public career. Tiberius, his successor, is believed to have caused the murder of the too popular and well-beloved Germanicus, his nephew, the idol of the army and of the people, and is known to have destroyed his two sons, Nero and Drusus, the heirs of his popularity and virtues, the one by famine in a distant island, and the other by poison in the imperial palace. He destroyed also the harmless and incompetent Agrippa Posthumus. Two sisters of Caligula were banished because of their immoralities, and a third, guiltier than either, remained in the palace, as if to prove that no conceivable crime should be wanting to the house of the Cæsars. In this imperial pile of the Palatine hill, resplendent with gold and beautiful with art, here is the crypt where Caligula was murdered; here the cell where Drusus died of hunger, gnawing the leather of his sandals, and cursing Tiberius; here the festive hall where Britannicus was poisoned, and the garden where Messalina perished. Crime kept pace with luxury, and was as exaggerated as the splendor with which it was associated; and in the language of Tacitus, Locusta, the female poisoner, became an instrument of Government.

Under Claudius, a dull and gross, but not cruel Emperor,—the tool of his freedmen and his wives,—crime held high saturnalia in the halls of the Cæsars. The names of Messalina and Agrippina, the last two wives of Claudius, and the latter his own niece, occupy a place of infamy in history which it would have been supposed could not have been equaled, if Poppea, the wife of Nero, had not subsequently appeared. It is a proof of the abjectness of Claudius' subserviency to his two infamous wives, to find that a grave historian of the empire gives, as the title of one of his chapters, "The Government of Messalina," and of the other, "The Domination of Agrippina." When we read the history of the former we seem to follow the adventures of one who is by turns a wild bacchante, incapable of thought, and an implacable fury; and the narrative sounds like an ill-constructed and incredible romance. The stolid Emperor, at last convinced of her guilt, after all Rome had known it long, commanded that she should be slain; and concluded his dinner when the news had been brought to him that his orders had been executed. The incident reminds us of Nero's turning upon his couch to see Britannicus carried out, convulsed with the poison that had been prepared in his own chamber, with the remark that his brother had been subject to epilepsy from his boyhood, and then resuming his meal. In the history of Agrippina, we find all the vices fearfully developed, but all mastered by a political craft and ambition which remind us of the policy which Machiavelli preached and Cæsar Borgia practiced. Such were some of the shapes which start up before us as we enter Cæsar's house.

There Nero reigns and revels, the last of the dynasty of the Cæsars. That dynasty indeed was not composed of a single family, but of four connected families, which by marriage and adoption constituted the imperial stock. The succession passed from them on the death of Nero and the accession of Galba. There is a singular illustration of the dying out of this guilty race mentioned by the historian Suetonius. Livia, the wife of Augustus, planted a laurel grove, whence each of the Emperors gathered the leaves for his triumphal crowns, and where each one planted a new tree. It was observed at the death of each of them that the tree which he had planted died also; and that a little before the death of Nero the entire grove perished. A stroke of lightning knocked off the heads of all the statues of the Emperors, and broke the scepter which the hand of that of Augustus held. It is also a curious fact, in this connection, that the beautiful statue of Augustus, which is now in the *Braccia Nuora*, in the Vatican, was found in the ruins of the villa of Livia; and that when I saw it, previous to its removal, it was lying as it was found, with its head off, and the arm which held the scepter broken by its side.

It is indeed a remarkable history, that of the dynasty of the Cæsars. In the genealogy of the Cæsars, by Lipsius, it is found that out of forty-three persons, of whom it may have been said strictly to have been composed, thirty-two perished by violence. From the death of Cæsar under the daggers of the conspirators, to the pitiable suicide of the craven Nero, no Cæsar died without crime, or the strong suspicion of crime. No Emperor had a son for a successor. The wretched end of the daughter and granddaughter of Augustus; the son of Tiberius poisoned by Sejanus, his grandson by Caligula, and his granddaughter by Messalina; the daughter of Caligula, but two years old, condemned to die; the children of Claudius, Octavia, Antonia, and Britannicus, all slain by their adopted brother Nero,—all this is in the direct line of the Cæsars. Of the sixteen wives of the five Cæsars, six perished by a violent death, seven were repudiated, three only, by a prompt death or a fortunate widowhood, escaped divorce or punishment. An historian has well remarked that there never has been such cruelty, because there has never been such power.

And now behold this lord of the nations, the last and most miserable of his race, free from the restraints of the early part of his reign, surrounded by the subservient ministers of his pleasures and his tyrannies, who smile and flatter him in his presence and tremble in his absence. The usual impression of Nero is that of a licentious, cruel, and brutal person, with all his evil portentously developed by the possession of power greater in fact than that which was attributed by heathenism to the gods, and by the absolute subserviency, flattery, and kindred depravity of all around him. This conception of his character is just, but insufficient. He was not a bold and brutal imperial gladiator, with low tastes and vulgar vices, like Caracalla; nor was he like Maximinius, a rude provincial soldier, carrying from the camp the taste and manners of a Goth into the palace of the Cæsars. He was a person of elegant tastes and manners. He gathered philosophers about his table. He wrote such verses as Seneca condescended to praise and quote. Architecture was with him a passion, and music little less than a frenzy. He was also, as Tacitus informs us, a painter and a sculptor. In early life his bearing conveyed an impression of modesty and timidity. He blushed easily, and shrank, seemingly more in mortification than in anger, from censure and dispraise. But, in fact, he had no good qualities; the worst blood of Rome was in him. He seemed to inherit and combine from his brutal father and dreadful mother all the worst male and female vices. His artist taste and habits exercised over him no humanizing influence; on the contrary, they stimulated him to wild extravagances and to personal and official degradation. When Rome was burning, he came up from Ostia on the third day, and gave orders that the flames should not be arrested. His artist nature enjoyed the magnificent terrors which could not harm him, and which he saw would enable him to indulge in new luxuries of architecture, and in the ornamentation and reconstruction of the city.

With this character and these tastes Nero grew up in the court of Claudius in the charge of a dancer and a barber, in a school of maternal and imperial pollution, a rapid pupil under elaborate masters, in all the arts of splendid vice. His seeming modesty was but the furtive and stealthy stealing away from observation which was appropriate to his essentially tiger nature. Cruel in heart, and yet a thorough coward, he dared not indulge in cruelty unless he could do it with perfect safety, and unless he was lashed into audacity by terror. He was not satisfied unless he could put more than one vice into a single action. His sensuality could not be fully gratified unless it were connected with the betrayal and banishment of a friend. Cunning by inheritance from his mother, and under her subtle training, he became an overmatch for her before he was twenty years of age, and imposed upon her by elaborate courtesies and filial kisses, when at Baii he assisted her into a boat which he had had constructed for her destruction; and yet, though cunning and remorseless, still so timid and superstitious, that after the news had been brought to him of his mother's murder in obedience to his command, he paced the floor of his chamber all night in the wildest terror, and fancied that he could hear the voice of his murdered victim in the sound of the breeze which came from the shore where the horrid deed was done.

From that period it would seem as if he could *enjoy* only when he made *others suffer*. Afraid, after this deed, to meet the senate and the people, he yet could not be content with their mere abject acquiescence, but must put upon them a pressure which would force the people, in craven fear, to come forth and meet him with processions, and garlands, and music, and the senate to address to him the most fulsome adulations. It was not enough that Seneca should not blame; he must compose a panegyric upon the deed. The craven tyrant must have the base gratification of feeling that how low soever he may sink in infamy, the senate and the people must sink still lower, and hold him up with their flattery and approbation. His relish of iniquity is heightened by the consciousness of the real abhorrence of those out of whom his power crushes praise. When he appears upon the stage to play upon the harp, he is not content to have broken down the old Roman sentiment, which made such performances, even in private, a degradation to a patrician, but a man of consular dignity must stand by his side to hold his harp, and a consul must bespeak the indulgence of the audience for the blushing candidate for their approbation; and he must set the whole proud aristocracy of Rome to fiddling and driving chariots, and even to wrestling with gladiators in the public arena. As an actor, he cannot enjoy the enforced applauses of the people of his poor squeaking singing, and all the crowns of victory which he brings from his trip as Emperor-actor from Greece, unless he murders his rival and teacher in music and companion in revelry, and hears Seneca praise his "*generosa vox*," his rich voice. His cruelty will be without a condiment sharp enough to please his palled appetite, unless he receives from Seneca a fulsome dedication to him of his treatise upon clemency. He has no other conception of hilarity than that which involved pain in others; for when he and Otho issue out in wild revelry at night, it is to rush drunken through the streets and to knock down and bruise unoffending citizens, while a guard attends not far off to save the imperial miscreant from harm.

At the period of which I write, this dreadful spirit, thus given up to evil self-will, and free from all its old restraints, is the master of the world. It developed rapidly in that career of unparalleled iniquity which culminated in the persecution of the Christians, the burning of Rome, the wild extravagances of the Golden House, and went out in the pitiful and reluctant suicide, which proved him to have been the meanest and most cowardly, as well in proportion to his capacities the worst of all the Cæsars. It was a fearful exhibition of what a writer forcibly calls the imperial *mania*, "a double excitement born of danger and of power, of desire without limits, and of fear without cessation, of the rage for enjoyment, and the dread of death."

And now there is no one to stand in Nero's way. Burrus, of whom he was most in awe, is dead, and his place is supplied by the supple Tigillanus, whose name is inseparably associated in infamy with that of his master. Seneca falls under a cloud. Courtiers whisper that Nero has been too long in tutelage to a pedagogue whose creed was indeed stoical, but whose practice was epicurean. They point out the extent of his villas and gardens and estates, and proclaim that his wealth and luxury approach too near the imperial standard for a subject. Seneca, alarmed, hastens to lay them all at the imperial feet, and to beg to be released from a service which his sagacity advised him would soon be taken from him; and the Emperor, playing his part in the comedy well, dismisses him with many compliments, and postpones his murder and the confiscation of his goods to another time. He retires to one of his humbler villas, and writes some of those admirable moralities and lofty sentiments of superiority. to fate and fortune which would have been more impressive if we did not know that they were written after a life of eager pursuit of wealth and honors, by one who, if he were not the counselor, as some believe, was certainly the apologist of the murder of Agrippina, and the ready flatterer of Nero whenever he fell short of being excessively atrocious.

But the evil inspiration of this period of his life was the beautiful, gifted, quiet, soft-spoken, graceful fiend,—shall I call her?—Poppea. Her portrait lives in ineffaceable colors on the page of Tacitus. To her there was nothing wanting, he declares, but virtue; the rarest beauty, the loftiest rank, with an equal fortune, were her inheritance. She was modest in manners, but utterly shameless in practice. Married to a Roman knight, she was divorced to marry Otho, who was subsequently Emperor. Nero, fascinated by her, sent Otho away as Governor of Lusitania, and wished her to be divorced. But her aim was to share the imperial throne, and ruling Nero to rule the world. She refused to be divorced until she could be sure of her victim, and prepared to clear the way for herself in the palace by the removal of Agrippina the mother, and Octavia the wife, of Nero. It was by her prompting that Agrippina disappeared. The divorce and destruction of Octavia, the wife of Nero, is one of the most mournful incidents of a reign full of tragic woe. The stern historian Tacitus becomes softened as he narrates the story of the young, beautiful, and virtuous Octavia; the only specimen of pure and lofty womanhood which the history of that period presents.

She was divorced and exiled by Nero at the bidding of Poppea. But this outrage was too great to be borne peaceably by even the abject Roman populace, by whom Octavia was beloved and honored, as Agrippina, the wife of Germanicus, had been in the reign of Tiberius. They made such clamorous and passionate cries for her recall about the palace, that the tyrant was alarmed, and she was brought back from exile. The news of her recall was welcomed by such a popular demonstration as increased Nero's fear. The people rushed to the Capitol to return thanks to the gods; some overthrew the statues of Poppea, others carried those of Octavia on their shoulders, crowned with flowers; the palace was besieged by joyful multitudes who had come to thank Cæsar for his clemency. His return for the unwelcome demonstration of gratitude was an order to drive them away with clubs and with the display of naked swords.

Then with simulated fears, with tears, with appeals to Nero's pride and passion, Poppea demanded the sacrifice of the innocent rival whom she hated intensely because she wronged her grossly in supplanting her and driving her from her home and throne. A charge of adultery was vamped up. Aniceta, the murderer of Agrippina, was the infamous instrument of the plot. Octavia's faithful slaves were in vain tortured to extort false witness against her.

"Never did an exile draw more tears from the eyes of those who were its witnesses. They remembered Agrippina banished by Tiberius, and more recently, Julia driven away by Claudius. But they were in the vigorous years of life. They had known some happy days. But Octavia's marriage day was fatal to her. The house she entered presented only subjects of mourning: her father poisoned, she, the mistress of the mansion, humbled before a slave, Poppea espoused for her destruction, and she the victim of an accusation more cruel than the death which was to follow. This young creature, in the twentieth year of her age, surrounded by centurions and soldiers, the presage of her coming destruction, could not resign herself to her doom. She was ordered to prepare herself for death in a few days. She entreated Nero, no longer as his wife but as his sister; she invoked their common relations to Germanicus, and employed even the name of Agrippina to induce him to spare her life. But in vain. She was bound with chains and her veins opened, and as the blood, arrested by terror, did not flow freely, she was thrown into a hot bath, by the vapor of which she was strangled. By a refinement of cruelty her head was cut off and sent to Rome and placed before Poppea. Then thanks and offerings were presented in the temples. And this I mention," says the historian, "in order that those who wish to understand the sorrows of this epoch, may know that after every execution, thanks were presented to the gods, a token formerly of prosperity but then a sign of slaughter and of woe." (*Tacitus, Annalium,* lib. xiv. 63, 64.)

One feels, after reading such a narrative, that the feigned avenging Nemesis of the heathen, which is God's real moral retribution, would have slept too long if she had not made Nero destroy Poppea by personal brutal violence, and at last driven him, a cowering and trembling wretch, consciously loaded with the imprecations of the world, to the cowardly death which he neither dared to meet nor shun, which overtook him in the poor coal-hole of his freedman Naon, while weeping and exclaiming— "what a great artist is about to die!"

Such were the master and mistress of Cæsar's house, surrounded by an army of guards and servitors and ministers of every luxury and pleasure. If one at that period should have passed up the steps of the palace, he would have found the *atrium* divided into many portions by large curtains. By dint of entreating the freedmen and bribing the porters, he might penetrate to the peristyle in view of the crowd that waited to pass to the private quarters of the Emperor. There Cæsar, such as we see him still in his busts and medals, might have been seen lolling perhaps upon a couch, or trifling upon his harp. All around him would be seen the statues of the ancient families, which made up the imperial stock—the Julii, the Domitii, the Claudii—and the little grotesque images of the household gods. Gathering near him a crowd of courtiers would be seen endeavoring to arrest his attention, elated at his least notice and turning pale at a glance or word of displeasure. There were patricians and freedmen, parvenu slaves and ruined nobles, lackeys converted into senators, and senators with historic and heroic names, and with spirits as abject as those of lackeys, all in search of profitable employment. There also was a crowd of astrologers, Jews, buffoons, philosophers, deputies from distant cities, ambassadors from the Parthians and Germans, tributary kings, music men, mimics, charioteers and gladiators, and nearest to him the watchful slave who carried a perfumed handkerchief to put below his mouth, when too rough a breath of air from the uncourtly Apennines came to put in peril the tone of the imperial voice which was that day to charm a delighted audience in the gardens of Adonis. Suddenly, from out the inner court of the palace, the Empress Poppea, radiant with pomp and with her conscious supremacy, swept through the crowd with her brilliant bevy of attendants, for a drive to some pleasure house upon the Campagna.

Such was the house, the household, and the occupations, and such the memories of guilt and splendor on that then scene of glory, but now of desolation, the Palatine hill.

III. What a contrast to the heathen household of Cæsar were the saints who were there, and the other saints in Rome! Who were the saints of Cæsar's house we are not informed. They were probably, for the most part, humble members of the household. They may have been the servants and soldiers of the Prætorium. It was probably through the soldiers that the knowledge of St. Paul was diffused through the household of Cæsar. Each one, as he came from the day's duty of guarding the Apostle, would speak of his preaching to the group assembled in his house, or of his personal appeals to himself. Each convert thus won, with the characteristic zeal of that early period, would communicate the fact of his conversion and repeat the message of salvation. St. Paul ascribes this precise influence to his bonds. "But I would that ye should understand, brethren, that the things which have happened unto me have fallen out rather to the furtherance of the Gospel; so that my bonds in Christ are manifest in all the palace and in all other places, and many of the brethren in the Lord waxing confident by my bonds, are much more bold to speak the Word without fear." (Phil. i. 14.) His bonds were known in the Prætorium and thence in all other places; brethren, encouraged by his success and impunity in preaching while thus bound, more boldly and openly proclaimed the faith. Doubtless it was chiefly among the servants and the humbler inmates of Cæsar's house that the first converts were to be found. "Ye see your calling, brethren," says St. Paul, "how that not many mighty, not many wise, not many noble are called."

An interesting coincidence of names with some of those in the close of St. Paul's Epistle to the Romans is found in the Columbaria of the Vigna

Codini which contains the ashes of many of the household of the Cæsars. There we find the name of Tryphena—the same as that of one of the women who labored in the Lord. The name of Philologus and Julia are also there, and "Amplias the beloved of the Lord" has also a namesake there. These correspondences, if they are no more, intimate at least that the Roman Church at that period consisted chiefly of persons of the humbler classes.

Saints in Cæsar's household! And if there were saints there then, it is evident that there is no place of temptation and of trial in which men may not be Christians. Every influence against becoming Christians, in fact and in profession, and each in its highest intensity, must have been exerted in the house of Nero. It is probable that no palace ever held more degraded and abandoned beings, and that in none were dependents ever compelled to more polluting services than those which then thronged the halls of Nero. The lust of the flesh, the lust of the eye, and the pride of life enjoyed there a perpetual saturnalia. Their habits must have made excessive self-indulgence and worldliness a second nature. All worldly interests were on the side of Paganism. Hatred, ridicule, and contempt must have been in such a scene a Christian's daily and hourly experience. The liability to the outbreak of fanatical hatred into bloody persecution must have been constant. In such a scene Christ's disciples must have known well what the Master meant, by taking up the cross *daily* and following him. Yet all these adverse influences were resisted by some. There were saints in Nero's household.

The scorn and contumely with which Christians

may have been treated in Cæsar's palace appear from the remarkable *graffito*, or rude sketch, made by a sharp stylus in the cement of a wall in one of the lower apartments of the palace of Tiberius, the quarters of the servants and the Prætorian guards, which has been transferred to the museum of the Collegio Romano. The sketch represents the figure of a man with the head of an ass; the arms are stretched upon a cross, and the feet rest upon a transverse support. On the right, and a little below, a man is represented in an attitude of devotion. The inscription in rude Greek characters is, "Alexamenos is adoring God." It is probably the work of an inmate or servant of the palace who thus ridicules the religion of his fellow-servant or inmate. The Jews were represented by Tacitus as rendering divine homage to the ass, and Christians were at this time considered as only a baser sort of Jews. This constitutes a singular and striking proof, in the very palace of the Cæsars, of the contumelies to which Christians were then exposed. It is also remarkable that the earliest authentic representation of Christ upon the cross should be thus rude and scornful. To take up the cross in Cæsar's household is thus proved to have been another name for exposure to ridicule and shame.

But there is no reason to doubt that *some* mighty and wise and noble connected with Cæsar's house were called to the faith of Christ. There are some patrician names among those to whom St. Paul sends his Christian salutations, in the Epistle to the Romans. Ecclesiastical history also confirms this fact. And what a lesson does the fact read to those who in public life in our day declare that it is almost if not quite impossible to be at the same time a statesman and a Christian; to serve at the same time God and Cæsar; to discharge the duties of public life and those of a strict and holy follower of Christ! Yet how evidently is their position less adverse to the claims of Christ than that of those who professed faith in Him in Cæsar's court! They were born in a Christian community. They inherit a Christian sentiment. They are surrounded by Christian influences. The government with which they are connected is nominally Christian, and its constitution and laws enshrine the principles of Christian morality. There is nothing in the occupation and duties of government in any of its departments which is *in itself* demoralizing. On the contrary, it is a most lofty calling. The application of the principles of justice to the government of a great people for their security, their development, their prosperity, and their happiness,—what human function can be nobler? What can be more directly in the line of the Christian's high vocation, who, while he works out his own salvation with fear and trembling, is also laboring to fashion and fix society in such a position as shall best fit it to profess and possess faith in the Son of God? Nay, the open and public Christian profession of a public man by no means robs him of public honor and regard. It only so restricts him that he cannot well work with those with whom politics is a trade, and the only trade in which dishonesty is not dishonorable. But the public honor him all the more for his profession of the Christian faith if it shows itself brave, genuine, and consistent. The public knows not how to express its huge delight when it finds a leader and commander of the people thoroughly honest, true, and staunch; and these are precisely the qualities which a real Christ-life in the heart produces. Christian men, fitted to adorn their country's history and promote their country's good, should not avoid public life on the ground that it is impossible to discharge its functions and remain true to Christian principle. The saints of Cæsar's household cry shame on their unmanly weakness.

Hence they are not to be heard or heeded, those godless and abandoned men with whom politics is gambling and political principles but the loaded dice with which they play the dishonest game. These flatterers and plunderers of the public, golden-mouthed orators, whose glittering rhetoric has been gilded in the public mint, warn and hoot Christian men from the ground of politics, crying out, "Keep off from our domains. We are sovereigns here; we have pre-emptive claims to this field. You have no right to come here with your strict Christian principles. You and they are in the way. Your scruples are a bother. Leave politics to us. We understand them. We have no troublesome misgivings. You are too good. Go and teach Sunday-schools. Sing psalms. We will take care of the government. You cannot be a Christian and a politician."

Oh! evil it is, and evil it has been, and more evil it will be, because these men are believed, and because they so often frighten or disgust God's men from the field. The greatest want of our times has been and is the want of saints in that divine institution, the state, who shall comprehend that they are placed as ministers of God for the punishment of evil-doers, and for the praise of those that do well.

IV. But there were other saints besides those in Cæsar's household or connected with Cæsar's court. "All the saints," says St. Paul, "salute you."

A goodly company they were! Many of them were soon to be enrolled among the noble army of martyrs. Most of those whom St. Paul had saluted a few years previous in his Epistle to the Romans, were probably alive and still at Rome. We know of some who were at that time there. Faithful and affectionate Epaphroditus, so tenderly and gratefully mentioned by St. Paul, (Phil. ii. 25–30,) was there. The bearer of pecuniary aid from the Philippians to St. Paul, he was sick at Rome nigh unto death, but seems to have been convalescent when the Apostle wrote his Epistle. Tychicus, a beloved brother and faithful minister and fellow-servant in the Lord, (Eph. xxi.; Col. iv. 17; 2 Tim. iv. 12,) was also at Rome during St. Paul's residence. Onesimus also is reckoned among the beloved brethren by the Apostle. It is interesting to observe the manner in which he is mentioned by St. Paul in his Epistle to the Colossians. He went with Tychicus, who bore a letter of St. Paul to the Colossians, himself bearing the remarkable letter of the Apostle to Philemon, his master. While the Apostle commits him to the justice of his master as a slave who had wronged him, he pleads for his kindness as a repentant and converted brother, who deserved not only his pity and forgiveness, but his esteem. And at the same time that Onesimus, a converted fugitive slave, of his own will returns to his master and takes this epistle, he is commended by St. Paul to the church at Colosse, in connection with Tychicus as equally deserving of their regard. "Whom," speaking of Tychicus, he says, "I send unto you for the same purpose that he might know your estate, and comfort your hearts; *with Onesimus, a faithful and beloved brother*, who is one of you. *They* shall make known unto you all things which are done here." (Col. iv. 7–9.) The Christian slave is put on a precise equality with another honored Christian brother in the Kingdom of God. It is a striking illustration of St. Paul's own exhortation to Philemon to treat him as no longer a slave, but above a slave, as a brother in the Lord, and exhibits the inevitably emancipating and equalizing power of the true working of the brotherhood of Christ.

We know also that Aristarchus was at Rome. He accompanied St. Paul there, (Acts, xix. 29; xxvii. 2,) and is mentioned as his fellow-prisoner. That bond of fellow-imprisonment, whether at Cæsarea or at Rome, does not appear, and the fidelity of which it was a proof, must have made him peculiarly dear to the Apostle. Justus, a converted Jew, is mentioned as one who had been a comfort to him as a fellow-worker unto the Kingdom. Epaphras, (Col. i. 7; iv. 12,) a minister of the church of Colosse, was evidently a person of unusual fervor. St. Paul calls him his "dear fellow-servant," a faithful minister of Christ, always laboring fervently for the Colossians in his prayers, and as having great zeal in behalf of those among whom he labored. Demas also (Col. iv. 14) is joined in the same salutation with Luke, the beloved physician. Afterward St. Paul speaks of him in those touching words in which there is much sorrow and no anger. "Demas hath forsaken me, having loved this present world."

But those in whom St. Paul must have taken most comfort at Rome were Timothy, his son in the Gospel, the beloved Luke, and Mark. We do not know the reasons for the absence of Timothy from the church of Ephesus, in the charge of which St. Paul had left him some years before; but that he was not about to return there, as to a settled and exclusive Episcopate, appears from St. Paul's declaration to the Philippians: "I trust in the Lord Jesus to send Timotheus shortly unto you, that I also may be of good comfort when I know your state." (Phil. ii. 19.) Timothy's residence at Rome and St. Paul's message to the Philippians prove that the apostleships and episcopates of that day were missionary rather than stationary. St. Luke it is believed, and with great probability, composed the Acts of the Apostles under the eye of St. Paul while they were together at Rome. If they had been written later, St. Luke would certainly have continued the history of St. Paul. Mark also was with the Apostle (Col. iv. 10,) when St. Paul wrote to the Asiatic churches. The disagreement which led to St. Paul's separation from him several years before seems to have been entirely forgotten. If to these we add some of the brethren mentioned by St. Paul in his Epistle to the Romans, and others like-minded and like-hearted not mentioned, we see the Apostle surrounded and cheered by much Christian fellowship, sympathy, and affection.

Great indeed must have been the strength and consolation which the Apostle derived from these brethren in the Lord. We know that sympathy is sweet in proportion to the bitterness of trials. We know that Christian fellowship is dear just in the degree in which one is surrounded by unchristian and uncongenial influences. Hence St. Paul, in bonds and living amid a most awfully polluted Paganism, must have richly relished the converse and sympathy, the mutual faith and prayer of Christian brethren and friends. Hence the terms of tender endearment and generous praise in which their names are mentioned. He speaks of them as "beloved," as "dear," as "faithful," as "those that labor," that "labor much," that "labor exceedingly in prayer," that exhibit "great zeal," and that "long after" their converts in Christ. We know not precisely where, but probably very near the place in which we now worship, these brethren met with St. Paul, or themselves preached and prayed. We know how and what they preached, and to whom they prayed. They preached Christ and him crucified. They prayed only to the Triune God. They labored in the establishment of a kingdom not of this world.

It would be difficult to conceive a greater contrast than that presented by the house and household of Cæsar on the one hand, and the saints there and the other saints in Rome on the other. It was Paganism in its utmost power, splendor, and corruption; and it was Christianity in its first feebleness, poverty, and purity. It was the setting of a lurid and baneful sun, and the rising of a pure and lustrous day-star. Nero and Paul represent, each in the highest degree, what the world and the Gospel can do for man. The one tormented by conscience in the midst of boundless luxury and power. The other joyful on the verge of martyrdom. The one possessing all things and enjoying nothing. The other having nothing and yet possessing all things. The one corrupted by power, and the other purified by suffering. The one driven by terror into the arms of death with a passionate love of life, and the horror of a doom to which nothing but the dread of a direr doom could have ever urged his coward soul. The other exclaiming, with calm eyes fixed upon the prepared altar of his martyr-sacrifice, "I am ready to be offered, and the time of my departure is at hand!"

Nero and his court, and Paul and the saints,—these are the parties for our choice which God is ever presenting to us all. The gain of the world, or the attempt to gain it, or the saving of the soul,—these are the alternatives.

"Choose ye this day whom YE will serve!"

LECTURE VII.

ST. PAUL'S POSITION IN REFERENCE TO ESTABLISHED CUSTOMS AND INSTITUTIONS.

The powers that be are ordained of God.—ROMANS, xiii. 1.

THE law's delay may be a modern phrase, but the fact which it expresses is old. It was exemplified in the case of St. Paul. He arrived in Rome in the spring of the year A.D. 61. His accusers were not there. The Jews in Rome had not even heard that they were coming. By the Roman law it was essential to a process that the accuser should be personally present. A trial might therefore be long delayed. An accused person might suffer more by delay than by an adverse judgment. Hence, personal malignity might hold one a long time accused, in restraint or imprisonment and obloquy, without trial. If he or his friends had not sufficient influence to bring the trial on, it might be suspended for years. When it was probable that the accused might be acquitted, it is evident that a malicious accuser might wish to delay the trial. By thus delaying justice, he might obtain what he sought—revenge.

This was probably the policy of St. Paul's accusers. The case was one which evidently had no Roman law to rest upon. Agrippa had openly declared that St. Paul might have been released if he had not appealed unto Cæsar.

But quite apart from the intent of his accusers, Paul's case was one which would be likely to be long delayed. Witnesses were to be brought from the remotest portions of the empire. The convenience or caprice of the Emperor in hearing the case was to be waited for. Tiberius was in the habit of putting off trials for years. Nero, immersed in guilty pleasures and frivolous pursuits, would not be likely to be more prompt.

But the period of delay was not lost or wasted by St. Paul. He had been sent by the Master to Rome to preach and teach Christ and his kingdom. Diligently and faithfully he discharged that mission. Many of his hearers were brought to the knowledge of the truth as it is in Jesus.

The case of Onesimus, the fugitive slave of Philemon, is one of peculiar interest. Converted by St. Paul to the faith of Christ, he was sent back to his master. It is a case which furnishes a proper occasion on which to consider the whole subject of St. Paul's views and feelings in relation to established customs and institutions.

The great principle on which St. Paul proceeded in reference to all established customs and institutions,—by which we shall be able to understand all that he did and all that he left undone in reference to them,—is one which is extremely simple and intelligible. It is this: he did not attack established customs and institutions, how much soever of evil sprang from them directly or indirectly, unless they interfered with, or prevented the personal duty, or personal access of the soul, to God. He attacked indeed, directly and vigorously, all heathen worship, because it was treason to God and a sacrifice to devils; because it robbed the soul of its privilege of access to its Heavenly Father, and prevented the discharge of its duties of love and service to him. He also attacked the doctrine of the present obligation of the abrogated Jewish economy, because it destroyed the Gospel. These were the interests of that spiritual kingdom which he came to administer. Everything which obtruded itself into this kingdom, as truth which was falsehood, as duty which was sin, as obligation which was a matter of indifference, he confuted, resisted, denounced, forbade. A law of man which should forbid him to profess faith in Christ and to perform his spiritual duties in the world, he would disobey, even under the penalty of death, because it was an unlawful intrusion of the power of a human government into the sphere of divine things, which would have compelled him to sin, and to omit the discharge of his highest obligations. While it was no part of his mission as an Apostle to define what *acts* of human governments were lawful within *their sphere*, it was his right and duty to resist and disobey such laws as would forbid him to discharge his duty in the higher sphere of the kingdom of God.

Hence those customs, and those established institutions, and laws of human society, which he found in existence, however evil in themselves or their results, he did not directly attack and denounce, and preach the duty of destroying. He denounced evil in all its forms, and in all institutions, whether of divine or human origin. Even those which were the outgrowth of human depravity, or the perversion of such divinely established institutions as the Church and State, he did not declare should be at once destroyed. He inculcated *principles* which, if practically and universally established, would destroy every evil custom and institution in the world. He knew that it would be useless to cut off the evil fruit and leave the tree evil, because its next growth would be the same; and because if the tree were made good, the fruit through all time would be also good. There were all around St. Paul at Rome vast structures of iniquity,—evil from their base to their summit,—and yet, what did he do? He preached the kingdom of God, and taught those things which concerned the Lord Jesus. There was at Rome the awful despotism of Nero; there was a system of concubinage; there were cruel gladiatorial fights; there were the horrible slaughters of beasts and men in the amphitheaters; there was a dreadful system of slavery; and yet not against one of them is there a denunciation in the Epistles which he wrote from Rome. But no doubt the presence of these awful iniquities added fervor to his earnest exhortations to the love of God and man, to purity, and righteousness, and mercy, before which all these pollutions and cruelties would flee away!

Let us examine the mode in which St. Paul treated some established customs and institutions while he sojourned at Rome. During that period he wrote the Epistle to Philemon, to the Ephesians, the Colossians, the Philippians; and during his second sojourn his second Epistle to Timothy. To these Epistles I shall particularly refer. And in order that we may have a complete view of St. Paul's mode of proceeding in reference to them, let the facts be borne in mind which we have already mentioned, viz., that the *general* description of St. Paul's work at Rome was that he preached Christ and the kingdom of God, and that, in the midst of customs and institutions which were utterly evil, he did not turn aside from his great work to denounce them, but inculcated principles and fostered feelings in the presence and ascendency of which they could not survive.

We will speak first of those institutions which were of divine origin and obligation.

I. The Jewish economy was of divine origin, and had been of divine obligation. Many of the Jewish Christians, as we have seen, still contended that its rites were obligatory. Now these rites, and indeed the whole Jewish economy, St. Paul contended had been done away and were no longer obligatory. Nay, he contended that it was wrong to observe them as of present obligation. In the Epistle to the Colossians, (ii. 16, 17,) he writes: "Let no man therefore judge you in meat, or in drink, or in respect of a holy day, or of the new moon, or of the sabbath days, which are a shadow of things to come, but the body is of Christ." To condemn this institution as of present obligation, was a duty which he owed to the Gospel, which he was commissioned to proclaim.

II. The *family* was a divine institution and of perpetual obligation. It was founded in Eden; it was regulated by the law; it was enjoined in the Gospel. Its one divine form was that of man and wife, and their offspring. To break the marriage bonds was one of the greatest of crimes. It was to violate a specific law of God; and it was to fill society with pollution, violence, and manifold evil.

During the Republic, and even in the age of Augustus, the utmost purity in the family relation prevailed among Roman citizens. The name of a Roman maiden was synonymous with purity and modesty, and that of a Roman matron with dignity and honor. The violation of the marriage bond between Romans was by law, and in fact, visited with death or exile. The guilty daughter and granddaughter of Augustus, as we have seen, were both banished to a solitary island,—a humiliation to the proud Cæsar which was a fit punishment of his own cruel licentiousness. But this stern jealousy of the purity of the Roman family had far more reference to the interests of the state than to morality. It was that the Roman stock might be preserved unmixed and unweakened, and that the state might always have fit citizens to uphold and extend the glory of all-conquering Rome. Outside of the Roman families great license prevailed. It was the purity of the Roman matron and maid, and not that of the Roman father or youth, that was so sternly guarded. Philosophers counted licentiousness within the limits of the law, to be rather unwise than wicked. Cato did not condemn it. Cicero apologized for it. Epictitus, the sternest of the Roman Stoics, regarded it as weakness and folly, but not as crime when it did not violate the law. So that even in the best times of the Republic, when the purity of the family relation was singularly preserved, it was on the grounds of civil polity and expediency, and not on those high grounds of inherent and divine and moral obligation, on which alone obedience is virtue.

But at the period when St. Paul was in Rome, society had become exceedingly corrupt. We have seen how, in the family of the Cæsars, there had been a frightful succession of adulteries, repudiations, divorces, remarryings, concubinages, legal murders, and secret poisonings, in the interests of monstrous lusts. The same spirit and practices were exhibited in the entire patrician circle. How little the sanctity of the marriage tie in itself, and irrespective of the law of the state, was respected even in the purer period of a hundred years before Nero, appears in the well-known case of Cato. No name in the Roman annals stands higher for lofty virtue, on the Roman model, than that of Cato. Yet when his friend Hortensius, desirous of an heir to his immense fortune and high fame, divorced his wife and was in search of another, Cato offered to him his own, with whom he had lived happily and in honor, and the offer was gratefully accepted; and after the death of Hortensius and the birth of children to him, his wife was remarried to Cato. "The virtuous Cato," said Cæsar, "surrendered his wife when she was young, and resumed her when she was rich." If such things could occur at that period, and among men of the high moral standing of Cato and Hortensius, we can readily suppose that in the days of Claudius and of Nero, the very saturnalia of the Roman history, corruptions of the most frightful kind must have spread through the whole structure of Roman society. The system of patronage and clientage which prevailed at Rome, inevitably forced the manners and habits of the Cæsars and of the patricians on the lower and dependent classes. Hence, as was to be anticipated, it is found that the marriage and family relations were in a state of corruption, contempt, and dislike, which were the sources of enormous crimes and evils. In vain did

Augustus endeavor to force and shame his subjects from celibacy, and from loose and licentious divorces, into permanent marriages and the family duties which they involved. The patricians, leading the life of the circus, the theaters, and the baths,—studying, reveling, and traveling,—having free play to every whim and passion,—could be induced to marry only from motives of ambition or of interest. Mecænas, the favorite minister of Augustus, in the face of his master's stern decrees against divorce, repudiated and remarried his wife not less than twenty times. From the palace of the Cæsars to the lowest quarters of the Aventine and the Suburra, the marriage and family relation, when St. Paul wrote, was in a frightfully corrupt condition. "The old Roman paternal despotism could not subsist under imperial despotism; the old laws of the family were too stern for effeminate Rome; too national for Rome, inundated with foreign elements; too patrician for Rome, governed by freedmen; and too little in harmony with the debased morality and philosophy of the age."

Now it was just at this period, when this family license and corruption culminated, that St. Paul lived in Rome. How did he deal with the subject in his letters to the churches, written when all this frightful corruption was passing under his eye? He explained the divine constitution of the family; the headship of the husband; the reciprocal duty of the husband to love and honor, and of the wife to love, honor, and obey; the duties of both to their children, and of their children to them. In the Epistle to the Ephesians, (v. 22-33,) he writes thus:

"Wives, submit yourselves unto your own husbands, as unto the Lord.

"For the husband is the head of the wife, even as Christ is the head of the church: and he is the saviour of the body.

"Therefore as the church is subject unto Christ, so *let* the wives *be* to their own husbands in everything.

"Husbands, love your wives, even as Christ also loved the church, and gave himself for it;

"That he might sanctify and cleanse it with the washing of water by the word,

"That he might present it to himself a glorious church, not having spot, or wrinkle, or any such thing; but that it should be holy and without blemish.

"So ought men to love their wives as their own bodies. He that loveth his wife loveth himself.

"For no man ever yet hated his own flesh; but nourisheth and cherisheth it, even as the Lord the church:

"For we are members of his body, of his flesh, and of his bones.

"For this cause shall a man leave his father and mother, and shall be joined unto his wife, and they two shall be one flesh.

"This is a great mystery: but I speak concerning Christ and the church.

"Nevertheless let every one of you in particular so love his wife even as himself; and the wife *see* that she reverence *her* husband."

The reciprocal duties of parents and children are thus enjoined, (Eph. vi. 1–4:)

"Children, obey your parents in the Lord: for this is right.

"Honor thy father and mother; which is the first commandment with promise;

"That it may be well with thee, and thou mayest live long on the earth.

"And, ye fathers, provoke not your children to wrath; but bring them up in the nurture and admonition of the Lord."

The same injunctions are repeated in the Epistle to the Colossians, (Col. iii. 18–21.)

Here we see that a divine and holy character is attached to the family relation, and that its duties are to be discharged "as to the Lord." The union of man and wife is like that of Christ and his church, and its reciprocal duties and affections are like the holy ones which spring from that divine relation. It is a beautiful and pure ideal placed in the midst of the awful practical corruptions of the age, whose realization was approached in the actual practice and experience of Christians. It was the pure family as it ought to be, in the midst of the polluted family as it was.

Now that to which I wish to call attention is the fact that St. Paul's mode of dealing with the corruption that prevailed in this divine institution, was to describe it and enjoin it as it was divinely constituted, and as it ought to be. He did not directly attack the prevailing and recognized laws and customs of the period, which were awful violations of the true purposes of the family, dreadfully corrupting to the individuals, and fearfully destructive of the public prosperity and peace. He attacked them only by enjoining as sacred and indispensable duties all that was opposite to them in the letter and the spirit. Those calm and solemn instructions, those words of passionless and weighty wisdom, intended for all ages and all nations,—one can scarcely conceive of them as written from the licentious Rome of Nero to the scarcely less licentious cities of Asia Minor. It may have been that as his hand, benumbed by the long and weary weight of his chain, was slowly and painfully tracing these words, he could see the gay thoroughfare on which he lived thronged with the chariots in which shameless patrician vice, as it is painted in the vivid pages of honest and indignant Juvenal, and as we cannot repeat it, flaunted by; or a louder rumor and a vast clinking train of eunuchs, players, pantomimes, and prætorian guards, might announce to him that the greatest and the guiltiest pair, the most powerful and shameless corrupters of all family ties and all remains of chastity and honor then upon the earth, Nero and Poppea, were approaching. Now what a proof it is of the large, divine, calm, world-embracing wisdom by which St. Paul was guided, that at such a time he could withhold his holy and indignant denunciations! Not all holy men could have refrained from denouncing directly and personally upon Nero as Imperator, and of charging upon established customs, and immunities, and laws of Rome, the frightful corruption that then prevailed.

But St. Paul knew that the source of all these evils was deeper—even in the depraved and fallen heart of man. He knew that the kingdom of God cometh not with observation. Its first work is in the soul. It penetrates, pervades, transforms institutions, by first penetrating, pervading, transforming the souls of those by whom they are fashioned and sustained. It changes the one as it does the other.

That which in the heart and life superinduced is evil, *falls;* that which is good in the design of God, *stands transformed.* That which is *evil in itself* in society, if society becomes holy, and in proportion as it becomes holy, disappears; that which is good, in the lower sense of prudential or mere moral goodness, remains, and becomes penetrated with a higher and holier goodness. Ambition, hatred, cruelty, and lust disappear from holy hearts, in the same measure as they are holy; nature's love for wife and child, and for blameless human and sensitive enjoyment, remains, *converted,* purified, exalted into holy affections, and into joys which are at the same time duties. Precisely such is the transformation of society. That which is evil in itself—such as the amphitheater with its inhuman slaughter, wars of aggression and ambition, licensed and protected licentiousness, the outgrowth of ambition, cruelty, and lust—will disappear among nations in proportion as they are holy. The family and the state, which are good in themselves and divine in their organization, but which have been degraded into instruments of human iniquity, will remain transformed and purified.

Such is the process and the work of holiness in individuals, and in the customs, laws, and institutions of the world. The institutions which are wholly evil do not fall by being battered, but by being undermined. They are not suddenly overthrown like the temple of Dagon by Samson, but they gradually melt away like the ice palace of the northern Czar. Such institutions as are conformed to man's true needs, or are of divine origin, are filled at length with purity, under the influence of Christian light and life, not as at midnight the world is filled with sudden and temporary light by lightning flashes, but as the day fills it, at first with the pearly radiance of the rising, and then with the full effulgence of the risen sun. Hence St. Paul could see the imperial *cortege* and the gay patrician crowds flash by in guilty revelry, and feel with profound sadness the awful desecration of the family institution, and could yet indite those calm and holy teachings to the Ephesians, in which there are no allusions to the scenes that were passing all around him. He wrote with loving tranquillity, for he wrote for all time and all the world, under the influence of that Holy Spirit whose emblem is the dove. "Wisdom reacheth from one end unto the other *mightily*, and *sweetly* doth she order all things." Divine wisdom embraces the whole course of time in her vigorous administration, and gentle and gradual as nature's growths and processes, are her moral and spiritual transformations. The form and structure of the vine is not changed when the sap recedes in winter and creeps upward in the spring; but the result of the one is a gradual transformation of the leafy and purple vineyard into bare and straggling sticks, and of the other into graceful and festooned foliage, which makes the hill-side laugh, and into precious and clustered fruit which makes glad the heart of man.

III. As is the family so also is the state a divine institution. It is so described by St. Paul in his Epistle to the Romans. Obedience to it is enjoined in the Lord, and as unto the Lord. It was when Nero was Emperor of Rome that St. Paul wrote to the Romans the most full and complete assertion and explanation of the divine constitution of the state, of the sacred character of the magistracy, and of the respective duties of the rulers and the ruled, that inspiration has produced. It certainly proves the universal applicability of these words to find that they were addressed to the horribly misgoverned citizens of Rome just at the period when a Claudius had ceased, and a Nero had begun to reign.

"Let every soul be subject unto the higher powers. For there is no power but of God: the powers that be are ordained of God.

"Whosoever therefore resisteth the power, resisteth the ordinance of God: and they that resist shall receive to themselves damnation.

"For rulers are not a terror to good works, but to the evil. Wilt thou then not be afraid of the power? do that which is good, and thou shalt have praise of the same:

"For he is the minister of God to thee for good. But if thou do that which is evil, be afraid; for he beareth not the sword in vain: for he is the minister of God, a revenger to *execute* wrath upon him that doeth evil.

"Wherefore *ye* must needs be subject, not only for wrath, but also for conscience sake.

"For for this cause pay ye tribute also: for they are God's ministers, attending continually upon this very thing.

"Render therefore to all their dues: tribute to whom tribute *is due;* custom to whom custom; fear to whom fear; honor to whom honor."

Here is a description of the state, as before of the family, as it is divinely constituted, and as it should be administered. Without any theories, or any explanations, as to how governments should be constituted,—whether as republican, oligarchical, or monarchical, or mixed,—he makes the broad and distinct announcement that the powers *that be*—*established governments*—are the ordinance of God. As such they are to be obeyed. Resistance to them is resistance to the ordinance of God. They are designed to administer justice, to be a terror to the evil, and to reward and protect the good. Hence also they must be obeyed, not from fear only, but from conscience. Hence also they must be sustained by the payment of dues and tributes. They must also be honored as well as obeyed, because established by God, and administering human justice by his authority.

It is to be observed that while organized society, with laws, protection, punishment, and rewards, is declared to be an ordinance of God, there is no prescription as to the *forms* which governments should assume, and no expression of preference for one rather than another. The precise form of the family —man and wife and their offspring—*is* designated, but not that of the state.

It is to be observed, moreover, that while obedience in general to parents and the state is enjoined, the limitations to that obedience are nowhere prescribed. In the case of the family, love, protection, nurture on the part of parents, and obedience on the part of children, are enjoined; but the contingencies in which they may or ought to be limited, suspended, or withheld, are not specified. It is certain that if parents enjoin crime upon their children, it is their duty not to obey, but to disobey. In like manner while the duty of magistrates is enjoined, the circumstances in which it becomes lawful or obligatory not to obey or to disobey, are not specified. It is certain that such circumstances may arise. The settlement of such cases is left to the individual conscience. By such means it is that conscience becomes purified and quickened.

Thus it was that St. Paul wrote to the Romans during the early period of Nero's reign at Rome. When he resided at Rome the second time, the public administration of Nero had become as atrocious as his private life. And yet in the letter to Timothy, which he wrote from Rome, there is no change and no modification of his teachings in respect to governments and rulers, and obedience to them. He did not then write anything to this effect: "When I wrote the Epistle to the Romans, enjoining obedience to the government as of divine institution, that government was then justly administered, under the direction of Seneca and Burrus. Now it has become an instrument of capricious cruelty and oppression. It has violated all the purposes for which a government is established; and therefore it has ceased to be worthy of obedience or honor; it would be lawful and right to overthrow it." He wrote no such words. He let his first teachings stand. As the inspired teacher of the Church for all ages, it was his office to declare the principles upon which governments should be on the one hand administered, and on the other obeyed. While such governments existed their laws were to be obeyed, unless they were such as compelled individuals to violate the laws of God. When it would become lawful, or expedient, or obligatory, for subjects to combine to overthrow such a detestable tyranny, he did not declare. He left such questions for the decision of Christian citizens on the principles which he had enjoined.

It is certainly all the more striking proof of the fact that it is not the mission of the Gospel and the church to assault and overthrow existing institutions, however evil in themselves or in their administration, but rather that it is their divine function to proclaim principles which shall, if really adopted, gradually undermine or transform them, to find that St. Paul wrote this remarkable description of the relative duties of governors and citizens at a period when the world was most tyranically, cruelly, and unjustly governed. It is true that when St. Paul wrote to the Romans, the government of Nero was mild and just. But St. Paul had known well the dreadful character of the two preceding reigns of Caligula and Claudius. He knew human nature well enough to be assured that such vast irresponsible power in the hands of one man was fearfully liable to abuses. All these abuses of power were known, and perhaps exaggerated, in the provinces. News from Rome, sent by officials, or carried by private hand, was posted in the Basilica, or in the Forum of all the cities of the Empire. The bulletin would announce that Nero had just escaped assassination by his mother, and offerings of gratitude for his safety would be offered in all the temples; but private letters and the gossip of travelers would spread abroad the fact that Agrippina was murdered at the suggestion of Poppea. Thus St. Paul in the provinces would not remain ignorant of the atrocities of the capital. He had known the cruel treatment of his countrymen by Caligula. He had known all the wild and capricious excesses of the two crowned furies, Messalina and Agrippina, in the reign of Claudius. And yet it was in the full knowledge of all this misuse and perversion of power, that he wrote that calm and complete delineation of the relation of the rulers and the ruled, whose first words are "Let every soul be subject to the higher powers."

The two points which seem singular to us in this doctrine of St. Paul are that the powers that be, however unjust in their origin and cruel in their administration, should be said to be ordained of God, and that the duty of obedience to them, without restriction or qualification, "as unto the Lord," should be enjoined. Yet there they stand in St. Paul's Epistles, too distinctly to be misunderstood. They have been used to sanctify cruel despotism, and to make resistance to them a crime against God. How are these teachings to be reconciled with the attributes of Him whose name is love and whose government is righteous, and who demands loyalty and obedience only to that which is just and good?

1. When St. Paul says that the powers which be are ordained of God, I understand him to mean that it is the will of God that man should live in organized society under governors and laws. He does not specify, as in the case of the family, any one *form* which states shall assume. The *form* of such governments is an ordinance of man. *The existence of government in some form* is an ordinance of God. Hence St. Paul was able to say, even of the government of the Cæsars, that it was of God. Does one who thinks of the government of Nero exclaim, "Can it be that this awful domination is of God?" We do not wonder at the question. Yet when one looks in upon the family where the husband is a

brute, and the wife a fiend, and the children the victims of their blended vices; or when one or all convert the family relations into a dreadful scene of cruelty, suffering, and pollution from which it is impossible to escape, and which it is a life-long agony to endure, he might ask the same question, "Can this be of God?" Not *this* certainly in the intention of God, in either case. In the one case justice and mercy on the part of the ruler, and reverence and obedience on the part of the people, and in the other case mutual affection and regard on the part of husband and wife, and loving obedience on the part of children,—*this* is the ordinance of God. It is none the less a right ordinance of God because man perverts it. With all its horror, the government of Nero is better than anarchy; and with all its woes, the family in its worst form is better than the lawless reign of lust and passion, which would soon convert what God created a paradise into a pandemonium.

2. If these institutions of the family and the state be of God, then obedience to them, "as to the Lord," logically ensues. That no restrictions to this duty are stated, should create no surprise. On the one hand, justice, mercy, and affection are enjoined on governments and parents, and on the other, reverence and obedience on the part of citizens and children. They are to go together. When we are bidden to obey lawful authorities, and when there is no specification of what we are to do when they cease to exercise lawful authority lawfully, it by no means follows that there is no limit to the obedience which we should render. We know one limit which is clearly and broadly marked. If either of

them bid us to commit a crime, we know that it is our duty to disobey. Other duties to self, to brothers and sisters, and to communities, may be paramount to the duties of parents or of governments when they transcend their powers. It is the province of the lawmaker to put forth precise and dogmatic laws concerning certain relations. It rests with those to whom they are addressed to determine when disobedience becomes duty.

Thus we see how they err who make man's path of duty to be *always* a straight and level way. It is, on the contrary, *often* rugged and winding, and not well defined, and to be discerned only by alert and earnest faculties. He climbs, he plunges, he wades, he dives, he deviates, he turns impossible precipices and leaps yawning gulfs, and when he shall reach the end of the journey, palpitating and weary, he will be developed in strength and capacity, and relish his success all the more because it was difficult to gain.

LECTURE VIII.

ST. PAUL'S POSITION IN REFERENCE TO ESTABLISHED CUSTOMS AND INSTITUTIONS.

WE have shown in our last how St. Paul dealt with existing institutions. He did not attack them directly, however evil they might be; but he inculcated principles, the adoption of which would destroy evil by introducing good. In the case of divine institutions which were perverted from their original purpose, he inculcated the duties and affections which were appropriate to them. He unfolded the duties of the marriage and family relation. He explained the mutual duties of rulers and subjects. He described the *"powers that be"*—existing governments—as ordained of God; and with Nero upon the throne, proclaimed disobedience to government to be disloyalty to Heaven.

We shall not be able fully to feel all the significance of this fact, unless we recall some of the incidents of those reigns, which will show us what sort of a government existed in Rome just previous to the period when St. Paul wrote his Epistle.

Every one has heard of what may be called the more personal extravagances of the reign of Caligula. His incestuous passion for his sisters; his claim to be a god, and to hold private conferences with the moon, and with Jupiter; the elevation of his favorite horse to the Consulate, and his wish that the Romans had but one neck, that he might destroy them all at a blow,—those imperial insanities are well known. We have alluded to his bridge at Baii, which drew to that point all the vessels of the empire, and called for thousands more,—an extravagance which strained the resources of the empire to the utmost for a mere imperial whim. We have spoken of the drunken frenzy in which, on the occasion of its inauguration, he consigned helpless and unoffending victims by the boat-load to the sea. We have described also his impious cruelty to the Jews. Even these wild violations of all the purposes for which a government is instituted, were outdone by the means which he adopted to replenish his exhausted treasury.

Seneca informs us that at one repast he expended ten millions of sesterces; and in a year two thousand and seven hundred millions of sesterces. These extravagances called for extraordinary means. Accordingly confiscations were multiplied. Caligula professed to find in the records of Tiberius proofs of the treason of those rich persons whose possessions he coveted; and they were cut off. He adopted a means, which subsequent tyrants largely practiced, of replenishing his treasury by getting himself appointed heir of the estates of his subjects. "If you wish a favor of Cæsar—make him your heir! If you wish to escape a charge of treason—make him your heir! If you wish to rescue a relative from the wiles of informers—make him your heir!" Such were the messages which his creatures gave to the trembling citizens. Even then, if the old man who had enrolled him as heir to the detriment of all his own relations, lingered too long in life, a delicate ragout was sent to him from the Emperor's table with his compliments, and with poison in it; and he died it was said of apoplexy, and the grateful Cæsar commemorated his virtues. If it was announced that one who was a stranger to him had left to him all his property, to the exclusion of all his own relatives, he declared that the sanctity of wills must be preserved; and took the money! If another who had received any benefit, by offices or contracts from the state, had forgotten him in his will, it was declared to be an infamous insult to the imperial majesty and beneficence; and he broke the will and took the money. If another died, and a friend of Cæsar informed him that the deceased told him that he *intended* to have made him heir—though his name was not mentioned in the will—the intention was held to be sacred, and Cæsar broke the will and received the money. Thus a vast source of supply was opened by a means which was at the same time absolutely unjust, and so cunningly cruel that it must have kept every wealthy citizen in a terror of anxiety, and all his relatives in a state of doubt and fear.

On the birth of a daughter the poor Cæsar affects to fear absolute ruin and destitution. How to provide for her support? He asks alms of his people. He seats himself in the vestibule of his palace on his throne, to receive their gifts. Consuls, the senate, patricians, goldsmiths, and merchants crowd, with hands and togas full of coins, and of precious gifts, and lay them at the feet of Cæsar. It is much, but it is not enough. The imperial beggar resorts to another device which sinks the Cæsar as low as the vilest imagination could place the most infamous creature of his household. As one now passes through the colossal substructions of his palace, recently uncovered, under the auspices of the Emperor of the French, the series of apartments is pointed out which, according to the statement of a Roman historian, Caligula rented out as the place of debauchery, whose patrons were commended by him for thus aiding their impoverished lord, burdened with the expense of an imperial baby.

But the supply is temporary and insufficient. He professes to find records which prove that his deceased sisters had been plotting against his life. Their effects are sold. Caligula attends the sale, and cries up the articles, and exhorts the purchasers to bid generously for the possession of goods which once belonged to the imperial family; and for the pressing needs of their poor bankrupt master. "Are you not ashamed, you misers! to be richer than I? See to what straits I am reduced!—compelled to sell the furniture belonging once to Augustus. Behold this choice utensil! Mark Antony once used this!—and Augustus this! For the love of history and of Roman glory, purchase this for the trifle at which it is offered,—only 200,000 sesterces! Crier! why do you not observe that Aponius nods his head in sign that he takes the thirteen gladiators at my price,—only nine millions of sesterces!" And Aponius, a corpulent man of consular dignity, who was asleep and nodding, awakes to find himself ruined, with thirteen voracious gladiators on his hands. And to all this ludicrous degradation of themselves and of their prince, the once haughty Romans, whose pride was always associated with dignity, tamely and unresistingly submitted.

For a time Caligula was again rich. His gold was strewn upon the floor of one of the rooms of his palace, and he handled it with greedy glee, and took off his sandals and walked over it, and even slept upon it. But golden bigas set with precious stones, and golden oats for his favorite horse, and his vast new palaces, and his bridge over the Forum, from the Palatine to the Capitoline hill, soon exhausted his means, and led him to resume his business of auctioneering on a still grander scale. The supply of his exhausted treasury was secured in the rich provinces of Gaul.

On his way to commence his ridiculous invasion of Great Britain, which he undertook only for the purposes of obtaining more money, he paused in Gaul and hastened to despoil its citizens. The people were subjected to new and onerous taxes. A conspiracy, real or pretended, at Rome, enabled him to destroy and to seize the possessions of some of its richest citizens. While in Gaul he sent, in hot haste, for what would be called, in modern phrase, the *regalia*, or jewels, and for many of the triumphal chariots and equipages of state, which he sold at auction. Every appliance of terror, and every species of trickery was resorted to, in order that an exorbitant price might be secured. He personally set forth the peculiar value of each article as it was offered. "This," he said, "belonged to my father, and this to my grandfather. This vase is Egyptian, and was used by Antony; and this is a trophy of the victory of Actium!" By this means he again accumulated enormous sums.

And this poor creature was the master of the world! This is the great Cæsar who insisted upon being worshiped as a god in the Temple at Jerusalem, at the same time that he officiated in Gaul as an auctioneer of the property of murdered citizens, and of the state. And it was in the full knowledge that the government of the Roman Empire had been committed to such hands, and was in hands as vile when he wrote, that St. Paul penned the remarkable declaration, "The powers that be are ordained of God."

In the reign of Claudius, the abuses of the government were scarcely less. He was not personally cruel, but he was a dull, inactive, learned gormandizer, and the administration of affairs fell into the hands of his freedmen and his wives. Pallas, who, once a slave, became the master of the master of the world, possessed in a few years a fortune of a hundred millions of francs, and saw all patrician Rome groveling at his feet. Narcissus, another freedman, his rival, was scarcely less powerful. These creatures, in league with Messalina, or mixed in tangled intrigues with each other, made the reign of Claudius, if less disastrous to the public, quite as atrocious in the palace as that of Caligula. Let me here adopt the words of one of the historians of the Empire.

"I here close my account of Claudius. Is it not strange that the Empire should have been subject in succession to Caligula, who mocked everything, and to Claudius, whom everybody mocked? Is it not horrible to think that this imperial power over life should have been seized and squabbled for by women, eunuchs, and valets, each drawing from the imbecile Emperor what he desired,—one a pardon, one an exile, one gold, and another a punishment? Murders were sold like the other prerogatives of power. These creatures passed over to each other the sword of the centurion or the poison of Locusta. Such were the exchanges of men who were to be murdered; the bargaining and bartering of lives. Under this reign, legal executions and murders were confounded. It was indifferently the assassin or the informer, as the case required, that was employed. Men were publicly invited to destroy themselves, or were poisoned by some exquisite dish sent from the table of the prince. If it were the Emperor and Messalina that wished to dispose of an enemy, or to fulfill a contract of murder, they carelessly turned to the centurion on guard and said to him, 'Go and destroy this man.' If it were a more timid freedman, he sent for Locusta, who proved her loyalty by first showing the power of her poison on a slave. I do not now speak of manners. If I should say half that history records upon this topic I should seem to say too much. But the fearful licentiousness of manners is forgotten in this license, this openness of murder. Think what must have been, in the presence of such crimes among the powerful, the morality of the people, and how readily they would, when they could, imitate the vengeance of their masters. Assassination committed in the name of authority is a public invitation to every species of crime."

These were the governments which immediately preceded that during which St. Paul wrote his Epistle. When he wrote his second Epistle to Timothy, Nero was in his high career of murder, dissipation, and boundless extravagance. Rome had been burned, the Christians martyred, the journey of Nero as imperial singer and fiddler to Greece had been completed, and he had returned with his eighteen hundred laurel crowns all reeking with blood; proscriptions and murders were multiplied; and St. Paul, in the midst of the mad and cruel misgovernment, knew that the hour of his own martyrdom approached, and wrote, "I am ready to be offered, and the time of my departure is at hand."

Now it must be admitted that if it were ever the function of the Gospel and the church to assail institutions and customs instead of vices of the heart and life, the occasion was presented to St. Paul. But his mission was not directly to attack the evil works of unregenerate men, but to bring men to the cross and to the washing of regeneration, that the fountain of evil works might be dried up. That he should have written and left on record only *principles* on which governments should be administered at a period when the world was more than ever misgoverned, and just at the moment when he himself was about to fall a victim to its cruelty and injustice, is the most striking evidence that could be furnished that the Gospel and church and ministry were intended, in their direct use and application, as the agency for building up that Kingdom of God which is not of this world. Hence in the Epistle to Timothy, so touching, when we recall the circumstances under which it was written, there is no escape from him of the personal feeling of righteous indignation with which we may well suppose him to have been filled; there is no denunciation of the perversion of the heaven-delegated powers of government, by which it had become a terror, not to the evil, but to the good; there is no calling down of fire from Heaven on the guilty rulers who had turned God's benificent institution for the protection of man into an instrument of cruelty and oppression. St. Paul writes for the Kingdom of God of all ages. He occupies himself in giving many and minute directions and exhortations to his son Timothy for the right ordering and establishment of the Church of God. Then, looking forward to his reward, he exclaimed: "I have fought the good fight; I have finished my course; I have kept the faith; henceforth there is laid up for me a crown which God, the righteous judge, will give me at that day."

And yet let not these statements of St. Paul's position be misunderstood. The church and the Gospel are not indeed agencies to be employed directly against evil institutions, or perversions of good institutions, but against the sins, and for the sanctification, of the human heart. Yet when in them and by them hearts are made new, and men made holy learn to do justly and to love mercy, then in all their relations they should strive to bring all institutions into conformity to righteousness and love. As citizens they should strive to bring down every citadel of wrong, every habitation of cruelty, by the use of such means as justice and righteousness approve. The statement that because a man is a Christian he should shut up all his sympathies and activities within the church, and allow wicked men all around him to build up their structures of iniquity and oppression without an effort to overthrow them, and with a saintly indifference to the sufferings and wrongs which they may inflict, is an insult to his Christian manhood. *Because* he is a Christian he is bound as a man and citizen, always indeed in the spirit of righteousness and truth, to resist wrong, whether it be individual or combined. He is not, it is true, to bring his church, designed for another purpose, to bear against these wrongs. But in that church, a separate spiritual kingdom in the midst of earthly kingdoms, the mountain of the Lord's house, he is to learn the lessons and imbibe the spirit which will fit him to come down into the midst of this bad world's evil, and do brave work for God and man, for righteousness and truth.

St. Paul, as an inspired teacher of the church, declared that the powers that be are ordained of God; but he did not declare that Nero's government was administered according to God's ordination, or that it was to be always tamely submitted to, and its oppressions borne, when it became excessively cruel and unjust, as a religious duty; and that it would be wrong for its citizens to overthrow it in any circumstances. The duty of the obedience of the citizen and subject is not more clearly announced than that of the just and righteous administration of the magistrate. When duties are reciprocal, it by no means follows that the one remains in undiminished obligation when the other has been wholly and grossly violated. We *have* the directions of St. Paul, the inspired teacher of the church, as to the duty of Christians toward established governments, so long as they continue to exert and perform their appropriate functions. But we have not, for reasons which have been developed in the previous discourse, his declaration or direction as to the duties or privileges of Christian citizens in reference to the reformation or overthrow of established governments, when they have become hideous and tyrannical perversions of all the purposes for which governments were ordained. These were subjects on which they were to decide their own duties on Gospel principles in the fear of God and in love to man. The principles upon which established governments should be administered and obeyed clearly stated,— the circumstances under which the revolution and overthrow of oppressive governments may be a right or duty left undefined and to be settled by the Christian conscience,—this is St. Paul's mode of dealing with the powers that be.

IV. The institutions hitherto enumerated are divine in their origin but utterly perverted in their uses. There were many other established customs which were exceedingly evil in themselves, and in their effects, and wholly inconsistent with the spirit and principles of the Gospel, and of wide-spread disastrous influences, to which St. Paul makes no reference in his Epistles. There were desolating wars of aggression and ambition; there was a system of concubinage recognized by the government; there were corrupting spectacles and cruel gladiatorial fights, and the slaughters of the amphitheater, to which the hard Romans, as if retaining the fierceness of the ancestral wolf, were passionately devoted. Of these I will mention briefly only some of those spectacles which were at once a sign and an instrument of the moral corruption that so frightfully prevailed.

The extent to which these spectacles were carried, and the frenzy of devotion to them on the part of the Roman people, seems incredible. One of the chief cares of state was to provide them. No consul could be popular, no edile could be tolerated, no candidate for the favor and offices of the people could be successful, who did not provide or furnish them on a scale of great magnificence. A memorable example of the bloody and cruel spirit in which these spectacles were conducted is furnished in the reign of Claudius.

Julius Cæsar had examined the Lake Fucinus in the gorges of the Apennines, and had conceived the project of draining it and recovering it for agricultural uses. It was in an elevated position, of wide extent, and subject to an irregular rise and fall and overflow. Augustus had examined the subject and rejected the project of draining the lake as impracticable. Claudius, however, undertook the task from which Augustus had recoiled. He attempted to pierce the Apennines, and to turn the water into the River Liris. For eleven years thirty thousand men worked incessantly at the task of opening a channel three miles long. When it was supposed to be finished, Claudius wished to celebrate the event by a great fete. He surrounded the lake with the Prætorian guards, and with a rampart provided with instruments of war. Within this inclosure, twenty-four vessels, divided into two fleets, had sufficient space to move, and upon these vessels nineteen thousand men, condemned to death, were embarked, and commanded to fight to the death for the amusement of the people. Vast multitudes from Rome and from the neighboring country thronged the shores and the circling hills. Nature had provided an amphitheater far more vast than the Coliseum for a spectacle of blood too wide to be crowded into any structure of human make. Claudius presided, with

Agrippina seated by his side. The historian mentions that her robe was of woven gold with no admixture of other material. A silver triton rose from the water and sounded his shell in signal that the combat should begin. Then the poor victims cried, "Cæsar, about to die, we salute you!" His unskillful and confused answer led some of them to cry out that he had pronounced a pardon. A clamor for mercy rose among them, and for a space they delayed the fight. Claudius, in a rage, threatened to burn them all alive in the ships, and by rebukes and entreaties persuaded them to return to what he called their duty. The horrible slaughter commenced. The excitement and applause was unbounded. They fought fiercely. All perished. Thus was inaugurated an enterprise which was not in fact successful, and was never completed. It has been reserved for a Roman prince, Torlonia, to complete what a Roman emperor in vain attempted. The blood-stained waters refused to leave their bed. But the brutal Romans had enjoyed such a holiday as no potentate but a Roman emperor could have furnished, and no people but the degraded populace of the Empire could have relished.

But the spectacles at Rome,—what a picture do they present of the tastes and feelings of the people! A father of the church has thus designated them: "The infamy of the circus, the indecency of the theater, the cruelty of the amphitheater, the atrocity of the arena, and the folly of the games."

At this period all taste for intellectual power or genius in the amusements of the people of every class had disappeared. The only poetry which remained was that of the machinist and the painter of the scenes. On the stage there must pass troops of horses, chariots, elephants, cavalry, and infantry. On one occasion six hundred mules passed over the stage, laden with the spoils of a captured city; and hundreds of warriors issued from the flanks of a gigantic Trojan horse. Gross reality; brute power; splendor without imagination and excitement of feeling only from the view of suffering;—these were the characteristics of this deplorable era.

A passion for pantomime pervades all ranks. Formerly forbidden at Rome, because of the facilities which it furnished for immorality, the professors of the art now teach it in the imperial and patrician halls.

But all this is frivolous amusement. The bloody arena of gladiators and beasts furnished the serious and stirring occupations of Roman life.

The more bloody the more acceptable. The combats of beasts with each other, and of men with beasts, constitute their deepest joys. They will sit twelve hours on the marble steps in order to lose no part of the absorbing performance. Pompey brings six hundred lions into the arena; Augustus four hundred panthers. In one day five hundred Gatulian prisoners fight against twenty elephants. Giraffes and rhinoceroses vary the scene. Augustus in one series of fights in the arena sacrifices thirty-five hundred animals. Trajan holds games for one hundred and twenty-three days, and on each occasion from one thousand to ten thousand animals are slaughtered. Under Titus, five thousand perished in a day. When blood and agony and death become the pastime and exhilaration of a people, homes must be brutal, the government must be despotic, and religion only the worship, because the dread, of power.

But more exciting than all the other Roman spectacles were the gladiatorial combats. It gave to Rome a taste of the excitements of war. The *Lanista* trained his gladiators in a school or gymnasium, and fed them with raw flesh, that they might be fierce and strong. What they were, or what they became, may be seen from the full-length delineation of some of the most celebrated of them in mosaic, which were found in the baths of Caracalla, and have been transferred to the museum of the Lateran. The view of those brutal heads and faces, and those brawny limbs, suggests a vivid and disgusting conception of the character of the Romans, who made heroes of those trained and stolid murderers. The Lanista bought the gladiators if they were slaves, or hired them if they were free. They bound themselves on the penalty of death never to fly or yield until absolutely overcome. In vain did Augustus endeavor to restrain this human slaughter. The Romans had surrendered to him their rights as citizens; but they refused to surrender to him the privilege of being cruel and remorseless. The art of slaying was diversified by pungent varieties of murder. The *Essedarii* fought in chariots; the Rhetiarii, on foot; the Andabatæ, with their eyes bandaged. The Roman people attended these spectacles as connoisseurs. They criticised a becoming agony as they would a representation of it in a statue or a painting. They applauded a good murder. They hissed a victim who fell awkwardly on the arena, or seemed afraid to die. All around the inclosure there was a confused noise of plaudits, cries of joy, sentences of death; bets won and bets lost; bravos for a wound or a fall; bravos for those who kill well and those who die well.

But enough. It suffices to know how largely spectacles, most of them utterly brutal and cruel, entered into the Roman life, and were cared for by the state, and to find at the same time in Paul's letter, written from Rome, no denunciation of them, to have an additional and striking demonstration of the truth that it was not directly against institutions, however evil, but against the evil heart of man, from which they sprang, that St. Paul directed his efforts.

I have adduced these extreme cases of wrong and evil in customs and institutions, against which St. Paul makes no direct assaults, in order to demonstrate the fact, strikingly and convincingly, that the Apostle aimed at reforming evil within, even in the hearts of those who administer evil organizations, and practice and profit by evil customs. St. Paul, after the Master, refused to interfere in the sphere of civil or social wrongs, which it belonged to the state or the family to regulate. But this by no means debarred him from denouncing the sins of heart which gave rise to such wrongs, and from exhibiting the evil effects of such sins in just such cases as he refused to interfere with or adjudicate. Even a wise human father will rather exhibit to his children the evil of the bad temper and passions from which their dissensions rise, and leave them to adjust them on the principles which he has inculcated, rather than settle them himself as an arbiter and judge. When one came to Jesus asking him to compel his brother to divide the inheritance with him, the Saviour, without pausing to inquire into the right or wrong of the request, abruptly refused interference, saying, "Man, who made me a ruler or a divider over you?" Yet if both those brothers had become true disciples of Christ, the most absolute justice would have been accomplished; for the one would not have withheld what was due, and the other would not have desired what was not just. Hence the Saviour, adopting the divine method of regulating the evils of the world, struck directly at the root of the dissension which had arisen between them, when he added, "Beware of covetousness." This example of the Master was followed by Paul and all the Apostles.

How sublime—nay, how evidently divine—is this procedure! He enjoins men, if subject to unjust laws, to obey them while they exist; but he enjoins rulers to make just laws and to govern justly. He tells the poor to be patient in poverty; but at the same time he tells the rich to relieve it. He bids the wife to obey the husband; but at the same time enjoins the husband so to love the wife as that her obedience may be spontaneous and joyful. He bids the slave to obey his master; and at the same time enjoins his master to treat him justly, kindly, and as a brother in the Lord. And that which is a most striking proof of the divine character and mission of the Gospel is that it reforms the world by the singular method of making all classes act against their worldly interests and their passions. It engages the master in the interests of the liberty of the slave, at the same time that it reconciles the slave to bondage. It enables the poor to avoid coveting or demanding the possessions of the rich, and the rich to give of them cheerfully and joyfully to the poor. Its revolutionizing principles are simply these: immense patience on the part of those who suffer; disinterested and voluntary sacrifice are the part of those who enjoy.

These are not abstractions: they teach us to commence the removal of evil from the world by removing it first from our own hearts; and they bid us to be diligent in the most efficient way in diminishing human wretchedness, by promoting divine purity and joy; and at the same time to be patient in the midst of the sorrows and wrongs which fall on others, and peaceful under the trials which befall ourselves.

LECTURE IX.

ST. PAUL'S POSITION IN REFERENCE TO ESTABLISHED CUSTOMS AND INSTITUTIONS.

For perhaps he therefore departed for a season, that thou shouldest receive him forever;
Not now as a servant, but above a servant, a brother beloved.—
PHILEMON, 15, 16.

WE have shown that St. Paul did not directly attack established evil customs and institutions, nor even perversions of institutions which were divine. He taught truth and duty. He attacked evil in the heart. He gave laws and directions for the right ordering of the kingdom of God. He fenced it off from all that did not belong to it. He taught in it the duty due in every divine institution, and in every sphere in life. He would not make the church *the direct agent* in beating down any established customs and institutions; but he inculcated principles which, by the grace of God, transforming the evil heart out of which all evil customs come, would undermine and displace all the structures of iniquity, and all the habitations of cruelty in the world.

This course of procedure is the more noticeable from the fact that he lived in an era of the world's history when crime was organized and established, and when it would seem to human view as if good could find no place in which to be planted, unless this gigantic growth of evil should be first cut down. All wisdom, except that which was inspired, would have commenced with lopping off the branches and hewing at the trunk of this world-wide upas tree of evil. The wisdom that is divine directed itself to evil in its seeds and in its roots.

There is another principle of the divine procedure with established customs and institutions which it is necessary that we should understand, before we can study intelligently the course of St. Paul in reference to the slave Onesimus. Divine wisdom does not only abstain from attacking some of those customs and relations, which are evil in their origin and in themselves, *but it even enjoins the relative duties which they involve*, so long as they continue to exist.

This principle had been already sanctioned by inspiration, speaking through John the Baptist. Nothing could be more adverse to the spirit and precepts of the Gospel than war. It is a guilty perversion of the purposes for which governments were established. Inspiration traces it directly to the lusts that war in our members. (James, iv. 1.) And yet when the soldiers came to John the Baptist, demanding of him what shall we do? (Luke, iii. 14,) he did not say, "Refuse to fight—abandon your trade of blood—leave the army—endure scourging or crucifixion rather than be the hired murderers of Cæsar;" but he said to them, "Do violence to no man, neither accuse any falsely, and be content with your wages." Here the duties of a relation whose origin is evil is enjoined. Government is divine. Magistracy is of God. The coercion of evil is the proper work of government. War, for purposes of aggression, on the contrary, is a perversion of its purpose; and yet as an established institution of man, he enjoined a faithful discharge of the moral duties, and the peculiar obligations which were connected with it. But it certainly does not follow from this fact that war is a divine institution, or that it met the approval of the Saviour.

The same principle appears in St. Paul's first Epistle to the Corinthians. He declares it to be unlawful for a Christian to marry a heathen. Yet if by the conversion of one party to Christianity, a Christian husband or wife is found to be united to a heathen, he does not enjoin separation. On the contrary, he recommends a continuance in that relation. "If any brother hath a wife that believeth not, and she be pleased to dwell with him, let him not put her away. And the woman that hath a husband that believeth not, and if he be pleased to dwell with her let her not leave him. For the unbelieving husband is sanctified by the wife, and the unbelieving wife is sanctified by the husband." (1 Corin. vii. 14, 15.) Here we see what may be called the sanctified common sense; the plain and practical wisdom of the ethics of Christianity. St. Paul forbids a certain relation; when, however, it is found in fact existing, without the guilt which would have arisen from its voluntary adoption, he does not declare that it should be broken, but prescribes the duties which it involves. His injunction of the duties which belong to the relation evidently constitutes no sanction or approbation of the institution.

By the light of these principles we see the error of those who have considered that slavery has received the divine approbation, and is as really a divine institution as the family and the state. The Scriptures indeed prescribe the duties of this relation. St. Paul often enlarges on the reciprocal obligations of master and slave. But we have seen that it is not the divine mode of procedure to attack human institutions which are the expression or the stimulant of evil; but to correct the evil heart out of which they spring, and while they exist to prescribe the mutual duties which arise in them. God from the beginning has enjoined the union of one man and woman as alone lawful, and proclaims the marriage of a second wife to be adultery; and yet when among the Jews concubinage, or secondary marriage, became established, God at the same time leaves the law unrepealed, and yet forbears to denounce as evil all who have adopted this evil custom. David receives many divine directions; but none that I am aware of to the effect that he should repudiate all his wives but one. And there is one remarkable record in reference to King Joash, which seems to show that this toleration on the part of God of an evil when it became established, had led even a prophet to suppose that because it had not been condemned after it had been practiced, it might be lawful to originate the practice. In the same verses which declare that Joash did that which was right in the sight of the Lord, it is announced that two wives were selected for him. "And Joash did that which was right in the sight of the Lord all the days of Jehoida the priest; and Jehoida took for him two wives, and he begat sons and daughters."

Wars are the outgrowth of human sin, and John the Baptist does not abolish the function, but prescribes the duties of the soldier. Christians should not marry heathens; but if they find themselves in that relation it is not to be dissolved, but rather the new and sacred duties which arise from it are to be discharged. In like manner slavery, an existing institution, protected by the laws and part of the constitution of the state, though cruel in its origin and unjust in its very nature, is not denounced as that which must be at once destroyed; but on the contrary, it is described as a relation which involves reciprocal and solemn obligations. We cannot, from this divinely wise and practical spirit in which Christianity deals with human evil, organized into systems and institutions, conclude that they are approved of God; and much less can we infer that they are divine in origin and obligation. We cannot turn back to *tolerated* polygamy, and say that it was *established*. We cannot enroll war among the duties of man, because John the Baptist specifies the moral duties of the soldier whose profession is war. Nor, in like manner, can we infer slavery to be approved or enjoined because the master is exhorted to be just and merciful, and the slave to be faithful and obedient.

We may advance a step further. The absence of condemnation is not to be construed as approbation. St. Paul was at Rome when the cruel sports of the amphitheater—the slaughter of beasts and men in combat—was an absorbing passion with the Romans. Yet in his letter from Rome there is not a word of condemnation of this enormous sin. It is absurd to conclude that this bloody pastime met with his approbation. We cannot conclude therefore that because St. Paul did not specially condemn slavery in his Epistles, that he regarded it as just and right.

In these two principles then, viz., that of not attacking evil institutions but the evil heart from which they come, and that of prescribing the duties of relations which are established, we find an explanation of St. Paul's treatment of slavery, and of Onesimus the slave.

I. In the Epistles which St. Paul wrote from Rome there are several exhortations to masters and slaves. "Servants, obey in all things your masters according to the flesh; not with eye-service, as men pleasers; but in singleness of heart, fearing God. And whatsoever ye do, do it heartily, as unto the Lord, and not unto men; knowing that of the Lord ye shall receive the reward of the inheritance; for ye serve the Lord Christ. "But he that doeth wrong shall receive for the wrong which he hath done: and there is no respect of persons." (Col. iii. 22–25.) Here Christian slaves are addressed as those who owe a duty to their masters; duty which should be rendered as unto the Lord and not unto men. They serve the Lord Christ; they shall receive from him reward; if they do wrong they shall be punished. Then follows an exhortation to masters. "Masters, give unto your servants that which is just and equal, knowing that ye also have a Master in heaven." (Col. iv. 1.) Here the reciprocal obligation of justice on the part of the master, and fidelity on the part of the slave, are clearly enjoined.

The same exhortations, in words almost identical, are repeated in the Epistle to the Ephesians. (vi. 5–9.)

II. In precise harmony with these injunctions

was St. Paul's treatment of the case of the slave Onesimus. He belonged to Philemon, a member of the church of Colosse. He may have known of St. Paul in his master's house. He may have resorted to the Apostle for the relief of his destitution. However this may be, he came to him and was converted to the faith of Christ and confessed his sins against his master. St. Paul seems to have been strongly attracted toward Onesimus. It should be remembered in this connection that slaves were frequently persons of education and refinement. St. Paul speaks of him as one who might be profitable to him in his work. He wishes to retain him in Rome as a fellow-helper. Yet he would not violate the law of the state which made him the property of his master. He would not assume, on the higher grounds of the religious obligations of Philemon, to *decide for him* that it was his duty to release his slave. He therefore sent him to his master with Tychicus, who was charged with the Epistle to the Colossians. It is in this very Epistle, which Onesimus, with Tychicus, carried to Colosse, that the most full exposition of the duties of master and servant contained in the New Testament are to be found. He intimated his wish to Philemon that Onesimus might be released for the sake of the church, but he left the decision of the question to his own sense of duty. The letter which he wrote by Onesimus is a model of delicacy, Christian moderation, and affection. A part of it, in the translation of Conybeare and Howson, I subjoin.

"Wherefore, although in the authority of Christ, I might boldly enjoin upon thee that which is befitting, yet for love's sake I rather beseech thee, as

Paul the aged and now also prisoner of Jesus Christ. I beseech thee for my son whom I have now begotten in my chains, Onesimus; who formerly was to thee unprofitable, but now is profitable both to thee and me. Whom I have sent back to thee; but do thou receive him as my own flesh and blood. For I would gladly retain him to myself, that he might render service to me in thy stead, while I am a prisoner, for declaring the glad tidings; but I am unwilling to do anything without thy decision; that thy kindness may not be constrained but voluntary. For perhaps to this very end he was parted from thee for a time that thou mightest possess him forever; no longer as a bondsman but above a bondsman, a brother beloved; very dear to me, but how much more to thee, being thine own both in the flesh and in the Lord. If then thou count me in fellowship with thee, receive him as myself. But whatsoever he has wronged thee of or owes thee, reckon it to my account. I, Paul, write this with mine own hand. I will repay it; for I would not say that thou owest to me even thine own self besides. Yet, brother, let me have joy of thee in the Lord; comfort my heart in Christ. I write in full confidence of thy obedience, knowing that thou wilt do even more than I say." (8–21.)

Let us now endeavor to deduce from this Epistle some of the truths and principles which it contains in reference to the institution of slavery.

1. There is no reason to infer, from the case of Onesimus, that St. Paul approved of the institution of slavery, or considered it to be in accordance with the spirit and precepts of the Gospel. There is no such approbation expressed. There is none im-

plied. The failure to condemn does not, as we have seen, conclude approbation. The exhortations to perform the reciprocal obligations of this relation, as we have also seen, do not imply that the relation itself is right and just, such as Christians should originate and perpetuate, but only that while it *does* continue, the moral duties which it involves should be faithfully discharged.

2. But there *is* a recognition of the right of Philemon, in accordance with the then existing laws, to claim the services of his slave. This is evidently regarded by St. Paul as the civil right of his friend. St. Paul does not raise or touch the question whether it ought ever to have become an established right. As a Christian teacher, he does not feel called upon to discuss the justice of the laws or institutions of the state, but only in a general way to enjoin obedience to the powers that be and the laws that are. Christianity, leavening minds and hearts and consciences and communities, will gradually remove unrighteous institutions and improve all human legislation. But in the mean time he recognizes the legal and vested right of Philemon to the services of Onesimus. This is implied in the fact that he sends him to Philemon, with the request that he would release him from the obligation. If it had not been a right on the part of Philemon, St. Paul would not have requested him to waive it. Had it been a civil right, yet religiously wrong in Philemon, under the circumstances in which he was placed, St. Paul would have forbidden it by his Apostolic authority. But he expressly forbears from commanding, and limits himself to entreating. So that while we have no evidence and no hint that he

approved of the institution in itself, we see that as one which existed and was protected by the laws, he recognizes its rights and duties.

3. Yet while St. Paul plainly admits the right of Philemon to the services of Onesimus, there is no reason to infer that he felt himself under a legal obligation to remand him to his master. This case has been singularly treated as if it were one in which St. Paul felt himself bound to send back his son in the Gospel to servitude, in obedience to some existing fugitive slave law, or from a sense of religious obligation to the institution of slavery. But of this there is not the shadow of a proof. Onesimus may have desired to return. He may have felt that he had been ungrateful to his master, and now as a Christian he may have desired to render due reparation. It is intimated by St. Paul that he had defrauded his master, and now as a sincere Christian he might wish to go and confess his faults, and to the best of his ability make amends. St. Paul might have approved and encouraged his purpose to return to his master on these grounds. He might have done the same thing if Onesimus had been an apprentice or a free laborer. It was no case of the rendition of a fugitive slave in obedience to legal or moral obligation, or in the interests of slavery. St. Paul may have sent Onesimus at his own request. It is certain that true religious principle should have made him desirous to return, and would have prompted Paul to encourage him to fulfill that desire.

4. And, moreover, though St. Paul evidently acknowledges Philemon's legal right to the services of his slave as aforetime, and though he does not expressly declare that it would be morally or reli-

giously wrong to enforce that legal right, he just as evidently did not send him back with the purpose or the expectation that he would be remanded to slavery. Much less is there anything to prove, as has been asserted, that the great object for which St. Paul sent back Onesimus was that the relation should be renewed and rendered perpetual. He did not say, "It is your religious duty, Onesimus, to go back and put yourself again in bondage; and it is equally your religious duty, Philemon, to keep him there." It is most evident that he had no such object. On the contrary, his object seems to have been, that inasmuch as Onesimus had now become a Christian, he should return to his wronged and defrauded master, and as a Christian, on Christian grounds, such as would have been obligatory if he had not been a slave but only a hired servant, put himself in a right relation to his master, and that his master should put himself in a right relation to his penitent and converted slave. If St. Paul had wished Onesimus to be remanded into bondage, he would have expressed the wish.

5. And yet it is quite possible, in view of St. Paul's exhortations to master and slave, to imagine a case somewhat different from what I suppose that of Onesimus to have been, in which St. Paul might have recommended the Christian slave to have returned into bondage, and in which he might have enjoined the Christian master to retain him in that position. I mention such a supposable case for the purpose of showing how different the *application* of the same principles may be when the circumstances differ. If, as in the case of Onesimus, a slave had defrauded his master, it would be his duty to return

when he became a Christian, and acknowledge his fault, and put himself in a right moral relation to him. And if, moreover, he was one who had become unfit for any other position, and unable to provide for himself and family, and if in his master's service he could have enjoyed good religious privileges, we can well believe that St. Paul might have recommended not only that he should return and confess his wrong, but also that he should return to bondage, and that the master should keep him in that position. In that case the Apostle might appropriately have repeated the exhortations which are found in his Epistles. This course of proceeding would have been in perfect harmony with the principles which we discern in his teachings and his conduct.

6. But it appears very plain that St. Paul did *not* consider that the institution of slavery remained on the same footing, when master and slave became Christians, as it was before. Its legal *status*, indeed, was not changed, but neither master nor slave took the same view as before of its prerogatives on the one hand, nor its duties on the other. That was not lawful in the eye of the master which was lawful in the eye of the law. That was not duty in the view of the slave which law and custom had enjoined as duty. On the one hand, the master did not feel it to be right to exercise cruelty, or to enjoin immoral and polluting services upon his slave. On the other hand, the slave did not feel it his duty to obey commands which would involve a denial of his Master in heaven, or a violation of the law of God. It is evident that this change in the moral position of the parties completely changed the character of the in-

stitution, and took from it just those elements which constituted it slavery, in contradistinction to other menial service. This fact appears from the language of St. Paul. Says the Apostle, "For perhaps he departed for a season that thou shouldst receive him forever, not now as a servant, *but above a servant*, a brother beloved specially to me, but how much more unto thee both in the flesh and in the Lord." Here St. Paul states explicitly that by becoming a Christian he had become a brother, and was no longer as a servant but above a servant. It is as much as if he had said to him, "I send Onesimus to you, recognizing your legal right, if, on the whole, you shall conclude to exercise it, to his services. Without entering upon any questions as to the justice of this relation, I have, as you remember, enjoined the reciprocal duties which it involves so long as it continues. They are, you observe, very different from what, on heathen grounds, have been hitherto accepted. The slave is not now to be regarded as merely an animated thing, to be used with no recognition of his rights as a man, and no recognition of his brotherhood. He is now above a servant, in the heathen sense of that term. As you are both Christians, both and equally the purchased possession of the Master, both redeemed and loved by the same God and Saviour, he is no longer a servant but a brother beloved. If you should still retain him in the relation of servant, lay to heart, as I have enjoined Onesimus to lay to heart, the injunctions which I have given to both parties who sustain to each other that relation."

7. Thus by sending Onesimus to his master, and therefore recognizing his claim to the services of his

slave—recognizing them still further by the earnest request that he would waive them for the sake of the church and from affection to himself, "Now Paul the aged," the Apostle yet speaks as if, although he *entreats* Philemon he might *command* him: "wherefore though I might be much bold in Christ to enjoin that which is convenient, yet for love's sake I rather beseech thee, being such an one as Paul the aged, and now also a prisoner of Jesus Christ." What is it that St. Paul claims he might have commanded? Not certainly that he should have emancipated his slave on the ground that it was a relation which it was wicked for him for a moment to sustain. This cannot be, because he had enjoined the reciprocal duties of that relation. It could not be, that he, as a ruler in the spiritual kingdom, possessed a power of abrogating, even in individual cases, the laws and institutions of states; for he had written, "let every soul be subject to the higher powers!" It must have been on some other ground that St. Paul claimed that he might have enjoined Philemon to release Onesimus. St. Paul was an inspired Apostle of the church, and specially designated to the Apostleship of the Gentiles. Philemon is called a fellow-laborer with St. Paul. Whether in the ministry or a layman, he had accepted the position as a laborer for the Gospel, under the guidance of the inspired Apostle. As such the Apostle possessed the right to enjoin upon him what was necessary for the prosperity of the kingdom of God, to whose interests he was consecrated. Philemon was at liberty to manumit his slaves. But St. Paul does not say that he was bound to do it on the ground of moral obligation, because slaveholding in all cases and circumstances is, like theft and adultery, always sin. At liberty, but not necessarily bound, on moral grounds, to manumit his slaves, Philemon might yet be under moral or religious obligations to do it from regard to the interests of the church. The freedom of Onesimus might be necessary that he might do service to Paul, or other service as a fellow-worker in the Gospel. It is on this ground that he claims that he might have been bold to command. But he prefers to *beseech*. "Whom I would have retained with me that in thy stead he might have administered to me in the bonds of the Gospel. But without thy mind would I do nothing; that thy benefit should not be as it were of necessity but willingly." St. Paul offers personally to pay whatever Onesimus may owe his master. "If he have wronged thee, or owe thee aught, put that on my account. I, Paul, have written it with my own hand; I will repay it." He thus removes in advance the obstacles which might make Philemon perhaps indisposed to accede to his request; and then concludes with the expression of his confidence that he will do even more than he has been requested.

Such, so far as I have been able to educe them, are the views and principles by which St. Paul was guided in the treatment of this remarkable case of Onesimus. As the subject is one of much difficulty, I beg leave to connect the points which I have made in one brief statement:

(1) St. Paul, in the case of Onesimus, neither expresses nor implies an approval of the institution of slavery as in accordance with the spirit and precepts of

the Gospel; (2) yet he recognizes the legal right of Philemon to claim the services of his slave, while (3) at the same time he does not admit any legal or moral obligation on himself to remand that slave to his master; nor (4) does he send him back in the interests of slavery, in order that his bondage may be renewed and rendered perpetual; (5) though St. Paul might, under some circumstances, have enjoined or recommended a servant to return into bondage, and the master to render it perpetual, yet (6) it is evident from his language in this case, that if this should be done, Christianity would have completely changed the relation of the parties from what it had been under heathenism, and that the slave was not to be regarded as a thing, or an animal for mere use and profit, but as a brother beloved in the Lord; (7) it appears also, that although St. Paul claims that he might have commanded what he requests, he does it, not on the ground of divine authority over human enactments, but by virtue of his Apostolic authority, and in behalf of the church of God.

To that impatient spirit which expects the kingdom of God to come with observation, this proceeding of St. Paul may seem to have been slow and circuitous, and scarcely consistent with that sincerity and godly simplicity which he himself so earnestly enjoins. It would even seem as if there were some good Christians who would have preferred that this Epistle had not been written. Yet if it were not in the Sacred Canon, we should be without a remarkable practical exemplification of the mode by which the Gospel removes the evils that prevail in the world. It is good gaining on and supplanting evil, as the light, by penetrating into, dispels and supplants the darkness. One might as well accuse the growing dawn of a compromise with darkness, as to charge upon St. Paul's Epistle to Philemon a Christian sanction to slavery. It is an Epistle eminently profitable for "*instruction in righteousness.*"

LECTURE X.

For perhaps he departed from thee for a season that thou shouldst receive him forever.
Not now as a servant, but above a servant, a brother beloved.—PHILEMON, 15, 16.

IN a previous Lecture I have explained the relation of St. Paul to the institution of slavery as illustrated in his treatment of the case of the slave Onesimus.

III. That St. Paul's proceedings in this case arose from his fixed principle that the kingdom of God was not directly to assault human customs and institutions and the laws of states, will appear beyond all question if we consider the condition of slaves at the period when Paul wrote from Rome. It would be an insult to the Apostle to suppose for a moment that he could have approved of an institution so utterly inhuman. It shows him to have been restrained and guided by a wisdom from above that he could have abstained from forbidding Christians from holding such a relation as that of master to a slave. Let us look at the institution of slavery as it then existed at Rome, and as St. Paul saw it beneath his eye when he penned his Epistle to the Colossians, and sent it by Tychicus and Onesimus.

The condition of the common plebeian or field slave among the Romans was excessively wretched. Placed upon the block of a slave dealer in the Forum, and exposed like any other merchandise for sale, he could be purchased for what in modern value would be five hundred francs, or one hundred dollars. The *janitor*, or door-keeper, was sold with the house. The *vicarius*, or servant of a slave, was not so much regarded as the animals of whose comfort he had reason to be envious. The master in some cases personally knew but few of the slaves that thronged his courts, and would condescend to communicate with them only through an agent, or by the medium of imperious gestures. The slave was not regarded as a man, and the Romans were accustomed to use neuter and abstract terms to describe him. He was not so often called *servus*, a servant, as *servitium*, service; not so frequently *homo*, a man, as *corpus*, a body, or *mancipium*, property. According to law he was only a thing. One of the common descriptions given of the slave was that he was an animated tool, and of a tool that he was an inanimate slave. If he injures the property of another, it is the master who must make indemnity. If he is injured or slain by another, indemnity is made to the master. As he is not regarded as a man, engagements with him are not considered binding, and he has no rights which a freeman is bound to respect.

It results from the same cause that he can have no wife, no family, no relations. His wife, if he is allowed by the gratuitous kindness of the master a quasi marriage, or *contubernium*, is not *his*, nor his children *his*, in any true sense of right or possession; for they belong absolutely to another, and can be taken from him, and used in any way the master pleases, at any moment. Among slaves there can be neither husband, nor wife, nor father, nor mother, nor children. Nay, the slave is not permitted to have a god. Cato the elder, with that rigid and remorseless logic which distinguished him, wrote that the master only could perform religious rites for the slaves, and that they must not presume to make any offerings to the gods without the permission of their master. This was the Roman right and law. A kind master, indeed, would permit his slaves to celebrate some low rites connected with religion, but they all bore the stamp of the debasement which belonged to his condition. The shepherds enjoyed their rude sacrificial rites, in which wild revelry and license prevailed. The slaves in the city were permitted to enjoy their *saturnalia* and the women their *matronales;* but all these were gifts and concessions from their masters, which might be at any time withheld.

Although it was not altogether impossible for slaves to purchase their freedom in peculiarly favorable circumstances, and on the indispensable condition of the good-will of the master, yet it was exceedingly difficult.

The Emperors Claudius and Augustus had attempted to limit the arbitrary and absolute right of the master over the person and life of the slave. But manners and habits proved stronger than laws. As the nation grew more cruel and more devoted to the sports of the amphitheater, and more careless of human life, it would not be likely to grow more kind and considerate to the slave. Juvenal, in a well-known passage, depicts a woman who, with no motive but caprice, consigns her slave to the cross. Pollio fed his eels with the flesh of slaves. The crosses upon the Esquiline hill, with the bodies of crucified slaves polluting the air, or with their ghastly skeletons rattling in the wind, constantly reminded the slave to beware how he provoked the omnipotence of the master. When the slaves grew old they were sent to an island in the Tiber, where the sick and infirm were deserted,—left, as it was said, to the care of Esculapius. Cato the elder said to a friend, "If you are a good manager, you will sell your slave and your horse when they are old."

The number of slaves held by the rich Romans was very great. They were counted by the hundred and the thousand. Seneca was opposed to any external badges being borne by them by which they might be designated, lest, perceiving their numbers and strength, they might rise and overpower the citizens. He mentions one house in Rome in which there were four hundred slaves. He describes Demetrius, a freedman of Pompey, and richer than his master, who built the theater which went under Pompey's name, as receiving every night, like the general of an army, an account of the effective force of his slaves. And yet they lived in constant terror of assassination. There was a Roman proverb, "So many slaves, so many enemies." True, slaves guarded their doors and corridors and chambers, but who should guard them against their guards? The usual resource of terror is cruelty, and it was most remorselessly applied toward the slaves. If a master was slain by a slave, the law provided that all the slaves of the household, innocent and guilty, should be punished with death. A shocking instance of this cruel injustice had occurred at Rome just previous to Paul's arrival. It had startled even the imbruted populace of Rome by its unusual horror, and led to a practical modification of the law. A man of consular dignity was slain by one of his slaves. Four hundred slaves, men, women, and children, passed along in mournful procession to execution. The Forum was agitated; the people were roused almost into a revolt; and the Senate House was besieged for mercy while the weeping train passed on to death. It was all in vain. The law took its course. Four hundred innocent persons perished for the crime of one.

That which added to the horror of this event was the vindication of it which was made in the Senate. Some of the Senators had recoiled before the execution of this horrible law in a case where so many persons were the victims. But an old and learned lawyer, Cassius, charged with the task of resisting these weak-minded innovators upon the sacred customs of their ancestors, spoke in the true dialect of all advocates of prescriptive wrongs. "Shall we seek for reasons against a custom which our ancestors, wiser than we, have established? Among four hundred slaves, if all were not in the plot, is it possible that not one suspected, not one knew, the guilty one? And if information had been given by that one, would not the murder have been prevented? But you say that many innocent persons perish with the guilty. That is true; but when an army is found wanting in courage, and is decimated, both brave men and cowards incur the chances of the lot. There is always something of injustice in every great example, but the wrong inflicted upon the few is compensated by the advantage of the many."

Such was slavery at Rome when St. Paul wrote

his Epistles from that city. Its condition was no better in Asia Minor, to which Philemon and Onesimus belonged. It is just as certain that St. Paul abhorred the system as that he hated sin. Thus abhorring it he might have pursued toward it another course. He might have denounced it and exhibited its hideous cruelty. The denunciation would have been just. He might have shown its utter inconsistency with the precepts and spirit of the Gospel. His demonstration would have been complete. He might have forbidden Christians to sustain the relation. He might have instructed the slave that he was free of the master, and the master that he had no right to his slave. What would have been the result? He would then have employed the church in the settlement of an affair of the state. He would have placed the church in conflict with the state. He would have falsified the Saviour's declaration that his kingdom was not of this world. He would have brought persecution upon the church, destroyed the master, and not benefited the slave.

IV. But now observe the divine wisdom of the course which he did pursue. He gave Christians such precepts, and bade them pursue such a course as would have destroyed the main evils of the institution while it continued to exist, and would have led to its speedy extinction. If Christians should have acted upon St. Paul's exhortations, then the institution, in all its essential peculiarities, would have been destroyed. When masters were told to remember that they should be such masters to their servants as God was to them, when they were bidden to give to them that which was just and equal, it is evident that the whole system of slavery would be destroyed in all its essential features by the practice of that simple principle. For the system was in its nature, and by its very definition, unjust and unequal. The slave was not a man; his feelings were not to be regarded; he had no rights to himself, his wife, or children; he might be overtasked, beaten, and killed, at pleasure. Now to give him what was just and equal would be to treat him as a man, to render for his services the same return that he would to any other man, to regard his feelings, to admit his rights to his wife and children, to punish him only for what was wrong, and in the measure proportioned to his wrong-doing. To have treated him in this manner would have been to have destroyed all that was peculiar in practice in the institution of slavery, and to have left only its name and its legal tenure of property in the slave. To have acted in this manner would have led Christians to perceive that the doing of that which was just and equal to the slave would inevitably lead to the duty of bestowing upon him freedom. This was in fact the logic and this the practice of the early Christians.

The practical operation of this principle is seen clearly in the case of Onesimus. St. Paul sent him back with the implied admission of Philemon's legal claims to his services as a slave. Yet he exhorts him to regard him no longer as a servant, but above a servant, as a brother in the Lord. *A brother in the Lord!* Then he was bound to give as much as he received. It was not possible for him at the same time to treat him as a Christian brother and a slave. It is not to treat one as a Christian brother to hold him as property, to deprive him of freedom, and to exact labor from him without compensation.

The man who treats another as a slave would not believe that he was treated like a Christian brother if he was subjected to that condition. St. Paul requests Philemon to receive and treat Onesimus as his own flesh, his own son. Now surely the Apostle would not have wished his own flesh, his own son, to be used and treated as a slave; nor would he have felt that he had acceded to his request if he had still kept Onesimus in bondage. And again, St. Paul begs Philemon to receive Onesimus as himself. Surely he would not wish or expect himself to be received and treated as a slave by his Christian friend and brother. These expressions make it perfectly evident that nothing was further from the intention of St. Paul, when he sent Onesimus to his master, than to remand him to bondage.

It is indeed impossible for a master to regard his slave as a Christian brother. The two relations are contradictory, the one to the other. Brotherhood implies equality of nature and of rights. Mastership implies inequality of one or both. Hence one cannot at the same time consider himself as a master and a brother, and look upon another as at once his brother and his property.

And here let me add that these principles were practically applied, and produced their legitimate results in Rome and in other portions of the world. Says the author of Christian Rome, "Soon, only a hundred years after the birth of Christ, a prefect of Rome, Hermes, freed 1250 slaves on the day of his conversion. Under Diocletian, another prefect of the great city, Cromacus, gave liberty to 1400 slaves, who received baptism with him. 'Those who have become the children of God,' he cried, 'ought not to be the slaves of a man.'" The same thought, it will also be remembered, had already been in the heart of the virgins Praxedes and Prudentiana, who emancipated their slaves. The Pagans smiled in pity. They reproached the Christians with admitting into their number abject and ignoble souls. "Have you not among you," they demanded, "the rich and poor, the master and the slave?" "No," replied Lactantius, "it is because we believe all are equal, that we employ the word '*brethren.*' Though there be a diversity of conditions among us, there is at least no place for slaves; and religiously we are all the servants of God."

The thought may have occurred to the minds of my readers, "If St. Paul did not directly attack slavery, is it right for you to enter upon this exposition, and to express the condemnation which he withheld?" The same thought has occurred many times to myself. But observe this distinction. St. Paul would not employ the church as the direct agent in beating down slavery. Nor would I. But the Apostle adopted a certain principle in dealing with this question. I would understand and explain this principle. St. Paul uttered certain exhortations to masters and slaves. I would study them and endeavor to comprehend their real purport and significance. This is what I have attempted. It is an *interpretation of Scripture* which I consider, criticise, and condemn. It has been—as I believe erroneously—explained to sustain slavery. I would show that it condemns slavery as a moral relation between Christians, and between man and man. I find that St. Paul announced principles which, if they were carried out, would certainly overthrow slavery; but that he refrained from applying them directly to that institution at a time when such an application would have convulsed the state, have led to a persecution of the church, and have made the condition of the slave still more deplorable. In like manner, in similar circumstances, before the rebellion, when the agitation of this subject tended to convulse the States, and rend the churches, and make the condition of the slaves worse than before, I refrained, together with most of my brethren of the church to which I belong, from making a direct application of these principles to the institution of slavery, as it exists in our country. But now I feel that I act, and that the honored fathers and presbyters of the church act, precisely in the spirit of St. Paul, when we make a direct application of these principles against slavery in our land; because the admission and the practice of these principles are the only means which can now give peace to a convulsed country, and harmony to divided churches; and because the word now uttered in behalf of the poor slave is not a blow to rivet, but a blow to break his fetters. That which it was a duty to abstain from doing before the rebellion, it has now become a duty to do.

V. It is impossible that the consideration of this subject should not have turned our thoughts to the system of slavery as it exists in the United States. In one respect I think it is much worse than Roman slavery; and that is in the subjection and degradation of a whole race. There were slaves of many nationalities and many complexions among the Romans; but no one nation or race was set apart as a lower species of the human family, as a *slave race*, fitted by their constitution for no other position.

In that which constitutes the *peculium* of slavery, viz., the possession of man as property, to be bought and sold as an animated tool, without the right of possessing his faculties, himself, his wife, or his children, the two systems were essentially the same. And though much of the legislation of the slave States is cruel in the extreme, it must be admitted that the law affords them a protection greater than that which they enjoyed under the Roman system; and that the same absolute right over the life of the slave is not recognized by law, however it may sometimes be practically exercised with impunity. Yet, on the other hand, it must be admitted that slaves among Greeks and Romans had opportunities to rise to positions of trust and favor, and even of honor in their masters' households, such as are not enjoyed under our system. There were slaves with every degree of culture. Mechanics, accountants, stewards, musicians, artists, scholars, teachers, and poets were found among them. There were no laws, as with us, against their instruction. Each master was at liberty to train his servants according to his will. He was the gainer by their accomplishments, and it was both a matter of pride and profit with him to develop their peculiar powers. In comparing the two systems, I think it may justly be concluded that their revolting features, though not precisely the same, were about equal; but that in their practical administration, the spirit of Christian charity, and the general sense of justice and humanity which it has diffused, has prevented to a large extent the practice, and to a still greater degree the toleration and approval of atrocious personal wrongs and cruelties among us which would have passed without comment among the Romans.

On the practical working of our system of slavery there is a great diversity of opinion. Heated feeling has led to extreme representations of its evil and its good. On the one side, slavery is described as administered in a mild, paternal, and Christian spirit, which counteracts in practice the evil of its theory; it is claimed that it proves to be the best and kindest arrangement which can be made for the colored race; and that cases of cruelty and hardship are rare exceptions. On the other side, it is contended that, separate from the perpetual cruelty of placing persons in the relation of being owned by others, constant cruelties are necessitated by that relation, and that what would be considered harshness and cruelty toward free servants is not so regarded when exercised toward slaves; and that when kindness is felt and attempted to be exercised in rare and exceptional cases, it is not, and cannot be so effective as to seem like kindness so long as the relation is sustained. Opinions are formed upon such subjects by the facts which are before the mind; and as one's position or prejudice places one set of facts exclusively or more prominently before the view, he will be likely to form one or other of the above opinions. It would be in vain for me here to attempt to discuss this immense question. I can only give the results of the working of my own mind on the subject.

When I went into the midst of a slaveholding community, more than twenty years ago, it was with a feeling of strong moral reprobation of slavery, and with a deep conviction of its actual enormities and horrors. Living in the midst of it, and learning to respect and love the high and genial character of many slaveholders; observing their personal kindness to their slaves; seeing the comfort which many of them enjoyed; knowing the institution only where it was presented in its more favorable aspects, I at first concluded that the system was less evil in its practical working than I had supposed, while I still felt as strongly as before its inconsistency with natural justice, and with the spirit and precepts of the Gospel. A longer residence, and a more extended observation, and a closer study of the evil effects of slaveholding on personal character, rendering it willful and imperious; a revelation of the inevitable hardships and cruelties arising from the system itself, even in kind and Christian families, and which no personal kindness could prevent; a knowledge of the smothered animosities in the hearts of servants which it often produces, and of the consequent state of suspicion and vague terror, which always engenders cruelty, which it awakens; an observation of the fact that the standard of justice and kindness was lowered in relation to the colored race, and that consequently that treatment was considered kind to a slave which no free-born servant would have been expected to submit to; an initiation into the more inner workings of the system in families, and of the frequent half-recognized concubinage, or worse temporary connections, between the masters and the masters' sons and female slaves; the knowledge of some horrible cases of the sale of their own flesh and blood, on the part of men who still retained a position in the community where the facts were well known or generally believed,—all these facts led me to a *more* profound conviction of the inherent and incurable evils of our system of slavery than my first vague and less-informed impressions had produced.

But whatever convictions a practical knowledge of the system may have produced on different minds, there are certain evils which all must and do admit to exist, which are so great and so immediately the result of the system, and so without remedy while the evil exists, that it seems singular that so many good and kind and pious persons can uphold the institution. Admit all that the evidence allows of the kindness of masters and mistresses,—and the amount of this kindness is very great; admit all the religious influence that has been exerted over the slaves,—and it is very large; admit the claim that multitudes of them are far better off and more advanced than their savage brethren in Africa—and the fact is undoubted,—and yet it remains true that Christian men buy and sell their fellow-men, as if they were merchandise or cattle; that they separate husbands and wives, parents and children; that the laws of inheritance and the pressure of financial difficulty often force the cruel sale and separation of closely related slaves, and consign those who have hitherto been treated well to a fearful fate, and that numerous cases of horrible cruelty go unwhipped of justice. It is still all too true that cruel, licentious, abandoned men, the worst which a community possesses, *have a right to hold as property, and therefore to wield an absolute irresponsible power over just so many men, women, and children as they can buy!* This last fact is alone sufficient utterly to condemn the system as inhuman and unworthy of a civilized and Christian nation. It is still true that the laws forbid that slaves should be taught to read. Add to this the fact that the laws make it impossible for good and kind masters to carry out such purposes of benevolence as may be in their hearts. A Roman master could do all the kindness to a slave that he desired. He could instruct him, educate him, emancipate him, set him up in the world; and it was possible for him to rise, as many did rise, to the best positions in society, and the highest offices of the State. Our system forbids a master, under severe penalties, to teach his slaves. In many States he cannot manumit them, except upon conditions which are almost impossible to be fulfilled, and which would leave a freed slave in a position worse than that of bondage. No career is opened to the freedman. Citizenship is denied him. Law, and public opinion more *exigeant* and cruel than law, watches and visits with its wrath the slaveowner who should attempt any other kindness to him than that of promoting his physical well-being, and of furnishing him with some oral religious instructions.

I think this must be admitted to be a very temperate statement of the evils of our system. If it is just, then no possible alleviations and advantages which it may possess are sufficient to counterbalance its enormous wrongs. Its relations to the Gospel must be essentially the same as that of Roman and Grecian slavery. St. Paul's exhortations to masters and slaves, while the system subsists, are as applicable to the one as to the other. If the master should render to the servant that which is just and equal, if he should treat his slave as a brother beloved, the whole system would be undermined and eventually destroyed. But unhappily the law, and a cruel and denunciatory opinion worse than law, will not permit him, as it would have permitted the Roman master, to carry out in their spirit and in their fullness those just injunctions. It must be admitted to be a singular and mortifying anomaly, that in a Christian land a system of slavery should exist, which, if not quite so evil in some of its features as that which prevailed among the hard and coarse-grained Romans, is yet more tightly riveted upon its victims, and less capable of amelioration.

VI. In the light of these principles evolved from the words and the example of St. Paul, we are able to discern some of the mistaken extremes which have prevailed upon the subject of slavery in our day.

1. It has not only been vindicated as right in itself, but it has been claimed that it has a divine sanction; it has been elevated into a divine institution on the authority of St. Paul. We have shown how this mistake has arisen from supposing that when St. Paul urges the faithful discharge of the duties of a certain relation while it exists, he necessarily approves of the relation itself, and sanctions its establishment and continuance.

2. On the other hand, others have contended that it is wrong *ever*, under any circumstances, to sustain the relation of master to a slave. St. Paul evidently did not so regard it. He did not assume this ground with Philemon. In the case of a Christian husband or wife, connected with a heathen wife or husband, he sanctioned the principle that it may be right, and even a duty, to remain in and discharge the duties of a relation which it would have been unrighteous to have originated.

3. Hence also it is a mistake and wrong to denounce all persons who hold slaves, as thereby shown to be evidently inhuman men, and as consciously upholding a system of cruel wrong and oppression. One who has long known and lived among them cannot but deeply feel the injustice of such a judgment. He will remember some of the most excellent and exemplary Christians he has ever known among this class. He will recall instances of the most painstaking and self-denying labors for the temporal and spiritual good of those committed to their care. He will be able to mention the conscientious convictions of duty which have prevented some persons from freeing slaves, who would gladly have avoided the care and responsibility of them by this pecuniary sacrifice if they had considered such a course lawful. He will see that such persons do not differ in Christian principles, or even Christian practice, from those good Christians who mistakenly denounce them; but only differ *as to the case which is actually presented to them.* If by upholding slavery and holding slaves they thought that they were robbing men of their rights, keeping them in ignorance, perpetuating their degradation, and preventing their advancement, they too would oppose the institution and emancipate their slaves. But *this is not the case* as it is presented to them. They think that they are taking care of a race who cannot take care of themselves; that it is a kindness to force them to labor, inasmuch as it is better for their health and morals and advancement, than the vicious idleness into which they would else inevitably lapse; that thus they can be advanced in morals and

intelligence and religion as fast as they are capable of advancing; and that their sufferings in servitude, some of which indeed are in consequence of hard laws, which they personally would desire to have removed, are not to be compared to those which would result from freedom. Such is the case which *is presented to their minds*. One may think that they are exceedingly mistaken in this view. One may suspect that they have been led to adopt it by influences of interest or of passion of which they are wholly unconscious. One may be surprised and grieved at the degree of indignation and animosity which they feel against those who wholly dissent from them, and yet one may admit, and feel constrained to admit, and ought to be ready cheerfully to admit, and if he has associated much among this class, feels bound emphatically to testify that among them are persons of the most saintly and lovely character. As one of those who disapprove and would have removed the institution to which they cling, I have been subject to many hard speeches and bitter feelings among Southern brethren with whom I once held sweet counsel, and walked together in the House of God as friends; but I remember their friendship with gratitude; I mourn over the delusions of feeling and opinion which have urged them into most unpardonable and causeless rebellion; I sympathize with the dreadful sufferings which they have brought upon themselves, and lament the humiliation to which as a subjugated people they have become, or will soon become, exposed; and with all these feelings blending into one emotion of sorrowful regret, I feel that however they may speak of me and of my brethren who have felt and acted with me, it is alike a pleasure and a duty to speak thus of many among them.

4. And it is an equal mistake, and less excusable, and one which rests on grounds less plausible, to denounce the friends and advocates of emancipation as enemies of a divinely constituted society, and to affix to them opprobrious epithets, and cast out their name as evil. That a Bishop of our Church, with all the lights thrown upon this subject by recent events, should commit himself to such statements is a singular and mortifying event.* It is indeed a strange anomaly that in a State, constituted upon the Gospel principle of human brotherhood and equality, they, whose only error it is admitted has been the too rigid application of a right principle without a sufficient reference to practical and complicated difficulties, in the midst of which,

"Right too rigid hardens into wrong,"

should be denounced as pre-eminently guilty. The treatment of abolitionists at the North has been a disgrace upon our country; and has been the principal cause of all the harm that has come from their existence. That they have not been wise is no sufficient reason that they should have been treated as if they were the vilest of the vile. It will read strangely in future history, that in a republican State, the first sentence of whose proclamation of independent existence is but another form of the Scripture truth, that God hath made of one blood all nations, there was

---

* Bishop Hopkins, of Vermont.

a period when to advocate the continued existence of a system of slavery, far worse than that of Tunis or Algiers, without any improvement or any provision for its ultimate removal, was to be among the vast majority that were regarded as conservative of right and just principles; and to plead earnestly for its immediate removal was to be among a despised minority, which was regarded as vile, and cruel, and unjust. I am thankful to remember that, although I felt their schemes were not wise, I never gave in to this unrighteous clamor against their character. I knew that among them were some of the purest Christians of our time; and that among those who were infidel and radical, were many of those noble natures whom the world's wrong drives to disbelief, and maddens into a blind and unwise indignation, but who are in the basis of their character far higher than many who, with the name of Christian, are the narrow, and mean, and selfish advocates of all prescriptive and profitable wrongs. Some of the best men of the free States have been denouncing as unchristian and inhuman some of the best men of the slave States; and they have hurled back these denunciations with an equal conviction of their truth, and an added turning sense of outrage and indignation. Both of these classes are beginning to find that they were both and equally mistaken.

5. In this matter we all have grievously erred and sinned, and God is scourging us for our sins, and at the same time removing the evil that has clouded our judgments and kindled asperities of feeling. There were those who did not believe it wise or Christian, both on grounds of Christian obligation

and on St. Paul's principles of procedure, to labor for the immediate emancipation of slavery in the Southern States. They hoped and prayed that it would be ultimately accomplished through the action of Christian feeling in the communities where slavery existed. In this position I think they were right. Having myself occupied it, I do not now see or feel that I was wrong. But in so far as the taking of this position led any of us to extenuate the evils of slavery, to shut our eyes to its manifold abominations, to vindicate it on moral or religious grounds, and to denounce all strong sympathy with the sufferings of the slaves, I think we were clearly in the wrong. Those who advocated immediate emancipation, irrespective of constitutional obligations and of all the deplorable consequences which might ensue, were, I think, unwise and in the wrong, and in conflict with the "peaceable wisdom" of St. Paul. They were no less wrong in the bitter denunciations with which many of them assailed those who advocated the policy of peace and patience. But they were right, as all our subsequent history has shown, in their vivid representations of the sins and cruelties and shames of slavery.

Of the state of feeling and thinking on this subject in the Southern States I do not wish to speak. It is a time when every instinct of magnanimity and Christian sympathy for their sufferings, the consequences of their mistakes, and admiration for their heroic energy, should lead us to dwell rather on our own sins than on theirs. God is making the wrath and sin and folly of us all to praise Him. He is exorcising the evil spirit which has hitherto possessed our body politic, and the convulsions which it suffers are but from the struggles of the reluctant demon to retain his place. God is bringing all classes, in every portion of our country, to relinquish some of the errors of prejudice and opinion which they have hitherto entertained, and to unite in what promises to be the well-nigh universal conviction that as slavery has been our sin and has found us out, so repentance for it should lead to the works meet for repentance in the elevation and the investment with the rights of manhood and of citizenship of the race that has been so unjustly held in bondage. My profound conviction is that in twenty years there will be no one in all the breadth of our restored and purified Union to rise up as a public advocate or apologist of slavery. The amiable and gifted Mr. Stephens, of Georgia, proclaimed slavery to be the corner-stone of the new confederation, but it is a corner-stone on which no superstructure can rest, for it is upheld by a revolutionary earthquake which will cast it crushingly on the structure it was expected to support.

If this attempt to expound St. Paul's relation to established institutions, and especially to slavery, and to apply his principles to slavery in our own country, is not successful, it is not because I have not sincerely and earnestly desired to give it a dispassionate consideration, and to apply to it the result of many years of the most anxious thought, and of careful and widely-extended observation. One important lesson we should all learn from this consideration of this difficult subject. It is, that inasmuch as most of the practical duties of life and of society lie not among the distinctly-marked right and wrong of things, but rather among mixed and blending rights and wrongs, the most conscientious mind, still subject to the infirmities of our poor fallen nature, may through unconscious bias greatly err, and still retain high moral integrity and a genuine Christian spirit. This great lesson of charity I have earnestly endeavored to apply to others, and conscious of my equal need of it, I invoke it for myself.

LECTURE XI.

ST. PAUL'S SECOND IMPRISONMENT AT ROME.

For I am now ready to be offered, and the time of my departure is at hand.—2 Tim. iv. 6.

The history of St. Paul subsequent to the last record in the Acts of the Apostles is exceedingly obscure. We have hitherto moved with confidence in the open and well-lighted path of authentic history. We are now to grope and wind our way through historical probabilities and deductions by the aid of scattered and feeble rays of testimony.

We conclude that St. Paul was liberated from his imprisonment at Rome from a passage in the Epistle to the Hebrews. He was then in Italy or at liberty, for he writes, "they of Italy salute you;" and he says of Timothy, "Know ye that our brother Timothy is set at liberty, with whom, if he come shortly, I will see you." This Epistle was written subsequent to St. Paul's two years' imprisonment. He was then in Italy, and he was at liberty to visit the Hebrews, to whom he writes, in company with liberated Timothy. This seems to be a clear proof that St. Paul's trial had either resulted in his acquittal or had been abandoned.

The strongest proof, perhaps, which we possess that St. Paul had been tried and acquitted, is the universal belief that it was so which prevailed in the ancient church. The proofs of the fact, as they come to us, are few and indirect. They may have been explicit and numerous to the early church. Few as they are, there appears to be no counter testimonies. Clement, the disciple of St. Paul, and afterward Bishop of Rome, writing from Rome to Corinth, asserts that St. Paul had preached the Gospel in the East and in the West; that he had instructed the whole world in righteousness; and that he had gone to the extremity of the West before his martyrdom. Now as we know that St. Paul had not visited the West *previous* to his imprisonment at Rome, it must have been after his release.

There exists a Canon of the New Testament called Muratoris Canon, compiled by an unknown author about the year A.D. 170. In this document, it is said, in the account of the Acts of the Apostles, that "Luke relates to Theophilus events of which he was an eye-witness, as also in a separate place he evidently declares the martyrdom of Peter, but omits the journey of Paul to Spain." The writer refers, we suppose, by the expression "in a separate place," to the Gospel of St. Luke. In that Gospel there is no account of the martyrdom of St. Peter. The writer may have regarded the Saviour's words, "Simon, Simon, Satan hath desired to have you that he may sift you as wheat;" and Peter's reply, "I am ready to go with Thee both into prison and to death," as a *prophecy* of his martyrdom, and may therefore have called it an *account* of his martyrdom. But, however this may be, his assertion is distinct to the visit of Paul to Spain.

Eusebius tells us that after defending himself successfully, it is currently reported that the Apostle again went forth to proclaim the Gospel, and afterward came to Rome a second time, and was martyred under Nero. Chrysostom mentions it as an undoubted fact "that St. Paul, after his residence in Rome, departed to Spain." St. Jerome also testifies "that Paul was dismissed by Nero, that he might preach Christ's Gospel in the West."*

The argument thus far goes to prove that St. Paul left Rome, and preached the Gospel in the West, and especially in Spain.

The Epistles to Timothy and Titus, called the Pastoral Epistles, are usually believed to have been written after his first imprisonment at Rome. Their date, in the received translation of the Bible, is placed beyond this period. We find from these Epistles that after his first imprisonment at Rome he was traveling and at liberty at Ephesus, (1 Tim. i. 3,) Crete, (Titus, i. 6,) Macedonia, (1 Tim. i. 3,) Miletus, (2 Tim. iv. 30,) and Nicopolis, (Titus, iii. 12,) and that he was again, for the second time, a prisoner at Rome. These facts concerning his journeys and his history, are all that can be collected from the sacred canons.

The internal evidences that the second Epistle could not have been written during St. Paul's first imprisonment at Rome, but that it is to be referred to a subsequent imprisonment, are quite clear and strong. They have been well stated in Barnes's Notes. I can but briefly refer to some of them. St. Paul evidently expected, in his Epistles to the Philippians and to Philemon, a speedy release and departure from Rome. "I trust in the Lord I shall

---

* These authorities are derived from Conybeare and Howson's "Life and Epistles of St. Paul."

come shortly," (Phil. ii. 24,) he writes to the Philippians. He requests Philemon to prepare him a lodging. (22 v.) But in the second Epistle it is clear he had no such expectation, for he says, "I am ready to be offered, and the time of my departure is at hand." (2 Tim. iv. 6.) Again, St. Paul says, "Erastus *abode* at Corinth." (iv. 20.) This implies a second journey to Rome. It implies that they traveled together, and that while Paul proceeded to Rome, Erastus remained at Corinth. It is certain that this language would not be appropriate if written during Paul's first sojourn at Rome. The same remark is applicable to what St. Paul says of Trophimus. "Trophimus have I left at Miletum sick." (iv. 20.) Paul, when sent by Festus to Rome, did not stop at Miletum. Nor could he have referred to his first visit to Miletus, (Acts, xx.,) five years before. He evidently refers to a recent occurrence. There would have been no propriety in informing Timothy that, five years before, he had left a fellow-laborer sick, as a reason why he should hasten to Rome as soon as possible. The fact, moreover, that certain persons are spoken of as present in the first Epistle who are mentioned as absent in the second, is a strong reason for supposing the second Epistle to have been written during a second imprisonment. Timothy was at Rome when St. Paul wrote his first Epistle, and absent of course when Paul addressed to him his second Epistle. The same remark is true of Demas and of Mark. These internal evidences, added to those testimonies to which we have referred, leave no just reason to doubt that St. Paul was imprisoned at Rome a second time. If they do not constitute a demonstration, they at least conclude the very highest degree of probability short of demonstration.

It would be extremely interesting to know the circumstances of St. Paul's acquittal at his first imprisonment. In the absence of any authentic testimony on the subject, we can only form some conjectures as to his trial, from what we learn of the mode of procedure that prevailed at that period. This has been so admirably done in Conybeare and Howson's Life of St. Paul that it would be a great injustice to withhold at least a part of the description.

"In the first place, after a long delay, St. Paul's appeal came on for hearing before the Emperor. The appeals from the provinces in civil cases were heard, not by the Emperor himself, but by his delegates, who were persons of consular rank. Augustus had appointed one such delegate to hear appeals from each province respectively. But criminal appeals appear to have been heard by the Emperor in person, assisted by his council of assessors. Tiberius and Claudius had usually sat for this purpose in the former; but Nero, after the example of Augustus, heard those causes in the imperial palace, whose ruins still crown the Palatine. Here, at one end of a splendid hall, lined with the precious marbles of Egypt and Lybia, we must imagine the Cæsar seated in the midst of his assessors. These councillors, twenty in number, were men of the highest rank and greatest influence. Among them were the two consuls and selected representatives of each of the other great magistracies of Rome. The remainder consisted of senators chosen by lot. Over this distinguished bench of judges presided the representative of the most powerful monarchy which has ever existed, the absolute ruler of the whole civilized world. But the reverential awe which his position naturally suggested was changed into contempt and loathing by the character of the sovereign who now presided over that supreme tribunal. For Nero was a man whom even the awful attribute of 'power equal to the gods' could not render august except in title. The fear and horror excited by his omnipotence and cruelty were blended with contempt for his ignoble lust of praise and his shameless licentiousness. His degrading want of dignity and insatiable appetite for vulgar applause drew tears from the councillors and servants of his house, who could, however, see him slaughter his nearest relations without remonstrance.

"Before the tribunal of this blood-stained adulterer, Paul the Apostle was now brought in fetters under the custody of a military guard. But to him all the majesty of Rome was nothing more than an empty pageant; the demi-god himself was but 'one of the princes of this world that come to naught.' Thus he stood, calm and collected, ready to answer the charges of his accusers, and knowing that in the hour of his need it should be given him what to speak."*

We have seen already that the charges brought against the Apostle could not be proved, and even if proved, would not have been a violation of the laws of the empire. Yet if the influence of Poppea, or the caprice of the Emperor, had been

---

* Conybeare and Howson's Life and Writings of St. Paul, vol. ii. pp. 465–67. It is not thought necessary to append the notes which confirm or illustrate the passages quoted.

turned against the Apostle, no doubt he would have been condemned. We are left wholly to conjecture as to the influences which determined his acquittal.

The causes and the circumstances of St. Paul's second imprisonment at Rome are as obscure as those of his first acquittal. There is no expression of his purpose again to visit Rome in his first Epistle to Timothy, or in the Epistle to Titus. Hence we infer that he was carried thither as a prisoner. By whom or on what charges, does not appear. But we know that a great change in the policy of the Roman Government and in the feelings of the people had taken place between his first and second imprisonment. The first imperial persecution had occurred, and the Christians had become distinguished in the popular apprehension from the Jews, with whom they had formerly been confounded. St. Paul might well anticipate his own martyrdom when he arrived in Rome, a prisoner for the second time, after the scenes of persecution which have been so graphically commemorated by the pen of Tacitus. The well-known passage should not be omitted in this connection.

"But neither these religious ceremonies, nor the liberal donations of the prince, could efface from the minds of men the prevailing opinion that Rome was set on fire by his own orders. The infamy of that horrible transaction still adhered to him. In order, if possible, to remove this imputation, he determined to transfer the guilt to others. For this purpose he punished, with exquisite torture, a race of men detested for their evil practices, by vulgar appellation commonly called Christians. The name was derived from Christ, who, in the time of Tiberius, suffered under Pontius Pilate, the Procurator of Judea. By that event the sect of which he was a founder received a blow which, for a time, checked the growth of a dangerous superstition; but it revived soon after and spread with recruited vigor, not only in Judea, the soil that gave it birth, but even in the City of Rome, the common sink into which everything infamous and abominable flows like a torrent from all quarters of the world. Nero proceeded with his usual artifice. He found a set of abandoned and profligate wretches who were induced to confess themselves guilty, and on the evidence of such men a number of Christians were convicted, not on the clear evidence of their having set the city on fire, but rather on account of their sullen hatred of the whole Roman race. They were put to death with exquisite cruelty, and to their sufferings Nero added mockery and derision. Some were covered with the skins of beasts and left to be devoured by dogs; others were nailed to the cross; numbers were burnt alive; and many, covered over with inflammable matter, were lighted up when the day declined to serve as torches during the night. For the convenience of seeing this tragic spectacle, the Emperor lent his own gardens. He added the sports of the circus, and assisted in person, sometimes driving a curricle, and occasionally mixing with the rabble in his coachman's dress."*

St. Paul in his second Epistle to Timothy makes no allusion to the charge upon which he was again remanded to Rome and to prison. In the recollec-

---

* Tacitus' Annals, xv. 44.

tion of the scenes described by Tacitus, he must have had a full persuasion of his own coming martyrdom. It is probable that, after the persecution described above, the profession of Christianity was forbidden by the laws, then newly enforced against new and unlawful religions. They had been applied on several occasions to the worship of Isis, and other Eastern gods, when the popular indignation had risen against them.

There appear to have been none of the alleviations and relaxations to this imprisonment which he had previously enjoyed. He was now not only in chains, but as a malefactor. "I suffer trouble," he says, "as an evil-doer, or malefactor, even unto bonds." (2 Tim. ii. 9.) He had previously been arraigned rather as a state prisoner,—as one who had violated a law of one of their provinces, Judea,—whom they were bound to protect. Now, he seems to have been presented as a culprit—a direct violator of the laws of the empire. He was not permitted as before to preach and teach. That it was dangerous and obnoxious to visit him, and difficult to find him, we infer from his grateful commemoration of the visit of Onesiphorus. "The Lord give mercy unto the house of Onesiphorus; for he oft refreshed me, and was not ashamed of my chain; but when he was in Rome he sought me out very diligently and found me." (2 Tim. xvi. 17.) The aged Apostle, now more aged by several years than when he used the expression, seems to have been deserted by all his friends and brethren, except St. Luke. "Only Luke is with me." (2 Tim. iv. 11.) "Demas hath forsaken me, having loved this present world, and is departed unto Thessalonica; Cressens to Galatia; Titus unto

Dalmatia." (2 Tim. iv. 10.) Added to this sense of desertion and loneliness, was the consciousness of being subjected to the wiles of malignant enemies. "Alexander the coppersmith did me much evil: the Lord reward him according to his works; of whom be thou ware also, for he hath greatly withstood our words." (14, 15.) When he is arraigned before the tribunal, there is not a solitary Christian friend to stand by him. "At my first answer no man stood with me, but all men forsook me; I pray God that it may not be laid to their charge." (16.) He evidently looked forward to certain condemnation and death; and in these circumstances of the desertion of friends, of loneliness, and of the weight of years, was enabled calmly to declare, "I am ready to be offered, and the time of my departure *is at hand.*" (6.) It is a touching incidental proof of his destitution, and of the absence of friends to minister to his necessities, such as he enjoyed during his first imprisonment, when he declared, "I have all and abound," that he should now write to Timothy, "The cloak that I left at Troas with Carpus, when thou comest bring with thee, and the books, but especially the parchments." (13.)

That in the circumstances in which St. Paul was placed he should have been able to have written the Epistle to Timothy, is a proof of the sublime power of the Gospel and the grace of God. It is no less remarkable for what it omits than for what it contains. Its solemnity, its tenderness, its calm elevation are befitting to the soul that is on the verge of heaven. But that, thus in prison, deserted of friends, surrounded by enemies, and about to die a cruel death, there should be no egotism, no querulousness, no crimination,—in this is to be found the divine and sublime beauty of the Epistle. He writes to animate his beloved son Timothy to be steadfast under the persecution which he foresaw would soon assail the churches. He commends his faith—the precious inheritance of his mother Eunice and grandmother Lois. And then, animating him to constancy, he writes these noble words, "For Gód hath not given us a spirit of fear, but of love, and of power, and of a sound mind." And then, his soul soaring toward his Saviour, in lofty peace he enters upon his teaching and exhortation.

Timothy must not shrink from suffering. He must not merely submit to it, and be crushed by it. He must work in the midst of it. So did the Master. He must be a busy and thorough workman in the Gospel. He must avoid foolish, speculative, barren questions; for some, as Hymenæas and Philetus, have been led astray by them to the denial of the first truths of the Gospel. Better to rest in plain saving truth and practical duty. For from neglect of this, in the last days, evil times will come in which men will join licentious practices to speculative errors.

Then follow exhortations to constancy, in which there is no gloom, no fearfulness, but, on the contrary, high-hearted joyfulness. He would have Timothy come to him speedily. He evidently trusts in his friendship and fidelity.

There are some names mentioned in the last verse but one of this Epistle, which possess much interest. "There salute thee Eubulus, and Pudens, and Linus, and Claudia, and all the brethren." Linus is probably the person who was afterward Bishop of Rome.

Pudens and his family have been made the subjects of many Roman traditions. Those traditions are minute and specific, but rest upon nothing that can be considered as historical testimony. We are told of the sojourn of St. Peter at his house. We are shown the mosaic floor of his house in the church dedicated to Santa Prudentiana, his daughter. It is astonishing how many and minute facts are stated and believed, on no other ground than that such is the tradition of the church. We are not only required to accept with unquestioning faith the traditions of the church, but we are required to believe that certain things *are* the traditions of the church, on the most meager and unsatisfactory evidence. There is undoubtedly a certain *prima facie* evidence in a general tradition, which states facts which are improbable or impossible, but it may safely be said that we are called upon to accept many things as traditions on individual testimonies that are not so. Hence, when anything is stated on Romish authority to be a tradition, we have two separate questions to ask: first, "is it a tradition?" and second, "is it true?" The names of Pudens and Claudia are patrician. There is an epigram of Martial, congratulatory and eulogistic, on the marriage of a Pudens and Claudia; but there is no proof that they are the persons mentioned by St. Paul. The salutations sent by these Christian friends to Timothy prove that, at the period when this Epistle was written, they had access to the Apostle. It is scarcely credible that St. Paul could have been in the Mamertine prison when he wrote this Epistle, and was able to communicate with some of his brethren in Rome.

On what charges Paul was tried we cannot learn.

It may have been on the charge of teaching a religion forbidden by the state. It may have been on Nero's false accusation that as a prime leader of the Christians he had instigated them to burn the city. But that it was not this time "before Cæsar," appears from the statement of Clemens Romanus that he was tried before "the presiding magistrates."* He describes his first appearance before them in these words: "When I was first heard in my defense, no man stood by me, but all forsook me. I pray that it be not laid to their charge. Nevertheless, the Lord stood by me and strengthened my heart." (2 Tim. iv. 16, 17.) At that time he was delivered from the wrath of the lion. But at a subsequent period we cannot doubt that he was condemned and executed, although we are left utterly in the dark as to his trial and his death.

Although we have no authentic testimony on this subject, we may yet follow with great interest the suggestions which have been made by the authors already quoted as to "the probable external features of his last trial." He evidently intimates that he had spoken before a crowded audience, so "that all the Gentiles might hear," and this corresponds with the supposition which historically we should be led to make, that he was tried in one of those great Basilicas which stood in the Forum. Two of the most celebrated of these edifices were called the Pauline Basilicas, from the well-known Lucius Æmelius Paulus, who had built one of them and restored the other. It is not improbable that the greatest man who ever bore the Pauline name was

---

* See Conybeare and Howson, vol. ii. p. 498.

tried in one of these. From specimens which still exist, as well as from the descriptions of Vetruvius, we have an accurate knowledge of these halls of justice. "They were rectangular buildings, consisting of a central nave and two aisles, separated from the nave by rows of columns. At one end of the nave was the tribune, in the center of which was placed the magistrate's curule chair of ivory elevated on a platform called the tribunal. Here sat also the council of assessors, who advised the prefect upon the law, though they had no voice in the judgment. On the sides of the tribune were seats for distinguished persons, as well as for parties engaged in the proceedings. Fronting the presiding magistrate stood the prisoner with his accusers and his advocates. The public was admitted into the remainder of the nave and aisles, which was railed off from the portion devoted to judicial proceedings; and there were also galleries along the whole length of the aisles—one for men, the other for women. The aisles were roofed over as was the tribune. The nave was originally left open to the sky. The Basilicas were buildings of great size, so that a vast multitude of spectators was always present at any trial which excited public interest."

If such were the circumstances of St. Paul's trial, we cannot doubt that he bore himself, as before Festus and Agrippa, with dignity and intrepidity and with all fidelity to his Master and his convictions.

From all that we have thus far adduced we may conclude, I think, with a good degree of certainty, that Paul was tried and acquitted at his first imprisonment; that he subsequently exercised his ministry for some years, both in the East and West;

that he was a second time prisoner at Rome; that at his first hearing he was acquitted, but that he subsequently was tried and condemned and executed. But though there be sufficient proof of his martyrdom, there is nothing, as we shall see, which can be relied upon as proof, as to the circumstances of his imprisonment, trial, and execution.

Here we might naturally conclude our account of St. Paul in Rome. But what is called the tradition of the church, minutely and confidently narrates his confinement in the Mamertine prison, and the circumstances of his death. Many Protestant authors are disposed to endeavor to separate from these narratives all that is miraculous and absurd, and to rest in the conviction that the Apostle was confined in the Mamertine prison and carried out upon the Ostian Way and executed at the point· three miles from the gate, where the church "San Paulo alle Tre Fontane" was subsequently erected in commemoration of the martyrdom. Now although there is nothing improbable in the statement, and no evidence against it, I am yet unable to feel, from any authorities to which I have had access, that it is either proved, or *by the evidence* made more probable. It may be probable in itself; but no evidence has been adduced which, to my mind, increases that inherent original probability. It seems to me a point neither proved nor disproved, and having no satisfactory evidence for it or against it. My reasons for this conviction can be briefly stated.

1. In looking into the authorities for these statements I find none that are contemporaneous, nor that are so near to the period as to be the evidence of witnesses. Clemens Romanus declares the *mar-*

tyrdom of St. Paul, but gives no account of the place of his imprisonment, nor of the mode and scene of his martyrdom.

2. In the absence of contemporary authorities, we are referred to others which testify at the same time to incidents and marvels and absurdities which it is impossible to accept. It may be said that we are at liberty to accept what seems to us probable, and reject what is impossible or absurd. But in that case we do not accept anything in fact on the testimony, but only our own mind's decision as to what we conceive might probably have happened. I do not object to the inherent probability that St. Paul may have been placed in the Mamertine prison, and executed on the Ostian Way; but to accepting as of any value what is presented as testimony to that effect. We are told that St. Paul was in the Mamertine prison, and are at the same time informed that St. Peter was there, and that a fountain sprang out of the rock and still remains there, at which St. Peter baptized his jailers. We are told that St. Paul was executed at the site of the "San Paulo alle Tre Fontane," but by the same authority we are assured that when his head was cut off, it was milk instead of blood that flowed from it, and that it bounced three times after it was off, and at every spot at which it fell a fountain was opened which still continues flowing. Now we do not deny nor assert that St. Paul was at the Mamertine prison, and was executed at the spot thus indicated, but we refuse to accept such testimony in the case. If a witness testify to three things, two of which we know to be absurd and false, he has disqualified himself for being accepted as a witness to the third

point, however reasonable or probable his statement may appear.

3. The testimony, or tradition, or whatever we may prefer to call it, which would lead us to consider it a *fact proved* that St. Paul was in the Mamertine prison, and was executed at the point indicated on the Ostian Way, would also compel us to accept the statements concerning St. Peter's Episcopate in Rome and supremacy over the churches, as well as the fact of his martyrdom and its accompanying marvels. How impossible it is for a mind which demands proofs before it gives its assent, to accept the statements on those points with which the supposed proofs concerning Paul's imprisonment and death are inseparably bound up, will appear, I think, from the following considerations.

(1) From the history of St. Peter, as it is found in the New Testament, there is not the slightest evidence that he ever came to Rome. There is only one passage which can even be supposed to furnish a proof that he had ever been in Rome. That this passage should have been employed for that purpose is a proof of the extreme difficulty of finding anything that looks like evidence to that effect. The passage in one of the closing verses of the first Epistle, "The church that is at Babylon elected together with you saluteth you." This is the only passage upon which Bellarmine relies to show that St. Peter was at Rome. He considers that by Babylon, pagan Rome was intended by St. Peter. It is scarcely necessary to enter upon an argument to show how groundless is this supposition. Neither he nor any other writer pretends to cite any other evidence

from Scripture in proof of the supposed residence of St. Peter at Rome.

It has indeed been denied that this Epistle of St. Peter could have been addressed from the literal Babylon of Mesopotamia, because it was at that time a desolate wilderness, a haunt of wild beasts. Strabo says that the great city had become a great desert. This author died in the reign of Tiberius, about the year A.D. 25. If then his description is to be literally received, the city must have been *then* an uninhabited wilderness. But according to Josephus, (lib. 18, chap. ix. § 38,) it was at that very time the abode of a very numerous colony of Jews. He states that a large number of Jews, *after* this period, (between A.D. 37 and 41,) migrated from Babylon to the neighboring Seleucia, to escape the persecutions of the Parthians of that city. He also adds that, within the same period, 50,000 of the Jews perished by the hands of the Seleucians. Hence we are compelled to infer that Strabo meant nothing more than to give a strong expression to the contrast between the former grandeur and the then comparative desolation of Babylon. Moreover, it is well known that down to the middle of the second century, vast numbers of Jews were gathered in the Province of Babylonia, and that in the reign of Hadrian, they broke forth in frequent sanguinary attacks, both against their Parthian and Roman oppressors. Within three centuries after Christ, the great seat of Rabbinical learning was fixed at Babylon, and then and there the famous Babylonian Talmud was produced.

This then was precisely the place at which we might expect the Apostle of the Circumcision to have sojourned. In the absence of any proof to the contrary, and in the presence of many concurrent probabilities of the fact, we must conclude that St. Peter dated his Epistle from the Babylon of Mesopotamia. Thus the *one* alleged proof from Scripture that Peter was ever in Rome falls to the ground.

(2) There is also a negative argument against the claim of St. Peter having been at Rome so strong as to be almost equivalent to a positive demonstration. It is the fact, that neither during St. Paul's first nor second imprisonment, neither in his letter to the Romans before he came to them, nor in his letters from Rome during his first imprisonment, nor in his last letter to Timothy during his second imprisonment, is there the slightest allusion to St. Peter as having, or ever having had, any connection with the Church of Rome. It is incredible that if Peter had been, as it is claimed, Bishop of Rome for more than twenty years, no allusion, even remote and incidental, should have been made to him, on either of these occasions. When we add to this fact that St. Clement, who speaks of St. Paul, makes no mention of St. Peter, we have a negative argument, an argument from silence, as strong as can be conceived.

(3) As the one passage relied upon in Scripture to prove that St. Peter wrote his first Epistle from Rome is thoroughly insufficient for that purpose, so is the one passage outside of Scripture, in proof of his coming to Rome in the second year of Claudius. The Roman historian, Suetonius, (In Claudio, c. 25,) mentions that, at that period, a Jew, by the name of Simon, came to Rome, and so stirred up his countrymen to quarrels and seditions that Claudius decreed that all Jews should be banished from the city. On

this statement rests the only proof of St. Peter's coming to Rome in the year A.D. 41, and his expulsion from it for a time. It is asserted without a shadow of proof or probability that this Simon the Jew was Peter the Apostle. This statement, and the salutation from Babylon in the Epistle of St. Peter, are all the contemporary evidence which is even attempted to be adduced for St. Peter's residence in Rome. On these rest the traditions. On the traditions rests the statement of the fathers. On the statement of the fathers rests the whole vast fabric of the Papal supremacy. It is such a feat in logic as it would be in mechanics to upturn St. Peter's and make it rest upon the cross that crowns its dome.

(4) How utterly one finds himself without a reason when he seeks authorities for the facts so minutely recorded concerning St. Peter and St. Paul, will appear from a few instances.

There is no higher authority in the Church of Rome than that of their great historian Baronius. He relates at length the imprisonment of St. Peter and St. Paul. St. Peter's escape from prison, and his meeting of Christ on the Appian Way, with the salutation, "*Domini quo Vædis?*" "Lord, whither goest thou?" and the Lord's reply, that he goes "to Rome to be crucified anew," and St. Peter's conviction and return; the conversion and baptism of their jailers by the Apostles; their incarceration for eight months previous to their martyrdom. But when we look for the authorities for all these interesting facts, we are referred to nothing better than the *Roman Martyrologies*, which were compiled centuries after the events which are thus confidently recorded.

And again, when we *have references* to authorities which promise to be more authentic and reliable, we are compelled to wonder at the insufficiency of proof and the absurdity of the reasonings based upon them, to which we are so boldly directed. We are told, for instance, by Baronius, that when the Apostles were taken from the prison they were scourged previous to their execution. He says that it might be a question whether Paul, a Roman citizen, was subjected to this indignity, but that the fact cannot be doubted, *because the column is preserved in S. Maria, in Trastevere, at which the Apostles were scourged!** When the most learned of the Romish historians resorts to a proof like this, we may well suppose that no proofs exist.

The want of good faith in the conspicuous exhibition of so-called proofs of the most important statements, which are elsewhere admitted by the highest authority to be worthless, is another painful feature of this gigantic structure of deception and delusion. Of this I mention but one instance.

On the Ostian Way there is a little chapel erected at the spot where St. Peter and St. Paul are said to have separated, the one to be crucified on the Janiculum, the other to be beheaded at the Acque Salvie. On this chapel there is an inscription in Italian, of which the following is a translation: "At this place St. Peter and St. Paul, on their way to martyrdom, separated from each other; and St. Paul said to St. Peter, 'Peace be with thee, thou (*fundamento*) foundation of the church and pastor of all the lambs of Christ;' and Peter said to Paul, 'Go in peace,

---

* Baronius, vol. i. p. 666.

preacher of good tidings and guide of the saints and of the just.'" As authority for this statement, reference is made on the tablet to "*Dyonisius in Epistolo ad Timotheum.*"

Now certainly so important a statement as this—testimony given by St. Paul to the supremacy of Peter at the last solemn hour of life—should not be obtruded on the public highway, unless the church, without whose sanction it would not remain there a moment, fully believed that such testimony, whatever its value, *had at least been given.* What is our surprise upon turning to Baronius, the most authoritative and accredited historian of the church, to find him declare this quotation from Dyonisius not to be authentic, and that the fact there recorded is to be believed *rather by tradition* than from any direct assertion of the ancient writers!* What can be more dishonest than this conspicuous testimony obtruded by the church on the highway, which is at the same time declared by the highest authority in the church to be a falsehood and a forgery?

One other instance of the failure to find the respectable support to an assertion which we are led to expect from the reference which is given, will suffice. Baronius, in narrating the fact of the beheading of St. Paul, of the flowing of milk from his neck, and that the severed head gave three long leaps, and that from each place where the head struck, a fountain sprung, refers the reader to the sixty-eighth sermon of St. Ambrose. Upon turning to this sermon we find the following observations: "When the executioner had cut off St. Paul's head

---

* Baronius, vol. i. p. 666.

with a sword, *it is said* that milk rather than blood flowed therefrom, which is not at all to be wondered at in the case of St. Paul. For what is there surprising in the fact that the nourisher (*nutritor*) of the church, he who said to the Corinthians, 'hitherto I have fed you with milk and not with meat,' should abound in milk? This is plainly the land which God promised to the fathers, saying, 'I will give you a land flowing with milk and honey.'"

Now when reference is made to a father in proof of *a fact* which occurred centuries before his time, and he introduces such an extraordinary exposition with the statement, *it is said*, we must be pardoned for considering the passage as little a proof of the reported fact upon which he comments, as it is evidence of his taste or judgment as an expositor.

After even this brief examination, we are not impressed by the imposing array of the names of the fathers as authorities for St. Peter's residence at Rome, and all the high claims which are connected with his alleged Episcopate and primacy. We see from an examination of those references which we have considered, of how little weight, in the way of historical testimony, would be the statements of Eusebius and Jerome, and twenty or thirty other fathers who lived from a century and a half to four centuries after Peter, as to the question of his residence, his life and death at Rome. They could but repeat the statements of those who had gone before. They could but assert, over and over, that such and such were the traditions of the church. How much credit would be due to traditions thus created we have already seen. For it would not be difficult to show that whatever weight may be due to that which may properly be called traditions, the alleged statements with regard to St. Peter are not in fact entitled to that name.

A tradition is a statement of fact or doctrine, which, originating at the time, or near the time of its occurrence, has been uninterruptedly handed down by a succession of witnesses. Let me illustrate this definition. Just previous to our Lord's ascension, Peter seeing John, said to Jesus, "Lord, and what shall this man do? Jesus said, If I will that he tarry till I come, what is that to thee? follow thou me. Then went this saying abroad among the brethren that this disciple should not die; yet Jesus said not unto him, he shall not die, but if I will that he tarry till I come, what is that to thee." Now if St. John had disappeared, and no one had known that he had died, the saying that went abroad among the brethren that he should not die, would probably have been handed down from generation to generation, together with the statement that, in accordance with this saying, he had not died. It would then have been *truly* a tradition, though a tradition of that which was *not true*. It would have originated from the Master's saying at the time it was said, and would have been handed down by successive witnesses. It is a singular testimony with regard to the character and value of traditions, *that the only one which originated with and prevailed among the Apostles was not true.* But the statements of St. Peter's residence and Episcopacy and primacy are not even *truly* traditions, quite independently of the truth of that which they profess to deliver. We find no contemporaneous witness saying that St. Peter was at Rome, nor even *saying that it was said*. We find no witnesses *near that period* making the assertion. It is not until several generations after his death that it began to be said that St. Peter had lived and been crucified at Rome. After it once began to be said, it matters not how many may have repeated the saying on the authority of those who went before. They do not add any strength to the testimony. The chain of testimony fails for the want of connecting links between the first witnesses and the facts alleged. Nothing is accomplished by adding a thousand links at the other end of the chain.

We have spoken of the absence of any contemporary testimony of St. Peter's residence and Episcopate at Rome. We have shown that the tradition to that effect is utterly wanting in the characteristics either of a true tradition or of a tradition that is true. We might add that neither Clemens, nor Ignatius, nor Irenæus, nor Justin Martyr, nor Tertullian, directly affirm the fact. And now it would not be difficult, we think, to indicate the origin of this asserted residence of St. Peter at Rome. It is well known that even before the Apostles passed away from earth, the Jewish and Gentile converts differed and disputed concerning the observance of the Mosaic Law. Paul was regarded as the champion of Gentile freedom, and Peter of a more Jewish and orthodox strictness. The Church of Rome consisted, no doubt, in a largely preponderant measure, of Jewish converts. They would be anxious to sustain the credit of their chosen leader, who they erroneously supposed differed from St. Paul. Pious fraud, as usual, came to the support of fanatical and intolerant error. At a very early period spurious writings in the name of Peter, or professing to give an account of Peter, appeared at Rome. Their whole tendency and effect was to exalt St. Peter as the authoritative *doctrinal head* of the Christians of the capital. The step was not long nor difficult from this species of doctrinal headship and supremacy in the church,—itself an invention,—to the story of his actual presence and Episcopate and primacy. "The preaching of Peter" and "The Itinerary of St. Peter" are of very early date. But that which produced the most effect was the romance of "The Clementines," together with "The Recognitions," and "Apostolical Constitution and Canons," with which they became associated as a decisive authority in matters of faith and fact and right. In this pseudo-Clementine system, St. Peter is brought forward as the representative of what is claimed as the original and pure Christianity; and the historical romance is elaborated in the scene of the conversion of the father, the mother, and the brothers of Clement. In these writings, St. Peter is reported as the sole speaker and instructor, or the President of the Apostolic College. Clement, one of the earliest presiding elders of the Roman Church, is the chosen recipient of the Petrine ordinances, and the scene is laid throughout at Rome. Now there is no reason to believe that any report or belief of the presence of Peter in that city, at a date anterior to these writings, existed in the Roman Church. It is just as reasonable to suppose that the tradition took its origin from these writings, as that they sprang from a previously existing and accredited tradition.*

---

* Cathedri Petri. Thos. Greenwood, M. A., Book iii. Preface, Herzog's Eccl. Cyclopædia, article *Clementines.*

Hence it is seen why, on the one hand, we rest in the secure conviction that St. Paul went a second time to Rome, and why we believe that he then suffered martyrdom; and why, on the other hand, we say to the claim of St. Peter's residence and Episcopacy and martyrdom at Rome, *not proven*, and why we add with a good degree of conviction, *not probable*. We have external contemporary evidence that Paul left Rome and returned and was executed. We have internal evidence from his Epistles, that he wrote a letter to Timothy during a second imprisonment, and expected soon to suffer death. These are solid historical testimonies. But we have no evidences, equally strong as we have seen, external or internal, to Peter's sojourn at Rome; and we have probabilities against it from the silence of St. Paul and St. Clement, which amount almost to a demonstration.

From all these reasons it is that we prefer to pause at the point where we are abandoned by clear historical light, and to be content with the conviction that St. Paul's anticipation of speedy death was verified soon after he wrote to Timothy, and that he *was* "offered" a victim and a martyr to his fidelity to his Master. If we accept the statement as *historically true* that he was incarcerated in the Mamertine and beheaded at the *Acqua Salviæ*, we must do it on evidence which just as positively asserts St. Peter's companionship in imprisonment and death, and all the puerile marvels which marked their sojourn in prison and their execution. It is believed not to have been without a solemn motive that the place of the burial of Moses remained unknown, and that the record of it was made in vague and general terms. "So Moses the servant of the

Lord died there in the land of Moab, according to the Word of the Lord; and he buried him in *a* valley of the land of Moab over against Beth Peor, but no man knoweth of his sepulcher unto this day." (Deut. xxxiv. 5-6.) It was probably with a view to prevent the superstitious reverence which would have been likely to have been rendered to the spot, and to the remains of Moses, that the place of his burial was designedly left unknown. And similar may have been the object of divine wisdom in the uncertainty which has been permitted to remain as to the death and burial place of him who may not improperly be called the Moses of the New Dispensation. A carnal curiosity; a low and superstitious and irreverent intrusion into things unrevealed; a manifestation of that unspiritual desire "to know Christ after the flesh," when through the higher knowledge imparted by the Spirit it becomes his disciple "to know" even "him" in that respect "*no more;*" a return from the privileges of those who were permitted to see the divine beauty and meaning of earthly and outward ordinances by the Spirit, to resting on ordinances for the Spirit;—this relapse of the church from the spirit of the Apostolic age, at once led it to corrupt the sublime and spiritual purity of St. Paul's doctrine, and to search, as if for the most precious of divine treasures, for his bones, and which, in the failure to find them, gradually converted conjecture into tradition, and superstitious wishes into history. If we will rightly view it, there is something august in the solemn shadows through which we vaguely discern the great Apostle, passing with majestic peace to martyrdom and heaven!

As he disappears, we seem to see him pause a

moment, and with solemn earnestness declare the truth which underlies all his teachings, and which the Church of Rome everywhere reverses, "The letter killeth, the Spirit giveth life!"

NOTE.

THE theologian at present in greatest repute in Rome is Giovanni Perrone. Immediately after the above lecture was delivered, a small work of 160 pages was issued by him, under the title "*S. Pietro in Roma, ossia la verita storica del viaggio di S. Pietro in Roma.*" It is evidently nothing more than an enlarged syllabus published in advance of an enormous work upon the subject, in the preparation of which he is now engaged. It is to be a companion to the massive production of Passaglia on the Immaculate Conception of the Virgin. It is intended as a final and full gathering up of all the testimony of all time in favor of this fundamental dogma. If such a question were to be settled by the *number* of authorities *adduced* without reference to their pertinency to the real point in question, this array would be indeed quite overwhelming.

It is an interesting fact, as illustrating the progress of opinion in Italy, that the work is prepared in confutation of another published at *Turin,* as recently as 1861, with the title "*The Historical Impossibility of the Journey of St. Peter to Rome demonstrated by substituting True for False Tradition.*"

Before noticing the sort of proof which Perrone adduces for the fact of St. Peter's journey to Rome, let us remember the importance of the alleged doctrine which rests upon the alleged fact. To the Protestant it is by no means a matter of importance to prove that St. Peter was not at Rome. It might be admitted, and not a single step be thereby made toward the demonstration of the claim made on his behalf to the Vicarate of Christ and the Primacy of the Church. But to the Romanist it is essential that he should prove that St. Peter presided over the Church at

Rome. On that assumed fact is erected the most important doctrine—next to that of salvation by the death of Christ—ever proclaimed to man. If true, it is a truth on which the salvation of myriads rests. If false, it is a portentous falsehood, the evil results of which no imagination can conceive. It rests on the fact that St. Peter was at Rome. If he was not there, it falls to the ground, a convicted and dead lie. Now it will be admitted that such a fact should have proof that is unimpeachable, abundant, and undoubted. God did not allow the proofs of Christ's crucifixion and resurrection to be few and feeble. They are abundant and overwhelming. If he had intended St. Peter to be his vicar to the world, with the seat of his principate at Rome, he would not have left the doctrine or the fact of so momentous an arrangement in doubt. Of the *doctrine* there is not a shadow of proof in the Word of God. If it is conceivable that it should have been left so utterly without proof, it is conceivable only on the supposition that *the fact* should appear with indubitable brightness.

Now the mere fact that the question is *raised* whether St. Peter was ever actually at Rome, preliminary to the question whether he was there as head of the church, is presumptively damaging to the claims of his Episcopate and Headship. And the attempted proof of this alleged fact is so incidental, inferential, remote, and vague, that even if one is constrained, on the whole, to accept the fact of St. Peter's journey and residence at Rome, he would be equally compelled to conclude that no important doctrine, certainly no doctrine of such transcendent moment as that of the Primacy of St. Peter and his successors, could be allowed to rest upon a point proved with so much difficulty and by processes of argument so recondite, subtle, inferential, and remote.

And now, turning to the work of Perrone, we find a chasm just where we need a bridge. Positive assertions of St. Peter's residence at Rome *from* and *after* Irenæus, about 180 A. D., we find in abundance; but the proof or the assertion of this fact, from intermediate authors, is altogether wanting. The attempt to *wring out* of expressions which are merely incidental in Clement of Rome, and Ignatius, such a testimony, is an utter failure. Clement, in the way of narrative and exhortation, in his Epistle to the Corinthians, uses the general expression that we have seen with our own eyes good Apostles suffer martyrdom. He does not say *which Apostles*. Nor does the language imply, of necessity, an actual ocular view by *the Romans* and by them alone. He is writing to *the Corinthians*, and he says, *we have seen among us*. Writing, as he does, in a practical way to the Corinthians, and using the words *we* and *among us*, the words may well be believed to mean no more than if he had written thus: "I have spoken to you of the example of the ancient faithful men who have died from persecuting hatred. But let us turn to our own times. In our own day, we, *i.e.* the men of this generation, have seen faithful Apostles martyred."

He then proceeds to speak of Peter. He suffered and died from persecution. But Clement does not mention *where* he suffered. On this exceedingly small basis rests the alleged proof of the one only testimony which is ever claimed to be contemporaneous, of the martyrdom of St. Peter at Rome. The alleged testimony of Ignatius is equally unsatisfactory.

That the importance of this fact to the Romish system has not been overstated, will appear from the declaration of Perrone himself. The author of the work which he attempts to confute, asserts that some Catholic writers have declared that St. Peter was never at Rome. Perrone says that this is impossible. None but apostate Catholics could have made such an assertion. And why? *Because they become apostate by making it.* "The reason of this fact," *viz.*, that no Catholic could have made this assertion, "is that the coming of St. Peter in Rome and the seat there established by him is connected as the indispensable condition with an article of our faith, that is, the primacy of order and jurisdiction belonging of divine right to the Roman Pontiff. *Hence it follows that he cannot be a Catholic who does not admit the coming, the Episcopate, and the death of St. Peter in Rome.*"— Page 32.

LECTURE XII.

THE CLAIM OF THE CHURCH OF ROME TO SANCTITY, INFALLIBILITY, AND UNITY CONSIDERED.

But he said, Yea, rather blessed are they that hear the word of God, and keep it.—LUKE, xi. 28.

ON Sunday evening last I heard, and some of you heard, disparaging reference made to the word of God, by the distinguished Romish divine who is now preaching a series of Lenten sermons in a neighboring church. Those Christians were—I was about to say—*ridiculed,* who believe in and *rely upon a book* for divine truth and life. At the same time that this reliance *upon a book* for authority in sacred things was censured, appeals were constantly made *to a book* as if it were a final and absolute authority upon all questions of faith and practice. The book against reliance upon which we were warned was the Word of God. The book which was quoted to settle our faith and secure our assent was one of St. Augustine. While cautioned not to rely upon the Word, we were invited to believe in the one holy, illuminated, infallible present Church of Rome. It was said to us in substance, "Deluded, miserable, without the covenant, without grace, without the promises, without the divine life, are those who rely upon the Bible. Hear and believe the teachings of the Papal Church."

Such were the words which fell on our ears on Sunday last. To-day, from the ascended Son of man, from the enthroned Son of God, from the founder and teacher of the church, from Him who is the truth as well as the way and the life, and from whom the Holy Spirit itself, which is to guide the souls of men into all truth, proceeds, who surely knew what we were to hear and upon what we should rely; to-day, in the Gospel for the day, these precious words come to our ears, and we take them to our heart of hearts, "*Blessed are they that hear the Word of God, and keep it!*" Dear Master! having thy blessing in hearing and keeping the Word of God, we need fear no man's ridicule or anathema for doing that which wins thy benediction. "I wot that he whom thou blessest is blest!"

The question of the relative position of the church and the Word of God is most interesting and important. It is so quite irrespective of the claims of the Church of Rome. It has often been inquired "which was first, the church or the Word?" and very important results have been supposed to depend upon the answer. If the reply is, "The church was first," then it has been inferred that it was the prerogative of the church to interpret the Word. If the answer be, "The Word was first," then it has been concluded that it is the office of the Word to teach the church. Now, although I do not see that these inferences logically follow their respective premises, and though I do not therefore attach much importance to the inquiry, yet, as a fact, I think it cannot be doubted that the Word was first, and that the church is the outgrowth of the Word, administered by the Spirit. When God called Abram, and he heard and kept the Divine Word—then in him, the father of the faithful, the germ of the patriarchal church was formed. The Word summoning, and through the Spirit creating the church,—such was the process. When God called Moses, and he heard and kept the Word—then by the Word was the Jewish church begun. The twelve became the founders of the Christian church by being first obedient to the words of Jesus. As the creation was evolved into order under light by the power of God, so the church assumed its form under the light of the Word, ministered by the Holy Spirit.

It is a question more practical and important—"What is the relation of the church to the Word?" To this question it seems to me there can be but one answer for him who takes for his authority the founder of the church, the Lord Jesus Christ. Its office is not certainly to disparage, not to hide, but to dispense the Word of God. The Saviour's last solemn commission to his disciples before his ascension was this, "Go ye into all the world and preach the Gospel to every creature. He that believeth and is baptized shall be saved; but he that believeth not shall be damned." St. Paul, taught of Jesus, said for himself that he determined to know nothing among his disciples but Christ, and him crucified; and his son Timothy he exhorted with intense earnestness, as if it were the one work which he was to do—"preach the Word; be instant in season and out of season; reprove, rebuke, exhort." And everywhere the conviction, illumination, and sanctification of the heart is made dependent upon the Word of God, administered by the Spirit. *Not* of the personal Word, the Son of God, as was said on Sunday last, but plainly of the *written Word* is it declared that it "is quick and powerful, sharper than a two-edged sword, piercing even to the dividing asunder of the joints and marrow, and is a discerner of the thoughts and intents of the heart." "Being born again," says St. Peter!! "not of corruptible seed, but of incorruptible, *by the Word of God which liveth and abideth* forever." St. Peter did not speak disparagingly of the Word. St. Paul commended the Ephesians to God, *and to the Word of his truth,* which was able to build them up. "The *Gospel* is the power of God unto salvation." Is one baptized? It is when listening to the Word he becomes penitent. Does one commemorate the Saviour's dying love? It is because he obeys the Divine Word which says, "Do this in remembrance of me!" Does one go into the house of God? It is that he may worship according to the teachings of the Word, and listen to that right dividing of the truth which will furnish him his portion of meat in due season. Hence, as the church is established for dispensing the Word of God, its function is gone when that duty ceases to be discharged. Established for that purpose, of what use is it when that purpose is not accomplished? The church, according to the definition of our article, is the keeper and witness of the Holy Writ. It is her privilege to keep, and her duty to dispense the Word. Hence, the Word is greater than the church, even when she truly keeps and truly proclaims it; and, of course, immeasurably greater when she neither holds nor dispenses the truth of God, but proclaims only error. When the Jewish church made void the law of God by its traditions, how did God regard it, and what did he do with it? He abhorred it, and scattered it, and destroyed it; but the Word of God liveth and abideth forever. That Word itself—the prophetic Word—smote the apostate Jewish church; and another prophetic word is hovering over, and will in its appointed time strike and destroy the second great apostacy.

Great and precious therefore as is the church of God, and high as is its function, as that which holds the water of life, and dispenses it for the souls of men, yet if, in some other way, that water of life shall reach some thirsty soul, that soul shall live. Far off in the mountains is the source of the "Aqua Claudia." If the citizens of Rome had no other supply of water but this, then how precious to them would be the aqueduct, and the reservoirs, and the conduits, which should convey it to them, and keep them from perishing by thirst. Then how gloriously grand would seem to them the far-stretching arches that conveyed it; and how exquisitely beautiful the castelli that inclosed it; and how musical and refreshing would be the flow, and the spray, and the sparkle of the fountains! But even then it would not be the aqueduct, and the reservoir, and the fountains, but the water, that would quench their thirst and save them from perishing. If the aqueduct should be destroyed and the water should be brought to them some other way, they would not perish. Such is the function of the church of God. It is the established agency by which the truth of God is brought to the perishing souls of men. It is lovely and majestic to the eye of those who drink and live. They walk about this Zion; they count its towers; they breathe upon it the blessing, "peace be within thy walls!" They love it for what it is; they bless it for what it gives. Its prosperity is their joy; its adversity is their sorrow. If it is broken down, they thirst, they faint, they pine; but if the water of life be brought to them in some other way, directly from the source, they do not die, but live. Thus is held, in most revered and loving estimation, the church of God, because it dispenses the living and life-giving Word. And when the church ceases to perform this, its appropriate function,—what is it? Behold the majestic ruins of the Claudian aqueduct, as it stretches its broken and picturesque and festooned arches over the Campagna, and climbs the imperial hill; behold the shapeless mass of the *Meta Sudens;* and in them, long dry, and empty, behold a symbol of the Church of Rome, as it stretches in broken grandeur over the centuries of time! Nay, the symbol is not complete; for from those arches no poisoning dew distils to blight the grass beneath; and from that silent fountain issue no pestilential vapors!

Such we believe to be, on the authority of Christ himself, the true relation of the church of God to the Word of God. But the system which prevails in the Church of Rome is quite another; and was stated on Sunday last in a way which, I am told, seemed to some minds plausible and attractive. So far as the discourse to which I refer expounded the relation of the three persons of the Sacred Trinity —so far as it explained, in general terms, the office of the Holy Spirit, in its procession from the Father and the Son, and in its sanctifying, illuminating, and comforting influences, it appealed to the conviction and experience of all true Christian hearts. But when the attempt was made to show that all the influences of the Holy Ghost were limited to the church, which was itself limited within the bounds of the Roman obedience; then who could fail painfully to feel the deplorable degradation to which the blessed Paraclete was subjected? How vain the attempt to show that, either in just theory or in fact, its broad and blessed agency is so cribbed, cabined, and confined! Ah! as well might the Pope and his cardinals and priests stand at the door of St. Peter's and gather the sunshine that irradiates the world into their hands, and put it in St. Peter's, and lock it up and leave the world in darkness—as shut up the light of the world, which Christ manifested by the Spirit, within the bounds of the Papal Church!

The assumption of the discourse was, that the Holy Spirit, acting only in and through the church, reproduces in her its own essential nature and characteristics. Being essential light, it conveys to the church illumination, and thus becomes the world's guide. The Spirit of Holiness—it makes the church, like itself, holy, unchangeable, and indefectible; it imparts to the church infallibility. One and uniform, it gives to the one church one system of sacred truth. "*Holiness,*" "*illumination,*" "*infallibility,*" "*unity, interior as well as exterior,*"—these are the gifts, the reflex and repetition of itself, which the Holy Ghost imparts to the church,—and that church is the Church of Rome! I do not know that it would be going beyond the extremely strong expressions which were used in this connection if it should be said that the representation of the doctrine was, that as God the Word was incarnate in Jesus, so God the Holy Ghost was embodied in the church.

Now if it were proved or capable of proof that the Holy Ghost was promised to produce such results in a body upon earth, called the church, it would be no difficult task to show that assuredly they have not been realized in the Church of Rome.

I. The *Spirit* whose name is *Holy* must transfer to the body its own holiness; and one prominent mark of the church is therefore claimed to be "*sanctity.*" What is holiness or the fruit of the Spirit? "The fruit of the Spirit," says the Word, inspired by the Spirit, sent from the ascended head of the church, "is love, joy, peace, long-suffering, gentleness, goodness, faith, meekness, temperance." But it is said that nowhere but in the church does the Holy Ghost pour its influences and produce its fruit. Only in the Papal Church may we find sanctity. The limb cut off from the body cannot partake of the life that pervades the body. Now in connection with this declaration, and the Holy Spirit's own definition of sanctity, some conclusions must be drawn which are fatal to the exclusive claims of Rome.

It appears as *a fact* beyond all possibility of denial, that the fruit of the Spirit, described by the Spirit, does appear in those who, according to Rome, are cut off from the body. Take the catalogue and compare it with what is found in the hearts of Christians, of various names, and you will find the living graces and the description to correspond. We know, and are agreed, as to what *Christian love*, as a grace of heart, is; for Rome and other churches do not differ in their definition of Christian love, as it is a subjective and individual grace; and that love is in your heart, my brother! and fellow-Protestant against the Church of Rome. "Joy, peace, long-suffering, gentleness, goodness, faith, meekness, temperance,"—I find them all, in a degree, equal surely to that in which they are found in the members of the Church of Rome, in the hearts of those who are, by Rome, said to be cut off from the body, and therefore without holy life. The *fact* is beyond all possible doubt or denial. What can be done with it by the Church of Rome? Let it be turned and dealt with as it may, it is, on any disposition which she can make of it, absolutely fatal to her claims.

(1) Does she *deny* that these graces of the Spirit *are in the hearts of Protestants?* Then is she wanting in truth and charity, declaring that what are graces of the Spirit in the hearts of Romanists, cease to be so when they are seen, in their same essential qualities, and in their same outward tokens, in the hearts of Protestants; and thus failing in truth and charity, which are the very elements of holiness, she is void of the most important mark of the church—*sanctity*.

(2) Or does she admit that these graces enumerated by St. Paul *are* in the hearts of those who are cut off from the body, but that they do not constitute holiness? Does she say that there are other graces different from these which constitute sanctity, and that these do not? and that these graces are implicit and submissive faith in the church, and others of the same character? Then does she make void the law of God by her traditions, and subject herself to the same withering rebukes of the Master, as those with which he visited the apostate Jewish church?

(3) Or does she admit that these graces may be in the hearts of those who are cut off from the body, through the rich, uncovenanted, overflowing mer-

cies of the compassionate Redeemer; while, at the same time, the church, *i.e.* the Papal Church, is the only appointed, authoritative, and sure receptacle in which they are to be found? Then the position is abandoned that the limb severed is necessarily dead; and the admission is made that divine life can be obtained apart from the body.

(4) Or again, is it, on the contrary, stoutly denied that sanctity can be found anywhere but in the church; the one body organized by Christ, and vivified by the Spirit? Then must we, who exhibit sanctity, *i.e.* the graces of the Spirit, which, according to the Spirit, constitute holiness, be in that body where alone that sanctity is found. If that body be not the Church of Rome, or she is not a part of it, so much the worse for her.

Thus, if we take this claim to exclusive sanctity for the body, which is all along claimed to be the Papal Church, in connection with the Holy Spirit's own definition of sanctity—a definition admitted in its application to the individual, by the Church of Rome, and which cannot be denied without blasphemy against the Holy Ghost,—we find that the Word of God, the disparaged Word, utterly annihilates the pretensions of the church. No wonder that it is disparaged.

The truth is, that this pretension of the Church of Rome to be the exclusive depository of the Holy Ghost, can be sustained only by denying the very nature of holiness, as it is defined by the Holy Spirit. It cannot be admitted to be what St. Paul describes it; for then must the fatal concession follow that it is found outside the church. Accordingly we find that it can exist as a nameless something when it is utterly void of all moral or spiritual quality. Grace, or holiness, conveyed by the sacraments, reaches, and is infused into all who partake of them. It is not in you who love God, rely upon your Saviour, enjoy spiritual communion with the Father of your spirit, and exhibit in your daily life, love, forgiveness, meekness, temperance,—it is not in you, because you are not where it can be obtained. But it is in the brigand, who is now watching for lives in the mountains of Southern Italy, because he is in union with the body, and draws from it this mysterious sanctity, and adores the Virgin, and obeys the church. *What* is it? A new spiritual nature? Nay, the first glimmer of it is not to be found in him! Is it knowledge? He is absolutely ignorant. Is it holy love? His heart is full of hate, and has only some instinctive natural affections. Is it joy, peace, long-suffering, gentleness, goodness, faith, meekness, and temperance? The dog that follows him has scarcely less of any of these qualities than he! I do by no means deny—I rejoice to be assured—that there is genuine spiritual life,—real sanctity,—in the hearts of many members of the Church of Rome. But this too—this nameless infused grace, which has no spiritual or even moral quality—which may exist, nay, which *must* exist, in the heart of this brigand-member of the church; this sacred galvanism which informs souls that are utterly vile and evil; this too *is holiness*, and the spirit exhibited by Henry Martyn, by Heber, by the Dairyman's daughter, was not holiness. Oh how strange it is that such astounding absurdities can be believed! How awful it is that such blasphemies against the Holy Ghost should be uttered by the church which professes to embody it, to be its sole organ of expression upon earth! How sad that such a system should entangle and bring down a high and gifted spirit, once honored and beloved in a pure and scriptural church! Alas! that we should be compelled of this bright and beautiful mind to reverse the language of the Psalmist: "Though ye were as the wings of a dove covered with silver, and her feathers with yellow gold, yet are ye now lying among the pots!"

II. But it is to the church as a whole, in her corporate capacity, that the Holy Spirit imparts its power, and therefore in its function as a church, we are to discover the most striking evidences of a sanctity that is but a reflex of the holiness of its source. The moon receives light from the sun, and none the less is it a pure and completed rounded light because some spots may be discerned upon the surface. Let us see!

The Saviour declared that "His kingdom was not of this world." Those of whom it was composed were, according to St. Peter, "a chosen generation, a royal priesthood, a peculiar people." The mode in which it was to be made a glorious church is thus stated by St. Paul. "That he might sanctify and cleanse it by the *washing of water by the Word*, that he might present it to himself a glorious church, without spot or wrinkle or any such thing." Said the founder of this kingdom, "If my kingdom were of this world, then would my servants fight." A kingdom not of this world; a peculiar, separated people; a body which would be made glorious by the washing of water by the Word; and in which there could be no exercise of civil power, even for self-preservation, without a perversion and degradation of its high and holy functions. Such was the holy kingdom of our Lord as described by himself and by those whom he inspired. This is now the holy church, the body in which the Spirit's sanctity resides, and from which it emanates. Is the Church of Rome in its corporate capacity and its action such a church?

St. Peter, in the context in which he dwells upon the separateness and sanctity of the holy nation, enjoins upon it submission to the civil powers. "Submit," says St. Peter, "to the king as supreme," and the pretended successor of St. Peter replies, "I am myself POPE-KING!" "Submit," says St. Peter, "to the king," and the pretended successor of St. Peter seems to have read it, "Make all kings submit to you." Hence his kingdom is, whatever else it may be, a kingdom of this world, which the Saviour declared that his kingdom was not. Again said the Master and the founder of the kingdom, "The princes of the Gentiles exercise dominion over them and they that are great exercise authority upon them. *But it shall not be so among you.*" It is so with that body which is claimed to be the exclusive depository of the Holy Ghost. It exercises dominion and authority precisely as the princes of the Gentiles do. It has assumed, in addition to its spiritual, civil functions. The church, which was to be made glorious *by the washing of water by the Word*, is glorious with church edifices, rich in marble and gems and gold; with glittering priestly vestments; with elaborate ceremonies; with gorgeous carriages and liveried servants; with palaces and basilicas and halls of art which put to shame the poor pomp of emperors and kings; with all the officials of a human court and with the armed servants that *will* fight that their master be not delivered up to his enemies. The bishops of this holy body, the successors of those to whom the Master's injunction was "teach and preach; give yourselves wholly to the ministry of the Word," many of them never teach or preach at all, but they ride in stately carriages; they take part in church and state ceremonials; they are at the head of, or in the council for managing the war department, the treasury department, the department of agriculture, and public instruction and the police; they superintend the administration of the lottery and the theaters. And this is the great appropriate work of the Holy Catholic Church! This is that power which she declares is essential to her existence and to the right discharge of her high functions in the world. And these are manifestations of the Holy Spirit from that one body in which it is enshrined and to which it is confined. Others, which it is equally difficult to recognize as breathings of that Holy Spirit, whose emblem is the dove, are found in those anathemas which sound so like angry maledictions; in those persecutions of heretics which are so little in the spirit of the Divine Master who poured his compassionate lamentations over infatuated Jerusalem; and in that withdrawal of the Word of God from the people, and that disparagement of its sacred and sanctifying office, which is a direct denial of the Master's saying, "*Blessed* are they that hear the Word of God, and keep *it.*" But while Rome remains what she is we wonder not that she does not love the Book! If this Word be true, if the Holy Ghost speaks through it to the world and to the church, then the voice which we hear from the Papacy is not the voice of the Spirit. She is compelled to claim a monopoly of holiness and to deny that there is any other in the world, or from the Bible, except as it is dispensed by her; for the Bible itself, and all else in the world which claims to be holiness, on its authority, unite in declaring that much of her boasted exclusive holiness is secularity and sin.

III. (1) It is claimed that the Holy Ghost imparts also to the one body its own illumination and infallibility. It makes the church infallibly to receive and infallibly to teach the truth. The body thus interpenetrated and assimilated by the Spirit cannot hold or proclaim error. Hence it always holds, and always must have held, all the truth, and nothing but the truth. This claim was advanced in all its fullness. And certainly if the premises be admitted, the conclusion cannot be denied. If the work of the Holy Spirit is not only to sanctify the souls of men and keep in the world a church against which the gates of hell shall not prevail, but also so to transfer itself to the church as to make it incapable, like itself, of error; and if the body to which it thus transforms itself is the Papal Church, then it indeed follows that the church thus illuminated is infallible, both in receiving and teaching the truth of God. I do not now pause to consider whether such a gift was promised to the body. It was, in the discourse alluded to, assumed that it *was;* and it might be as readily assumed that it was *not.* It is sufficient to show that, whether promised or not, it is not in the possession of the body by which it is claimed. If the Holy Spirit transfers itself to the church in its full illumination, then as the spirit never holds only a part of truth, and never progresses in knowledge, but is always the same, yesterday, to-day, and forever, it must of necessity have at once led the church into all truth. There can be no place for doctrines of development and of gradual illuminations in connection with such a statement. We take it in its full and emphatic and unlimited form in which it was made. If, indeed, the church is claimed to be made infallible, that claim of itself involves the ever-present possession of all the truth. Hence this body, the Papal Church, must have always held precisely the same one complete faith once delivered to the saints.

(2) What a singular claim to be made for the Church of Rome! The Emperor Augustus said that he should think that two Augurs meeting together in the exercise of their pretended functions of divination from the entrails of sacrificed victims, must needs laugh in each other's faces. One would suppose that an advocate of the Church of Rome could scarcely advance this pretension without a smile. For from the days of the first Clement, Bishop of Rome, from his own pure and Paul-like Epistle to the Romans, to the days of the present Pope, the student of history can trace every succeeding step of the Church of Rome in error until the church of the nineteenth century becomes as little like the church of the first and second centuries as the worship of the High Places by apostate Israel was like that of the tabernacle in the wilderness. He can run his hand down the chart of history and mark the successive steps from bad to worse. Here commemoration *of* the dead became prayers *for* them. Here what had commenced as honors for the saints and mar-

tyrs became prayers *to* them. Here commenced the celibacy of the clergy. Here the claims of the Pope to the headship of the church were first hinted and here they were advanced. Here Purgatory. Here transubstantiation. Here masses for the dead for money. And here, last of all, the Immaculate Conception. And yet, in the face of historical monuments which verify these changes, which are just as authentic as anything in history, the claim is gravely advanced that the Papal Church has always been unchangeable, because infallible. All the time infallible, and yet not teaching in one century an article of faith essential to salvation which she proclaimed as such in the century following. All the time infallible, and yet one infallibility at Rome and another at Avignon, and both infallibilities infallibly anathematizing the other; and the church not yet agreed as to who was truly Pope. But we need not go back to history to show how infallibility has faltered and been at fault for eighteen centuries! Look at the new column of the Immaculate Conception!* Listen to its testimony! What does it say? It gives distinctly to the churches and world this testimony: "I proclaim that for eighteen hundred years, the church which professes to hold and dispense all truth, has been without this saving article of faith, this article necessary to be received on the pain of damnation. The body which accepts truth from the spirit has waited eighteen hundred years before it has accepted this. The children of the church have been robbed for centuries of this essential truth. Who knows how many other essential truths necessary to salvation there may be which the Spirit has

---

* Piazza di Spagna.

been struggling to present, and which the church does not yet accept, and may be eighteen hundred years more in learning!" So does that column, intended to commemorate the Immaculate Conception, stand a perpetual witness to the falsity of the pretensions of the church to changelessness and infallibility. And oh! if the marble lips of the image of the Virgin Mother which crowns that column could speak, if her spirit could visit earth and be heard from the elevation to which an idolatrous homage has lifted her, even above her divine Son, how would she cry out in the anguish of deprecation to her infatuated followers to cease that awful idolatry of a lowly creature, who mingles with the throngs that cast their crowns before the throne; and was highly favored on earth only because she was permitted to be very near in love and service to her divine Redeemer Son; is blessed now in heaven only in that she can sing with all the ransomed the new song to Him who has washed her and redeemed her in His blood! There is a feeling of inexpressible tenderness, sympathy, and reverence among Protestant hearts toward the Virgin Mother of our Lord; because they know that if she could be cognizant of what transpires on earth, and sorrow could enter heaven, her holy and loving heart would be torn with anguish at the awful idolatry which renders to her the homage due only to her divine Son and Lord.

(3) This pretended infallibility of the church is *assumed* on the ground of its *necessity*. A living infallible teacher for the church is announced to be a self-evident need. The Master says not so. The Word administered by the Spirit—this is provided,

and no intimation is given that anything more or other is needed. It seems to be considered that if infallibility is granted, then all difficulty in the way of right and sure knowledge and belief vanishes. Nothing more imposes on minds that have been in doubt, and crave an absolute certainty, than the claim of the church to be a present, inspired, infallible teacher of the truth. But it will be seen that this is a mistaken apprehension.

In the first place, we remark that it is not an infallible teacher that is needed, but an infallible learner. An infallible teacher will avail nothing unless the learner be equally infallible. Moses and the prophets were infallible teachers; but the Jews did not therefore learn from them and retain the truth of God. Jesus and the Apostles were infallible teachers—authenticating their authority to teach by signs and wonders—and yet how many did not believe, and how many who did believe, believed amiss! No additional perfection in the teacher, if that were possible; no multiplication of infallibilities, if they could be multiplied, would secure the soul of the taught in truth and holiness. The great difficulty is found in the sin, and blindness, and unbelief of the heart to whom the truth is addressed. We have already an infallible teacher in the inspired Word, administered by the Spirit. This, while it does not secure all who seek the truth from every error, does lead the believing, and honest, and earnest soul into all truth which is necessary for salvation and for spiritual life. Now it would not secure absolute exemption from all error, and certain introduction into all truth, if a present infallible interpreter were added, to make known the meaning of the present inspired Word, any more than when the Apostles were, under the very teachings of Christ himself, the inspired interpreters of his words: the disciples were kept within a rigid mechanical uniformity of faith and dogma, and secured as by a physical necessity from falling into error. Even then, if we should grant that the church were an infallible interpreter of the infallible Word,—if we *could have* such a guide,—it would avail little to save the soul from error. Without humility, penitence, and faith, it could not, even then, accept the truth; and with them it can accept it now. The Word is truth, and the Spirit, sought and used, will lead us into all truth necessary for salvation and for life.

But this infallible teacher that is promised us—where is it to be found? There is one who can authoritatively assure us where it is, and what it is. We are promised an infallible teacher in the church; and lo! we need another infallible teacher—and he does not come—to teach us where the Teacher is. Some of the doctors of the church declare that it is in the Pope alone; some that it is alone in the General Councils; some that it is in both combined; some that it is in neither singly nor in their combination; but that it is in the voice of the collective church. If we seek it in the Popes we find them frequently in direct conflict on points of prime importance. If we go to the Councils we find Constance against Trent, and both against Nice. To obtain a consentient teaching, from interconflicting Popes and Councils, or from the General Church of all ages, would be to evolve ordered music from the broken and tangled strings of a shattered harp. How then is the case of a Protestant practically improved in reference to his assurance of being under a perfect guide, by this promise of an infallible teacher, whom he cannot locate and cannot find? And if he could find the teacher, could he understand the teaching? For it is a curious fact in connection with this claim to be an infallible teacher of the truth, that the Roman Church professes to interpret Scripture, not in the independent exercise of the gift of the Holy Spirit which dictated the Scripture, and which is, in herself, but in accordance with tradition. And what is tradition? The consentient testimony of the fathers. Now how is the condition of the private Christian improved who has been accustomed to rely upon his Bible, under the teachings of the Spirit, and in connection with the prayers of the church and the ministry of the Word; how is it improved by having an infallible teacher who, after all, only gathers and repeats the opinions of the uninspired fathers of the church, some of whom were foolish, and who, not singly infallible, cannot possibly be infallible when combined? The case is not improved to a thoughtful mind, by the assurance that the teachings of the church are compacted into a little catechism which a child can learn and comprehend; for the suggestion constantly occurs that he has no assurance, that by whomsoever composed —by doctor, or Pope, or Council,—they are absolutely infallible, for he cannot ascertain that infallibility resides in either or in all. Oh! vain the attempt to obtain a better or surer teacher than the Holy Ghost, which the Saviour, before his ascension, promised to all his disciples; vain the hope of a higher blessing, in connection with the search for the truth, than that pronounced by the Master:

"Blessed are they that hear the Word of God and keep it!"

IV. Time will not permit me to enter at the same length upon the other claim of unity in the body, outside of which there can be no life, and schism from which must be inevitable death. This unity was described to be not only exterior in organization, but interior in holy charity, and in the universal possession of one faith and one doctrine. The question was asked, "How can that be the one body, informed by one Spirit, in which so many heterogeneous doctrines and sentiments prevail?" Without entering now upon that large question, of the unity of the church, it is sufficient to remark that the same series of questions, and the same train of observations, which were supposed to be conclusive against the claims of all religious bodies outside the Papal Church to belong to the one body of Christ, would be equally conclusive against that church herself. "How," we may ask,—taking up that mode of argument,—"how can that be one body, informed by one Spirit, in which one party locates the vast and momentous prerogative of infallibility in the Pope, another in the Councils, another in both, and another in neither, but in the church universal of all ages? How can that be one tree from one root and homogeneous, which bears on one branch the doctrine of the Jansenists, of justification by faith; and on the other the doctrine of the Jesuits, of justification by works and by grace infused? How can that body be pervaded by Spirit, whose fruit is love, which was rent by the fierce discords of Jansenists and Jesuits, Dominicans and Franciscans? How can the same illuminating spirit teach, at the same time, Transmontane and Cisalpine doctrine to different portions of the one body? How can the bishops and priests in Rome and Southern Italy claim the temporal authority of the Papacy to be a divine prerogative or a sacred duty, and 10,000 priests in Northern Italy regard it as an usurpation and degradation, and treason to the great head of the church, and yet both be under the teachings of the same Holy Spirit, and united by him in the same holy body? How can the priests who, in the Southern States of America, vindicate slavery as sanctioned by the Word of God, and in the Northern States denounce it as utterly at variance with the teachings of the Bible and the church, be of one body and taught of one Spirit? And so we might proceed with many more and similar contrasts. Surely no diversities which prevail among Protestants are greater or more fundamental and vital than these; and if *their* variations conclude them to be not under the teachings of the Spirit and not in the body of Christ, these variations of Popery no less prove her to be in the same situation. The truth is that there is more diversity of sentiment and more difference of opinion on fundamental points within the church, whose boast is that of absolute uniformity of faith and feeling, than prevail among the great body of Protestant Christians of various names. There is, at this moment, in this room, among the various churches here represented, which Rome would describe as the warring and discordant sects, more of the unity of the Spirit under the bond of peace, and more substantial agreement of opinion on points of prime importance, pertaining to life and godliness, than there is among the Romanists now at Rome!

I have thought it well, my Christian brethren, to prove that the claims of the Church of Rome to be the one body of Christ, with the exclusive life of the one Holy Spirit, as evidenced by sanctity, by infallibility, and by unity of faith and feeling, are utterly without foundation; by showing that she has *not* superior holiness, that she has *not* and *cannot* have infallibility, and that her boasted unity is but the enforced external union of warring elements. This train of thought may be useful to those who are impressed with the abstract and plausible argumentation to the effect that there *must be* this unity and infallibility in the church, on the ground of the inconveniences which arise from their absence, and the advantages which they would bring. The argument that they *must be*, on the grounds of their need and usefulness, may well be met by the demonstration that they *are not*. If a man contends that a certain thing really *is*, because it *must needs be*, then the *must needs be* falls to the ground when it is demonstrated that the thing is not. Such is the nature of the argument. When Rome dwells upon the varieties of religious opinions which prevail outside of her communion; when she depicts and exaggerates the dissensions of Protestantism; when she paints a beautiful and attractive picture of the one church of God, pervaded and taught by the one Spirit, the home of superior sanctity, where all are bound together in one golden bond of love, where the teacher speaks with divine authority and where the disciple cannot err, where all doubts and questionings as to what is truth, and all misgivings as to ultimate salvation are forever hushed to rest; when she thus appeals to minds and hearts that are not at peace through simple faith in the Lord Jesus Christ, she seems to promise that for which they yearn; and for persons in such a position it may not be useless as a preventive and a preliminary to show to them that these pretensions are utterly fallacious; that she does not possess that of which she boasts, and cannot give what she promises; and that the reality to the experience of the convert will be hideously unlike the promises held out to the hope of the inquirer.

But, indeed, these claims can seem to have the least plausibility only to those who permit themselves to dwell much on the real or the exaggerated diversities of opinion among Protestants, or to be troubled by doubts arising from the action of their own unaided and not very earnest speculations, and who do not keep their minds in habitual contact with the Word of God. They who devoutly read the Word of God with faith and prayer, and drink in the spirit of its teachings, cannot be accessible to the fallacies which would persuade them that it is unintelligible or injurious to their souls without an infallible human interpreter. Nor can such persons be entangled in the net-work of interminable argumentations and sophistries upon unity and infallibility and their connected falsehoods, because they can cut their way right through them with that sword of the Spirit, which is the Word of God. What need to climb up this elaborate pagoda and take apart, piece by piece, its twisted fret-work, and unloose its jingling bells, and painfully and slowly tear off its painted pasteboard ornaments, when single blows from the hammer of the Lord will at once knock away its foundation stones? The devout reader of the Word of God is furnished with principles which enable him at once to set aside the claims and pretensions of the Papacy, without the need of following her in her line of argumentation into details which confuse the mind by their complexity and weary it with their number.

Take, for instance, the doctrine that we are not to read and accept for ourselves the teachings of the Word of God. Nothing could be more absolutely conclusive than the words of the Master, in the Gospel for the day, against this most false, most injurious, and to Him, the great head of the church, who has expressly declared the opposite, this most traitorous dogma. Jesus, the great teacher, the head of the church, declared that "Blessed are they that hear the Word of God and keep it." Yea, rather blessed, or more blessed, was it to hear and keep the Word of God than to have been his human mother. What a double testimony is this against the idolatrous exaltation of his mother and in honor of the Word of God! Now whatever else may be true or false, this is true on the infallible testimony of Christ himself, that not deluded, not disobedient to his authority, but "blessed," and acting in accordance with his own holy will, are they that hear and keep that Word. Now as by this one word of God, this claim of the Papacy is at once destroyed; so by other words, in their spirit or letter, are all its distinctive dogmas to be annihilated. If the Word of God be in the mind and in the heart, the confutation of all the claims of the Papacy is then already in advance. They can find no entrance and make no lodgment in your mind. Let me entreat you, therefore, to make it the subject of your habitual and prayerful study and meditation. God's Spirit, on God's Word, which is truth, will lead you into all saving truth. Let me entreat you to keep away from instructions which may beguile you into forgetfulness of those foundation principles which are a perpetual confutation of all the errors of the Church of Rome. A practiced dialectician, a skillful orator may thus lay you open to its delusive and flattering claims, if he gets you off from the simple rock of faith in Christ Jesus, revealed to you in the Word, confound and perplex you with subtleties which you cannot answer, but which would not have disturbed you for a moment if you had been living close to God, through the communications of his word and the fellowship of his spirit, and had been able to have answered all sophistries, with the assurance which is the same time experience, "I know whom I have believed."

My friends, let me assure you as a pastor who knows something of the mental torture of those who have passed into Romanism from Protestantism, that if you are again entangled in this yoke of bondage you will find that it is such as you will not be able, as our fathers were not able, to bear. Its promises of assurance to the doubting mind, and of rest to the agitated heart, are most delusive. It cannot be with those who go out of Protestantism into Romanism, as it is with those who have been trained in that system from childhood. There will be the memory of a happier past to throw deeper gloom on the gloomy present. There will be a higher moral and spiritual culture to create a revulsion of the soul as it is admitted further into the exemplification in practice of dogmas and rites and ceremonies which were fascinating in the theory. What does it offer for those whose privilege it is in simple faith to receive from the Lord Jesus a complete salvation, an indwelling comforter, a guide in the Word which is a light to our feet and a lantern to our paths in all difficulties and doubts, and beyond, a heaven of rest when we fall asleep in Jesus? For this precious and full and present salvation, what does it offer? It invites you to a system in which your soul will be perpetually tortured with fear that your sins cast you out from God's favor, and that your good works are not sufficient to bring you back; in which you will be perpetually vibrating between a state of condemnation and one of forgiveness, the one inevitably induced by the frailty of your nature, and the other dependent upon the forgiveness of the priest; and then at last on the death-bed, when the body is fainting with anguish, it will have no better comfort to speak to your poor trembling soul than of a dim, far distant heaven, to be reached after uncounted ages upon ages of awful purgatorial fire. "Oh, my soul! come not unto their secret; into their assembly be not thou united!"

THE END.

www.ingramcontent.com/pod-product-compliance
Lightning Source LLC
Chambersburg PA
CBHW031330230426
43670CB00006B/298